PRIYADARŚIKĀ OF ŚRIHARṢADEVA

श्रीहर्षदेवविरचित:

प्रियदर्शिका

Priyadarśikā

of

Śrīharṣadeva

Edited with an exhaustive Introduction, a short Sanskrit Commentary, Various Readings, a literal English Translation, copious Notes and useful Appendices

M.R. Kale

MOTILAL BANARSIDASS PUBLISHERS
PRIVATE LIMITED • DELHI

First Edition: Bombay, 1928
Reprint: Delhi, 1977, 1999

ISBN: 81-208-1679-x

Also available at:

MOTILAL BANARSIDASS

41 U.A. Bungalow Road, Jawahar Nagar, Delhi 110 007
8 Mahalaxmi Chamber, Warden Road, Mumbai 400 026
120 Royapettah High Road, Mylapore, Chennai 600 004
Sanas Plaza, 1302, Baji Rao Road, Pune 411 002
16 St. Mark's Road, Bangalore 560 001
8 Camac Street, Calcutta 700 017
Ashok Rajpath, Patna 800 004
Chowk, Varanasi 221 001

PRINTED IN INDIA
BY JAINENDRA PRAKASH JAIN AT SHRI JAINENDRA PRESS,
A-45 NARAINA, PHASE I, NEW DELHI 110 028
AND PUBLISHED BY NARENDRA PRAKASH JAIN FOR
MOTILAL BANARSIDASS PUBLISHERS PRIVATE LIMITED,
BUNGALOW ROAD, DELHI 110 007

PREFACE TO THE FIRST EDITION

This edition of Śrī Harṣadeva's Priyadarśikā is prepared on the same lines as my editions of the Ratnāvalī and the *Nāgānanda* that have been already published, with a view to supply the University student with a text-book that will meet all his requirements. Care has also been taken to make the book useful to the general reader as well. A brief but sufficiently explanatory new commentary in Sanskrit has been added containing the solutions of difficult compounds, derivations of difficult words, etc. etc. Another feature of this edition is the Introduction wherein all that is necessary to be known about the author and the play has been succinctly put together for ready reference and systematic study. The figures of speech and the various technicalities of Sanskrit dramaturgy are not given (except in a few cases) as they are not of much use to the junior University students. I have used the editions of Jivananda Vidyasagar, V. D. Gadre (1884), Pandit R. V. Krisnamachariar (1906), T. V. Sreenivasachariar (1908) and that published by the Columbia University 1923; and I am beholden to the editors of all these for help of one kind or another derived from them, specially to those of the last mentioned work. My thanks are also due to Mr. L. S. Bhandare B.A.S.T.C. who helped me in writing out the later part of introduction. Any suggestions as to improvement etc. will be gratefully received.

Bombay
June, 1928.

M. R. KALE

CONTENTS

INTRODUCTION.

I THE SANSKRIT DRAMA.[1]

We shall begin with a brief outline of the general structure and arrangement of the Sanskrit Drama, without a knowledge of which the technical remarks on the construction of the present play here, as well as those made in the Notes, will not be intelligible to the general reader.[2] Poetry in Sanskrit, from its inherent nature, as apart from its intrinsic merit, is divided into two kinds—दृश्य 'what is capable of being seen or exhibited' and श्रव्य 'what can only be heard or chanted.' The drama falls under the first division. 'Rúpaka' is the general term in Sanskrit for all dramatic compositions, which also comprises a subordinate class called *Uparúpaka*. The Rúpaka,[3] which has Rasa or Sentiment for its substratum, is divided into ten classes, *viz.*, नाटकं सप्रकरणं भाणः प्रहसनं डिमः । व्यायोगसमवकारौ वीथ्यङ्केहामृगा इति ॥. Of the Uparúpakas or Minor Dramas there are eighteen species, the most important of which are *Nâṭikâs*, such as the Ratnâvalî, Viddhaśâlabhañjikâ &c., *Troṭakas* such as the Vikramorvaśiya, &c.

Having thus disposed of the divisions into which the whole of the scenic art is capable of falling, we turn to the principle of division among the *Rûpakas* themselves, which is

---

1 The first Section is the same as that prefixed to my ed. of the Ratnâvalî.

2 The information given here has been mainly culled from the Daśarûpaka. The minor particulars not noticed here will be found in my Sâhityasârasamgraha (Nir. Ed.).

3 अवस्थानुकृतिर्नाट्यं रूपं दृश्यतयोच्यते । रूपकं तत्समारोपाद्दशधैव रसाश्रयम् ॥ D.-R. रूप्यतेऽभिनयैर्यत्र वस्तु तद्रूपकं विदुः । नाटकाद्यैर्दशविधम्. *Nâṭya* is another and perhaps a wider term for the drama or the dramatic art, and is so called because it represents the different situations in (the scenes presented by) life. The sage Bharata is the founder of the science of music and dramaturgy and his work is styled the *Nâṭya Sâstra*. *Nâṭya* is also called *Rûpa* inasmuch as it has *dṛiś'yatâ* or the capability of being seen, and *Rûpaka* inasmuch as its subject-matter is represented by actors assuming particular characters.

threefold[1]—(1) वस्तु or the Plot of the play; (2) नेता or the Hero; and (3) रस or the Sentiment. These three are the essential constituents, nay, the very life-blood, of every dramatic piece. Each of these we shall succicly deal with in its order.

---

1 VASTU OR THE PLOT.

Vastu is primarily of two kinds: आधिकारिक or 'principal' and प्रासंगिक or 'accessary.' The Principal is that which relates to the chief characters or the persons concerned with the essential interest of the piece, and pervades the whole arrangement. The Accessary is that which appears in furtherance of the main topic, and is concerned with characters other than the Hero or the Heroine. This latter is of two kinds, *viz*., *Patâkâ* and *Prakarî*. *Patâkâ* or 'banner' is an episode by which the progress of the plot is illustrated, furthered or hindered (so as to give additional interest to it). It is of considerable length and sometimes extends to the very end of a play. The *Prakarî* is also an episodical incident—of limited duration and minor importance—one in which the principal characters take no part. Besides these two, there are three other elements requisite for the development of the plot. These are बीज or the seed, बिन्दु or the drop, and कार्य or the final issue. *Bija*[2] is the circumstance leading to the ultimate end briefly stated, which, as the plot develops, bears multifarious results and which is, as it were, the seed of the plot. *Bindu*[3] is what cements a break in the plot caused by the introduction of some other incident. *Kârya* is the final object of the plot which being attained the whole is finished. These five are technically called Arthaprakṛitis (अर्थप्रकृतयः).

The *Vastu*, which is thus divided into five classes, may again be divided into three classes according to the source of its derivation. It may be borrowed from history or tradition, or it may be fictitious, or mixed, *i. e.*, partly drawn from history and partly the creation of the poet's fancy. A *Nâṭaka* belongs to the first class, a *Prakarana* to the second.

As regards its development a dramatic plot has five stages or conditions called *Avasthâs*. They are (1) आरम्भ beginning

---

1 वस्तु नेता रसस्तेषां भेदकः ।.

2 स्वल्पोद्दिष्टस्तु तद्धेतुर्बीजं विस्तार्यनेकधा ।.

3 अवान्तरार्थविच्छेदे बिन्दुरच्छेदकारणम् ।.

or setting on foot of the enterprise,(2) यत्न effort, (3) प्राप्त्याशा prospect of success, (4) नियताप्ति certain attainment through the removal of obstacles, and (5) फलागम obtainment of the desired object. While these five stages are in progress there must be some links to connect them with the principal and subordinate parts of the main action (the episodes and incidents). These are called the *Samdhis* or junctures. They are five in number, answering to the five *Arthaprakritis*, each of which they join with its corresponding stage, *viz.*, मुख (Protasis or the opening juncture) प्रतिमुख (Epitasis). गर्भ (catastasis), अवमर्श (Peripeteia), and निर्वहण (Catastrophe), also called उपसंहृति or उपसंहार). Thus *Mukhasaṃdhi* is the combination of the Bîja and Ârambha, *i. e.*, wherein the seed is sown, so to speak, with all its *Rasas*. In the *Pratimukha* there is the means (*yatna*) to the chief end, as originally implied by the Bija in the Mukha which herein sprouts up. In the *Garbha* there is attainment and non-attainment of the desired end, implying a further sprouting up of the orginal Bîja. There are impediments, but the main plot gains ground under resistance. The *Avamarshasaṃdhi* is that in which the seed attains a more luxuriant growth than in the *Garbha*, being accompanied by *Niyatâpti* of the end, but whose final result is postponed further off by fresh impediments of various sorts, as in the Śàkuntala the King's forgetting Śak. after marriage owing to Durvásas' curse. The *Nirvahaṇa* or consummation is the harmonious combination of all the aforesaid parts in the final catastrophe.

The subject-matter, whether historical, fictitious, or mixed, is from its inherent nature capable of a twofold division. It is divided into (1) सूच्य–deserving to be suggested or implied only, as being of a dry and otherwise unfit character; and (2) दृश्यश्रव्य–fit to be represented and heard as being highly sentimental and pleasing. The suggestions or implications are made in five ways—विष्कम्भचूलिकाङ्कास्याङ्कावतारप्रवेशकैः।. (1) For *Vishkambha* see Notes, Act I. (2) *Chúlikâ* is the suggestion of some incident from behind the scenes (नेपथ्ये). (3) An अङ्कास्य[1] । is one wherein is suggested by the actors at the time of their departure the connexion between the Act finished and the one to be commenced, which otherwise would look disconnected, as the speech of Kámandakî and others at the

1 अङ्कान्तपात्रैरङ्कास्यं छिन्नाङ्कस्यार्थसूचनात् ।.

end of the 3rd Act of the **Mâl.-Mâdh.** (4) अङ्कावतार[1] consists in implanting the seed of the subject-matter of an Act in the previous Act before it has drawn to its close, so that the Act following is a continuation of the one preceding; *e. g.*, the sixth Act of the Śâk., the germ of which is cast at the end of the fifth Act; Mâlav. II. and Mâl.-Mâd. II, are other instances. (5) For प्रवेशक see notes Act IV.

The subject-matter is further divided into three kinds— सर्वश्राव्यं or प्रकाशं, अश्राव्यं or स्वगतं and नियतश्राव्यम्. The last is of two kinds, जनान्तिक and अपवारितक (अपवार्य which is explained in the Notes). Independent of these divisions there is one called आकाशभाषित (आकाशे) or Speech from the void.

The styles or modes of action (वृत्तयः) to be followed in a drama are four in number, *viz.* शृङ्गारे कैशिकी वीरे सात्वत्यारभटी पुनः । रसे रौद्रे च बीभत्से वृत्तिः सर्वत्र भारती ॥. Of these the Kaiśikî (used in the Nátiká) consists of music, dancing and love-sports, assisting the development of Śringára, and is delightful by that, and by the fascinating dresses worn by women. (See S. D., VI. 124). It has four *angas*, *viz.* (1) नर्म or polite pleasantry, (2) नर्मस्फूर्ज (०स्फञ according to D.-R.) or development of love, (3) नर्मस्फोट or the distant indication of love, and (4) नर्मगर्भ or covert action for the furtherance of love (यथा मालतीमाधवे सखीरूपधारिणा माधवेन मालत्या मरणव्यवसायवारणम्).

2 NETA OR THE HERO.

The Hero is required to be modest, decorous, comely, munificent, civil, of sweet address, eloquent, sprung from a noble family, &c.[2] Heroes are mentioned to be of four kinds, *viz.*, धीरोदात्त, धीरललित, धीरशान्त and धीरोद्धत. *'Dhîralalita,'* or Hero who is graceful and firm, is defined as निश्चिन्तो मृदुरनिशं कलापरो धीरललितः स्यात् (Sáh. D. III. 23) *i. e.*, one who is free from cares ever gentle and always given to the arts, like Vatsarâja. We are not concerned with the other three classes of Heroes

1 अङ्कावतारस्त्वङ्कान्ते पातोऽङ्कस्याविभागतः ।. The distinction, however, between an Ankâsya and an Ankâvatâra, is considered by some as merely imaginary. Viśvanâtha actually supplants the latter by Ankamukha which he defines as that where in one Act the substance of all the other Acts is suggested.

2 नेता विनीतो मधुरस्त्यागी दक्षः प्रियंवदः । रक्तलोकः शुचिर्वाग्मी रूढवंशः स्थिरो युवा ॥ बुद्ध्युत्साहस्मृतिप्रज्ञाकलामानसमन्वितः । शूरो दृढश्च तेजस्वी शास्त्रचक्षुश्च धार्मिकः ॥ भेदैश्चतुर्धा ललितशान्तोदात्तोद्धतैरयम् ॥.

here. Each of these Heroes may be of one or other of four sorts. He may be दक्षिण or 'gallant,' *i. e.*, equally devoted to many women, though principally attached to one; or शठ 'sly' *i. e.*, one who being attached to one lady, covertly acts in a way unpleasant to her; or he may be धृष्ट 'bold,' openly making his professions to another, and not ashamed even when reproached; or lastly he may be अनुकूल 'favourable,' devoted to one Heroine only. The धीरोदात्त Hero has eight manly qualities—शोभा, विलास, माधुर्य, गाम्भीर्य, धैर्य, तेजस्, लालित्य and औदार्य.

Among the assistants of the Hero the principal is पीठमर्द, the hero of the Patâkâ or episode, clever in discourse, devoted to his master, and a little inferior to him in qualities. Next comes the Vidûshaka, his constant companion, whose business consists in the repartees of wit, in helping his friend in his love-intrigues, and thus assisting in the general *dénouement* of the play. The third, and of equal rank with the Vidûshaka, is Viṭa, who knows one art only and is thereby useful to the Hero. The Hero thus equipped may still take into his service ministers of state and ministers of religion, ascetics, allies &c., as well as eunuchs, mutes, barbarians (Yavanas) &c. Sometimes there may be a Rival-Hero called प्रतिनायक who is avaricious, bold, impetuous, criminal and of evil conduct.

The Nâyikâ or the Heroine who must be possessed of qualities similar to those of the Hero is of three kinds. She may be the wife of the hero (स्वीया), as Sîta in the Uttar.; or one belonging to another (अन्या or परकीया), or a common woman (सामान्या or साधारणस्त्री) as Vasantasenâ in the Mṛich. The परकीया may be a maiden (so called because she is in the power of her guardian) or the wife of another. But the latter must not be introduced as the Heroine in a play[2]. The maiden's love, however, better helps the *rasa* and is, therefore, the most favourite theme with many Sanskrit poets. Further divisions and subdivisions of the *Nâyikâ* are not introduced here, as they have very little to do with the construction of the drama. For her assistants the Heroine

1 स्वान्या साधारणस्त्रीति तद्गुणा नायिका त्रिधा ।.

2 अन्यस्त्री कन्यकोढा च नान्योढाङ्गिरसे क्वचित्. "We may observe however, to the honour of Hindu drama, that the *Parakîyâ* or she who is the wife of another person, is never to be made the object of dramatic intrigue; a prohibition that would have sadly cooled the imagination, and curbed the wit, of Dryden and Congreve" Wilson: Select Specimens. Vol. I. p. 45.

may have a सखी, दासी, धात्रेयी, प्रतिवेशिका and others, possessing qualities corresponding to those of the friends of the Hero.

---

3 RASA OR SENTIMENT.

Rasa is that lasting impression of feeling produced to his overwhelming delight in a man of poetic susceptibility by the proper action of the *Vibhâvas*, and *Anubhâvas*, as well as the *Sâttvika* bhâvas and the *Vyabhichâribhâvas*[1]. Bhava (भाव)or 'feeling' is the complete pervasion of the heart by any emotion, whether of pleasure or of pain, arising from the object under sight. Vibhâva (विभाव) or an Excitant is that which being perceived nourishes the main sentiment. It is divided into (1) *A'lambana*, that which is, as it were, the support or substratum of the Rasa—the person or thing with reference to whom or which a sentiment arises—such as the Hero or the Heroine, and (2) *Uddîpana* or what excites or enhances(adds to the development of) the sentiment, such as the moon, the beauties of the vernal season, &c.; beauty, decorations, &c. of the principal characters, in the case of शृङ्गार. *Ânubhâva* or an Ensuant is the outward manifestation of the internal feeling through the eyes, face &c. The Sâttvika or natural *bhâvas* are a subdivision of *Anubhâva*, and are mentioned as eight in number—स्तम्भप्रलयरोमाञ्चाः स्वेदो वैवर्ण्यवेपथू । अश्रुवैस्वर्यमित्यष्टौ ।. The *Vyabhichâris* or the Accessaries are those *bhâvas* which are not strictly confined to any *Rasa*, but appearing and disappearing, like waves in the ocean, they serve as feeders to the prevailing sentiment and strengthen it in different ways. *Sthâyibhâva* (स्थायिभाव) or the Permanent Sentiment[2] of a composition 'is one—the ocean melting all salt into water—which not being interrupted by any sentiment contrary or akin to its nature occurring at intervals, converts all of them into its own nature.' Now a *Rasa* would prove contrary to another if the आश्रय or substratum of both were the same. But as अङ्गी (principal) and अङ्ग (subordinate) a रस may be mixed with one or more of others.

---

1 विभावैरनुभावैश्च सात्त्विकैर्व्यभिचारिभिः । आनीयमानः स्वाद्यत्वं स्थायी भावो रसः स्मृतः ॥ सुखदुःखादिकैर्भावैर्भावस्तद्भावभावनम् । ज्ञायमानतया तत्र विभावो भावपोषकृत् ॥ आलम्बनोद्दीपनत्वप्रभेदेन स च द्विधा । अनुभावो विकारस्तु भावसंसूचनात्मकः ॥.

2 विरुद्धैरविरुद्धैर्वा भावैर्विच्छिद्यते न यः । आत्मभावं नयत्यन्यान्स स्थायी लवणाकरः ॥.

There are eight Sthâyibhâvas, रति, हास, शोक, क्रोध, उत्साह, भय, जुगुप्सा, and विस्मय on which are based respectively the sentiments—शृङ्गार the Erotic, हास्य the Comic, करुण the Pathetic, रौद्र the Furious, वीर the Heroic, भयानक the Terrible, बीभत्स the Loathsome, and अद्भुत the Marvellous. There is a ninth sentiment, that of शान्त the Quietistic, having शम or tranquillity for its Sthâyibhâva. But it is not suited to dramatic purposes and rarely occurs as a main sentiment in a drama. Of these eight sentiments शृङ्गार and हास्य, वीर and अद्भुत, बीभत्स and भयानक, and रौद्र and करुण are akin to each other as they proceed from the same condition of the mind. As we are here mainly concerned with the Erotic, that being the prevailing sentiment in most Sans. plays, we will say something about it here. शृङ्गार is mainly divided into विप्रलम्भ or Love-in-separation and संभोग or Love-in-union. The former, the Daśarûpaka sub-divides into two kinds, अयोग the Non-consummation of marriage, and विप्रयोग the separation of the lovers deep in love after marriage. The former, which arises from the dependent position of one or the other of the parties or through distance or through the intervention of adverse fate, has ten stages, अभिलाष, चिन्ता &c. mentioned in the com.; विप्रयोग occurs through मान, प्रवास or some such cause; मान 'jealous anger,' arises from a breach in the duties of love (प्रणयभङ्ग) and may be on both sides (rarely, however, the Nâyaka is *Mânî*). This मान has several varieties, such as ईर्ष्यामान, आनुमानिकमान &c. It is capable of being dispelled in six ways: साम्ना भेदेन दानेन नत्युपेक्षारसान्तरैः—and is called गुरु, लघु or मध्यम according to the greatness or the smallness of the effort required to make the Nâyikâ give it up. संभोग is when the two lovers are in the enjoyment of each other's company, engaged in looking at each other, kissing each other, &c.

4 THE GENERAL CONDUCT OF THE NÂTAKA.

Every dramatic piece opens with a Prelude or Prologue (प्रस्तावना) which is itself introduced by what is called the *Nândî*. This *Nândî* according to some must suggest the gis. of the whole plot. The Sûtradhâra may sometimes retire after the recital of the Nândî, in which case another actor, called स्थापक (for he *establishes* as it were the topic of the play), takes his place. In the Prelude, which may begin with a brief allusion to the poet's literary attainments, his genealogy, &c., the Sûtradhâra or the Sthâpaka suggests the subject in the form of the Bîja, or by a simple beginning, or by naming the character about to enter, as in the Sâkuntala. He must please the audience with sweet songs descriptive of some season and couched in the Bhârâtî vṛitti. The प्रस्तावना is of two kinds—(1) प्ररोचना as in the Rat., and (2) आमुख, in which the Sûtradhâra holds conversation with the actress or his assistants, bearing on the subject to be introduced. This latter is of three kinds, of which one is प्रयोगातिशय. When the entry of a character is directly indicated by the Sûtradhâra, saying 'Here he enters,' that is Proyogâtiśaya.

The Prelude being over, the piece is commenced, being hereafter arranged and exhibited in the manner indicated in the three foregoing Sections. The whole matter should be well determined and divided into Acts and Scenes. A Nâṭaka may consist of from five to ten acts. The Hero should be of the Dhîrodâtta class. The Sentiment should be शृङ्गार or वीर (or sometimes करुण), others being introduced as conducive to its development. Nothing should be introduced into the play which either misbeseems the Hero or is discordant with the main sentiment. An Act must not be tiresomely long, should be full of *Rasa,* and introduced by *Vishkhambaka,* &c., according to necessity. Its close is marked by the exit of all characters. Such incidents as journeys, massacres, wars &c., should not be represented in a play; they may only be indicated. The death of the Hero must never be exhibited. This accounts for the somwhat monotonous character of Sanskrit plays, and the absence of tragedies in Sanskrit[1]. The play should end, as it began, with a Benediction or

1 Wilson observes—They (the Hindu plays) never offer a calamitous conclusion, which, as Johnson remarks, was enough to constitute Tragedy in Shakespeare's days; and although they propose to excite all the emotions of the human breast, terror and pity included, they never effect this object by leaving a painful impression upon the mind of the spectator. The Hindus in fact have no Tradegy.........The absence of tragic catastrophe in the Hindu dramas is not merely an unconscious omission; such a catastrophe is prohibited by a positive rule. The conduct of what may be termed the classical drama of the Hindus is exemplary and dignified. Nor is its moral purport neglected; and one of their writers declares, in an illustration familiar to ancient and modern poetry, that the chief end of the Theatre is to disguise, by the insidious sweet, the unpalatable, but salutary bitter, of the cup.

prayer, called the Bharatavâkya, which is repeated by the principal personage, not in his dramatic character but as a member of the dramatic party (भरत), and contains an expression of their wishes for general prosperity and happiness. The unity of interest or action must be maintained throughout.

As regards the language to be used in a piece, the Hero and the higher characters speak in classical Sanskrit, while females and the minor characters speak in the different Prákrit dialects.

The student will see from the foregoing sketch, that the characteristic peculiarities of the Indian Drama are mainly three—(1) Its peculiar structure; (2) the absence of the distinction between Comedy and Tragedy; and (3) the diversity of language to be spoken by the characters. The above-mentioned general characteristics of a Nâṭaka belong with certain modifications to the other divisions of the Rûpaka as well.

Of the Uparûpakas we are concerned here with the Nâṭikâ alone. We, therefore, give below its special features.

The Náṭikâ:—This is defined by the Sâhitya-Darpaṇa as:—नाटिका क्लृप्तवृत्ता स्यात्स्त्रीप्राया चतुरङ्किका । प्रख्यातो धीरललितस्तत्र स्यान्नायको नृपः ॥ स्यादन्तःपुरसंबद्धा संगीतव्यापृताथ वा । नवानुरागा कन्यात्र नायिका नृपवंशजा ॥ संप्रवर्तेत नेतास्यां देव्यास्त्रासेन शङ्कितः । देवी भवेत्पुनर्ज्येष्ठा प्रगल्भा नृपवंशजा ॥ पदे पदे मानवती तद्वशः संगमो द्वयोः । वृत्तिः स्यात्कैशिकी स्वल्पविमर्शाः संधयः पुनः ॥ The Nâṭikâ should be based on an invented story, should consist of four Acts, and abound in female characters. Its Hero should be an illustrious king and of the *Dhîralalita* class. The Heroine should be a maiden of royal family (or a celestial one)[1] newly touched with Love, and should be either connected with the inner apartment (as an attendant of the Queen), or engaged in musical performance. The Hero should proceed in his love affair cautiously from fear of the Queen. The Queen should be a grown up lady, bold, and also of royal family. She should display her indignation at every step, and the union of the lovers should depend on her consent. The Kaiśikî, with all its four parts, must be the *Vritti* employed, and of the *Sandhis* the Vimarsha should be partially introduced. The Das. R., however, does not sanction this. It says the Sandhis may be as in a Nâṭaka (कैशिक्यङ्गैश्च-

1 नायिका तादृशी मुग्धा दिव्या चाथ मनोहरा । अन्तःपुरादिसम्बन्धादासन्नाश्रुतिदर्शनैः ॥ *Das'a-Rúpka.*

तुर्भिश्च युक्ताङ्कैरिष नाटिका ।) The principal *Rasa* should be Śriṅgâra.[2] It should be named after the Heroine according to the precept नाटिकासट्टकादीनां नायिकाभिर्विशेषणम् ।

The points of difference between a Nâṭaka and a Náṭiká are-:—(1) The plot of a nâṭaka should be well-known, *i. e.* derived in its main features from history, while that of a Nâṭikâ should be mainly invented. (2) In the former the Hero is Dhîrodâtta, while in the latter he is Dhîralalita. (3) While a Náṭaka should have many males engaged in important affairs, the Nâtiká should have many females. (4) The former should have one principal sentiment, which may be either शृङ्गार or वीर, or करुण, while the latter should have शृङ्गार only. (5) A Náṭaka may consist of five, seven, or even ten Acts; a Nâtîkâ of *four* only.

II. THE POET.

(1) (*A Short Sketch of the Life of* Harsha *also called* Śri-Harsh or Harshavardhana)

A century after the destruction of the Gupta Empire by the inroads of the Hunas, it fell to the lot of a petty rájah of Tháneshwar, named Prabhakara-vardhana, to lay the foundation of a new great Hindu Empire in Northern India. Prabhákaras vardhana, by his victories over the Hunas, Gurjaras, Mâlvas, and others, rose to such a power in Hindustan that he assumed the title of Mahárājādhirājā Parambhattāraka' towards the close of the sixth century. He had two sons Râjya-vardhana and Harshavardhana, and a daughter named Râjyas'rî. Harshavardhana or Harsha was born about the year A. D. 590, 'in the month of Jyeshtha, on the twelth day of the dark fortnight, the Pleiads being in the ascendant, just after the twilight time.' Both the brothers grew up 'admantire' in the hardness of their frames and were trained in all the martial exercises of the time. In 604 A. D. when the Hunas again invaded the north-western frontier, the king sent his elder son, Rājyavardhana, to drive them away. Harsha accompanied his elder brother but engaged himself in hunting in the forests at the foot of the hills. In the meanwhile the king was suddenly seized with mortal illness and died. Harsha returned in time to be present by the

---

2 शृङ्गारोऽङ्गी सलक्षणः । D.–R.

bed-side of his dying father. Harsha's mother, Queen Yas'omatī immolated herself on the funeral pyre of her husband. Rājyavardhana who had defeated the Hunas, returned as soon as he heard of his father's death. He was at once proclaimed king though his own desire was to turn out an ascetic, leaving the throne to his younger brother. Misfortunes still dogged the footsteps of the two brothers. Their brother-in-law, Grahavarmā, the ruler of Kanauj, the husband of their sister Rājyas'rī, was slain in battle by the king of Malwa. The widowed queen was most cruelly treated and kept a prisoner at Kanauj. Rājyavardhana at once marched with a picked force against the king of Mālwa and succeeded in his campaign of vengeance by inflicting upon him a crushing defeat. But Rājyavardhana was lured into a private conference and treacherouly murdered by Sasāṃka, the King of Gauda (Central Bengal), the ally of the Malava King. The nobles unanimously chose Harsha as their sovereign and he assumed the reins of government in 606 A. D., a date which is marked as the beginning of the 'Harsha era.' Harsha, who was in deep grief owing to a succession of domestic misfortunes, accepted the throne with great reluctance. He did not assume the title of 'king' for some years, but called himself simply Rajaputra Sīliāditya (Sun of Virtue). Mr. C. V. Vaidya says that Harsha was not reluctant to ascend the throne of Thaneshwar but he had scruples to accept the throne of Kanauj, since the rightful heir to that throne was his widowed sister, Rājyaśri. Harsha was only sixteen when he assumed the responsibilities of governing a large kingdom. He had first two great duties to accomplish, the recovery of his widowed sister and avenging the murder of his elder brother. He succeeded in rescuing his sister who had fled into the Vindhya forests and was at this time contemplating suicide. She afterwards assumed the yellow robe and became the devoted companion and counsellor of her royal brother. As regards his second object of punishing Sasámka, king of Gauda, he seems to have succeeded in so far that he forced him to acknowledge his suzerainty. For nearly six years after his accession Harsha was engaged in incessant warfare with a view to bringing the whole of northern India under one domination. When Harsha had subjugated the whole of upper India, except the Punjab, he was formally crowned and assumed the title of Mahārajādhirája. For the next thirty-five years Harsha devoted most of his energy and time to the arts of peace and works of piety. But he did not enjoy complete peace or respite from war. In 620 A. D. he advanced against Pulakesin II, the great Chalukya king of the Deccan, but was defeated on the banks of the Narmadā. This was the only failure in Harsha's career of unbroken military successes. After this Harsha was content to accept the Narmada as his southern boundary. His last military exploit was the conquest of the district of Ganjam on the coast of the Bay of Bengal in 643. Harsha's empire at the time of his death extended on the west up to the Valabhi kingdom in Saurāshtra (Kathiawar) and on the east to the borders of Assam. Its southern boundary was the Narmadā while in the north it included the whole of upper India except the Punjab. His suzerainty was acknowledged by the powerful rulers of Kámarupa (Assam), Valabhî (Gujarat) and Nepal. His court became well known in distant Buddhist countries and he exchanged embassies with the Chinese Empire. Harasha was a strong, vigorous and benevolent ruler. Like Asoka he was indefatigable in the discharge of his duties and was always touring through his dominions, supervising the work of his servants. Education was widely diffused and Buddhistic monasteries at Naland and other places, and *ashramas* of learned sages were liberally endowed by the King. He built numerous monasteries and erected stupas in his dominions. He also built rest-houses throughout his dominions, where not only food and drink were provided to the people, but doctors attended upon the sick.

Harsha was naturally of a religious bent of mind and devoted several hours every day to religious exercises. He was originally a worshipper of Śiva but in the latter part of his life he was strongly inclined to Buddhism. His widowed sister Rájyasrî, who had embraced Buddihistic faith, exercised great influence on his mind. But he divided his patronage between Brahmanism and Buddhism and did not enforce his religious views on his subjects. He was tolerant of all faiths. He prohibited the slaughter of any living animal and the use of flesh as food on pain of death.

A Chinese pilgrim named Hsuan Chuang or Hieun Tsang, who visited India during the reign of Harsha, in quest of

Buddhistic scriptures, stayed in Harsha's dominions for 8 years (635–643). In his account of his travels this Chinese Buddhistic monk has graphically described the life and work of Harsha and the religious, social and political condition of India at the time. Harsha fell under the spell of Heun Tsang, in whose honour he held a grand assembly at Kanauj, the capital. The object of holding this assembly was to proclaim the doctrines of Mahayan Buddhism, as expounded by Hieun Tsang, called the Master of the Law. At the conclusion of this assembly Hieun Tsang was invited to another great assembly held at Prayāg at the confluence of the Ganga and Yamunā. This was the sixth of the quinquennial assemblies in which Harsha gave away his accumulated treasure to all the holy men of the various Indian religions, Buddhist, Bráhmanical, and Jain and to the poor and the destitute. It was Harsha's custom to give away freely his accumulated wealth every five years. This assembly held in 643 was the last, since Harsha did not live to hold another such celebration.

Harsha was not only a great warrior, an able administrator and organizor but also an accomplished scholar and man of letters. He wrote three plays, Priyadarsika, Ratnāvali and Náganand and a few minor poems. He was a most liberal patron of learned men and authors. Prominent among those who received patronage from Harsha and flourished at his court were the poets Báṇa and Mayura. Báṇa, in his historical romance 'Harsha-charita' has given an account of the early life and deeds of his patron. Harsha was also a master of calligraphy, as is evidenced from his signature inscribed on the well-known Banskhera plate.

Harsha chose the town of Kanauj for his capital and turned it into a magnificent city, adorned with lofty buildings, tanks and gardens.

This great monarch died in A. D. 648, worn out with the toils of constant warfare and the cares of governing a vast empire, before he had reached his sixtieth year. Harsha was the last great Hindu king of Northern India. He left no heir behind him and his empire broke up after his death.

2. Harsha as an Author.

(Controversies regarding his Authorship.)

The three plays, Ratnâvali, Priyadarśiká, and Nagānand are attributed to Shri Harsha or Harsha-deva of Kanauj. But Harsha's authorship has been questioned by some scholars Indian as well as European. In the first place some even doubt whether the same author wrote all the three plays. Now a perusal of the three dramas ought to lead every one to the conclusion that all the three plays are the product of the same mind. The prologues in the three plays are exactly the same in wording, barring slight variations necessitated by the fact of the plays being different. In the prologue of each play Shri Harsha-Deva is mentioned as the author of the play-श्रीहर्षदेवेन अपूर्ववस्तुरचनालंकृता रत्नावली नाम नाटिका कृता—श्रीहर्षदेवेन अपूर्ववस्तुरचनालंकृता प्रियदर्शिका नामनाटिका कृता—श्रीहर्षदेवेन अपूर्वरचनालंकृतं विद्याधरजातकप्रतिनिबद्धं नागानन्दं नाम नाटकं कृतम्. Besides the closing benedictory stansa in Priyadars'ika and Rátnâvalî is the same and two identical stanzas occur in Priyadarsiká and Nâgánanda (Priyandars'ikâ, III–3, Nāgānanda IV–1; Priya III. 10, Nāgā. I. 14). In addition to these we notice similiarity of style and tone, parallels in situations, repeated phrases and expressions which unmistakably prove the common authorship of the three plays.

Now the next question is who is this Śri-Harsha-Deva that is mentioned in the three plays ? Mr K. M. Pannikar in his monograph on Shri-Harsha of Kanauj mentions five Harshas as being known to ancient Indian History. The first is the half-mad tyrant of Káshmir who ruled that state from 1089–1101. The second is Shri-Harsha, the grand father of king Bhoja, of Dháránagar. The third is Vikramaditya Harsha of Ujjain, at whose court Mátṛgupta lived. The fourth is the author of Naishadhiya–Charîta, and the fifth, the author of Kávyapradipa.

(1) Harsha-Deva, King of Kâshmere cannot be conceived of being an author of any literary work, judging from his career and character. Besides no literary work is attributed to him. (2) Shri Harsha of Dhārānagar and grandfather of Bhoja lived in the earlier half of the 10th century. Damodar Gupta in his work called *Kuttanimata* gives at length the story of

Ratnávali, quotes the 24th verse of the 1st Act and praises it as a work of great merit.* Now this Damodar Gupta lived under Jayāpîda of Káshmir (A. D. 779–813). The play of Ratnávali seems to have been widely known at this time, that is, the eighth century. It is impossible, therefore, that a king who lived in the 10th century could have written a play which had become fairly old and attained celebrity in the 8th century. This argument can be advanced with equal strength against the authorship of Harsha-Deva, king of Kashmir.

(3) Vikramaditya Harsha of Ujjain cannot be the same as Shri-Harsha, the author of the three plays, because the latter is uniformly known as Harsha without the title Vikramáditya, If the author of the plays had possessed the title he would surely not have neglected to assume it. Besides Harsha Vikramáditya was an orthodox Bráhmana, while the author of the three plays shows a strong Buddhistic leaning in the Nāgānanda.

(4) (5) With regard to Shri Harsha, the author of Naishadhiya Charita, and Harsha, the author of Kâvyapradîpa, Mr. Pannikar dismisses them summarily on the ground that time places them out of the controversy. Harsha, the author of Naishidhîya Charita, who flourished under Jayachandra of Kanauj, lived about 1150 A. D. Among the works which he mentions as being composed by himself he does not mention any of these three plays. Besides his style, which is marked by crookedness of expressions, overstraining of words and distressing artificiality, is a marked contrast to the simple and elegant style of Ratnāvali and its sister plays. Besides Harsha of Naishadhîya-Charita was not a king but simply a poet who flourished under the patronage of the king of Kashmir and afterwards of the king of Kanauj; while the Harsha of Ratnàvali and its sister plays was a Sovereign Lord, 'with princes from various kingdoms dependent on his lotus-like feet.' See note or राजसमूहेन &c. p. 2.

Now there remains Shri Harsha or Harsha-vardhana of Kanauj (606–648 A. D.) A careful examination of both the external and internal evidence leads us irresistibly to

---

* आश्लिष्टसन्धिबन्धं सत्पात्रसुवर्णयोजितं सुतराम् ।
निपुणपरीक्षकदृष्टं राजति रत्नावलीरत्नम् ॥

the conclusion that this Shri Harsha of Kanauj must be the author of these plays. First, Bâṇa, a great court poet of Shri Harsha, in his biography of his master (हर्षचरित), speaks in eulogistic terms of his learning and poetical genius—"(1) काव्यकथास्वपीतममृतमुद्वमन्तम्" (2) "सर्वविद्यासंगीतगृहमिव सरस्वत्याः" &c. Allowing for the partiality of a protége for his patron and poetic exaggeration, it cannot be doubted that Shri Harsha was a scholar and author of some works. Secondly, the Chinese pilgrim I-tsing, who visited India in the last quarter of the 7th century, writes about king Shri Harsha, "King S'îladitya (*i.e.* King Harsha) was exceedingly fond of literature... ...He versified the story of the Bodhisatwa. Jimûtavāhana (Cloud-borne) who surrendered himself in place of a Nāga. This version was set to music (*lit.*—string and pipe); he had it performed by a band accompanied by dancing and acting, and thus popularised it in his time." (Takakusu, *I-tsing*, p. 163). This statement clearly shows that the author of the play Nāgānand is king Harsha, who lived in the 7th century. *Thirdly*, as we have pointed out before, Damodaragupta who flourished at the court of Jayāpida of Kâshmir (A. D. 779–813), quotes verses from Ratnāvali, and praises the play as a work of great beauty, in his work called Kuttanimata. The play is ascribed by him to a king, who, it is quite clear, must be Shri Harsha, who lived in the 7th century. *Fourthy*, Soddhala, who lived in the 11th century A. D., in his Udayasundarikathá, mentions Harsha along with Vikramáditya, Munja, and Bhoja, as being both भूपाल (king) and कवीन्द्र (prince of poets) presiding over a literary court (सभा). In another passage Soddhala punningly refers to Harsha (Joy) as 'the glorious Harsha' (श्रीहर्ष) whose 'joy lay in words (श्रीहर्ष) in his own assembly (निजसंसदि). The passage runs as follows:–श्रीहर्षेत्यवनिवर्तिषु पार्थिवेषु नाम्नैव केवलमजायत वस्तुतस्तु। गीहर्ष एष निजसंसदि येन राज्ञा संपूजितः कनककोटिशतेन बाणः॥ *Fifthly*, the famous poet Jayadeva, who lived in 11th century A. D. mentions Harsha as a poet with the earlier poets Bhāsa and Kālidās, and with his contemporaries Bāṇa and Mayúra. He punningly calls Harsha the joy of Poetry. Sixthly, Madhusudan the editor of Mayûra S'ataka, writing about A. D. 1654, says that Bâṇa and Mayúra were the court poets of Shri-Harsha and calls Harsha 'The chief of the race of poets and the author of the Nātikâ called Ratnávalî., Sixthly, in several Sanskrit anthologies, such as

'Subbāshitúvatî' and 'Sādhûktikarnāmrta' stanzas under the name of Harsha are quoted. Seventhly, there are epigraphic records which prove that Harsha was an author who not only wrote dramas, but also stray verses. The inscriptions on the well-known Banskhera and Madhuban plates are indisputably his own compositions. In the Banskhera plate (628 A. D.) which bears Harsha's own signature we find—"It is the own hand of me, the Paramount Lord, the Glorious Harsha (स्वहस्तो मम महाराजाधिराज-श्री-हर्षस्य)." Among the verses inscribed on the plates. there is one which is very beautiful and runs thus :—कर्मणा मनसा वाचा कर्तव्यं प्राणिने हितम् । हर्षेणैतत् समाख्यातं धर्मार्जनमनुत्तमम् ॥ Lastly, two short Sanskrit poems on Buddhistic spirit are attributed to Harsha. One of these is named, सुप्रभातस्तोत्र, a morning hymn in praise of the Buddha and the other is called अष्टमहाश्रीचैत्यसंस्कृतं स्तोत्र, a hymn to the eight Great Buddhist Shrines. These poems thoroughly harmonize with Harsha's acceptance of Buddhistic doctrine in the latter part of his life.

It is, however, necessary, to mention and refute the theories started by some scholiasts that Harsha did not himself write these plays but got them written for him by a court poet of his, who was amply rewarded for his labour. This theory is based upon a sentence in the Kâvyaprakāsha of Mammata, who lived about 1100 A. D. Mammata speaking of काव्य or poetry says that it leads to the acquisition of wealth, as in the case of Dhāvaka and others from Shri Harsha and the like—श्रीहर्षादेर्धावकादीनामिव धनम् ।. Several commentators have interpreted this text to mean that a poet, Dhāvaka wrote a play by name Ratnâvalî for Shri-Harsha and obtained wealth from him. The commentator Nâgoji Bhatta comments on the sentence thus.—धावकः कविः । स हि श्रीहर्षनाम्ना रत्नावलीं कृत्वा बहु धनं लब्धवानिति प्रसिद्धम् । " In the manuscripts of काव्यप्रकाश found in Kâshmir, the passage is read thus:—'श्रीहर्षादेर्बाणादीनामिव धनम." The original text of Mammata, "श्रीहर्षादेर्धावकादीनामिव or "श्रीहर्षादेर्बाणादीनामिव धनम्'' if interpreted naturally without reading into it any pre-conceived idea, would mean that poets like Dhâwaka or Bâṇa obtained wealth from their patron, Shri Harsha, for their literary works. In other words these poets were liberally rewarded by their patron, King Harsha. This interpretation is natural and correct and is in conformity with the tradition which ascribes Ratnāvalî and its sister plays to Shri Harsha. The interpretation of the commentators, who lived several centuries after the dramas had been written, does not satisfy a historical or critical test. There is no positive evidence in favour of the statement that Dhāvaka is the author of Ratnâvalî. No literary work under the name of Dhāvaka has come down to us. Besides nothing is known about Dhāvaka. So the theory that Dhāvaka is the author of Ratnâvalî is not tenable in the face of the overwhelmingly strong evidence in favour of the authorship of Harsha of Ratnâvalî and his other two plays. Another theory, that Báṇa is the author of Ratnâvalî is based on the variant reading of the passage in Kâvyaprakâsa; "श्रीहर्षादेर्बाणादीनामिव धनम्" This theory which was set forth by Dr. Hall in his introduction to Vāsavadattā is not tenable either. In the first place Báṇa's style, as it is seen in his great works, Kâdambarî and Harsacharita is quite dissimilar to that of Ratnāvalî. Besides Ratnâvalī nowhere betrays that high kind of poetry which is abundantly seen in Kādambarī or Harshacharita. It is also difficult to believe that Bāṇa sold Ratnāvali of all his works when he could have struck a much better bargain by selling his Kādambarî. Then again it has been proved that the author of Ratnāvali is also the author of Nāgânanda and it is impossible that Baṇa who was a strict Brâhmaṇa wrote Nágānanda which glorifies the Buddhistic doctrine. There is yet another theory which attributes these plays to Bhāsa, who is praised by Kâlidâsa and whose plays have been recently discovered and published. This theory was first propounded by Mr. Nârâyan Shâstri of South India and afterwards upheld by Prof. S. M. Paránjpe of Poona. Mr. Shâstri bases his theory on a passage from the कविविमर्ष of राजशेखर. But as the passage quoted by him seems to be spurions and its authenticity cannot be proved, his theory based upon it topples down. Mr. Paránjpe does not rely on this passage but argues independently to prove that Bhása is the real author of Nāgānanda and the other two plays. His whole position is based upon some parallel ideas, similar grammatical peculiarities and literary devices, which he has picked out from Bhása's plays and the two plays Nāgānand and Priyadārśiká. But mere similiarity of ideas and sentiments, and of grammatical and literary peculiarities has little value unless it is supported by other convincing arguments. Parallel ideas, and parallel literary devices or peculiarities even occur in the works of authors belonging to different ages and to different countries. So this argument of similar ideas, and of similar grammatical and literary peculiarities is not sound, especially when we find that the style of Bhāsa is widely different from the style of Priyadarśiká and its sister plays. The style of Bhása is crude and is not elegant or graceful; while the style of Ratnāvalî and its sister plays is refined and graceful. The plays of Bhása evidently belong to a more distant age. The similarity of ideas &c. can be explained on the ground that the author of Ratnāvali and the two plays might have read Bhása's plays, as he did Kálîdásás also, and tried to imitate him in certain points. So this theory about Bhāsa's authorship of the three plays in question, is also untenable. See also our Introd. to the Ratnâvalî.

We have thus disposed of all the theories about the authorship of the three plays, Priyadarsikā, Ratnāvali, and Nāgānand. We have also examined the internal as well as the external evidence that is available to us and we are led to the irresistible conclusion that Shri Harsha of Kanauj, who reigned from 606–648 A. D., is the author of Ratnāvali and the other two plays.

---

(3) HARSHA AS A POET AND DRAMATIST.

Harshás merits as a poet and dramatist are certainly great. But he can be placed only in the second class among Sanskrit authors. Like many other playwrights he does not show originality in the invention of the plots of his dramas nor great skill or delicacy in the portraiture of character. But he shows considerable skill in the creation of incidents and situations necessary for dramatic effect* He has neither the imagination, the fancy and the grace of Kâlidâsa, nor Bhavabhûti's loftiness of thought and depth and force of passion. As a dramatic artist and master of the language also he is inferior to either of them. But he has the great merit of simplicity of expression and thought. His style is free from the artificiality, overstraining of words, exaggeration of thought and sentiment, which characterise later Sanskrit literature. His Sanskrit is elegant and precise and his use of figures of speech and thought, is on the whole restrained and in good taste. Coming as he does after Kàlidása

* See *infra*. our remarks on the source of the plot

he does not, altogether escape the temptation to use long and difficult compounds and alliterations, *cf.* for instance Vidû.'s speech at p. 6, the passage and अविरतपतद्विविध कुसुमस्तबकभारशिलातलोत्सङ्गस्य &c. in the description of the palace, garden *Priyadarsika*, Act II. And for alliterations the stanzas, 'पाताले पत्तिरेव प्रथमतरमुरःक्षेपमात्रेण पिष्टा &c. (*Ibid* Act. I. 5); 'उर्वीमुद्दामसस्यां जनयतु विसृजन् वासवो वृष्टिमिष्टामिष्टैस्त्रैविष्टपानां &c.' (*Ibid* Act IV. 12); and for the jingling collocation of words, लीलामङ्गलमज्जनोपकरणस्नानीयसम्पादिनः (Ibid Act I, II); क्षामां मङ्गलमात्रमण्डनभृतं मन्दोद्यतालापिनीम् ; *Ibid*, Act, II, 1. He also occasionally indulges in puns, as घनबन्धनमुक्तोऽयं कन्याग्रहणात् परं तुलां प्राप्य &c. *Ibid*, Act I–5 ; घनबन्धनसंरुद्धं गगनं दृष्ट्वा मानसं नेतुम्—*Ibid*, III –8. For instances from the Rat. see our Introd. to the play, p. 32. Harsha's descriptions of gardens, the forest, the fountain, the mountain, the spring festival, the evening, the mid-day &c. are admirable. He undoubtedly took Kâlidâsa for his model, as is evidenced from many reminiscences of that great master in his plays. He has copied several ideas, literary devices and situations from Kalidasa's plays, most of which have been pointed out in the notes. Harsha calls himself a skilful poet (निपुणः कविः) and we think that his estimate of his own merits is correct. His place is among the second-rate poets and dramatists in Sanskrit literature.

II THE PLAY.

1. The Plot of the Priyadarsiká.

The Priyadarśikâ is a romantic comedy in four acts and is named after the Heroine, the daughter of Dṛdhavarman, king of Anga, as required by the rules of dramaturgy. To enable the student to understand the story of the play before he reads the text we give its general outline below.

Act I—The chamberlain of Dṛdhavarman, king of Anga. appears and narrates a series of events. From his narration we learn that Dṛdhavarman, had a very beautiful daughter whose hand was repeatedly sought by the king of Kalinga. But Durdhavarman promised her in marriage to king Vatsa of Kauśâmbî. Stung by the rejection, the Kalinga-king made war upon Dṛdhavarman, ravaged his kingdom, and made him his captive. Dṛdhavarman's daughter Priyadarśikā is carried in safety by her father's faithful chamberlain and placed in charge of his ally, Vindhyaketu king of the Vindhya forest. The chamberlain then goes to bathe at a holy place close by; but on his return finds that Vindhyaketu has been attacked and slain by some unknown enemy. The whole region is consigned to flames and no trace of the princess, Priyadarsikā, is to be found. The chamberlain further says that he has learned that king Vatsa, who had been held a prisoner by king Pradyota of Avanti, has escaped, carrying off the latter's daughter, Vāsavadattā with him. The chamberlain then declares his intention of going to his master Dṛdhavarman and serving him. The next scene is at King Vatsa's palace at Kauśāmbî. The King appears with his companion, the Vidûshaka. While they are talking Rumanvat, the minister, and Vijayasena, the cammander-in-chief, arrive. Vijayasena, who had been sent to attack the forest-king, Vindhyaketu, gives an account of his victory, not omitting to mention how bravely and desperately Vindhyaketu fought and fell like a true soldier. He then informs the king that he has brought with him as a captive, a beautiful maiden, supposed to be Vindhyaketû's daughter, who was found lamenting in his palace. The King at once gives orders that the girl be placed in charge of his queen Vāsavadattā, and instructed in all the arts befitting her high rank. He further directs that he should be reminded when the girl attains marriageable age. As the Act closes the King expresses his intention of sending Vijayasena to extirpate the King of Kalinga

Act. II —Queen Vàsavadattá is observing a vow attended with a fast. The king, who is temporarily deprived of the Queen's company, goes to the palace-garden with his companion, Vasantaka, to divert his longing. While walking there he happens to see A'raṇyikā who has come there at the command of the Queen in the company of one of the Queen's attendants Indîvarikā, to gather lotuses for an offering to be presented to the sage Agastya. The king is struck with her matchless beauty and hides himself with his companion behind a cluster of trees to overhear the conversation between the two girls. From their conversation the King learns that the beautiful maiden is the daughter of Vindhyaketu, who has now attained marriageable age. In the mean-while A'raṇyikā is assailed by bees, rushing out of the cluster of lotuses which she was plucking. She covers her face with her upper garment and cries out to Indîvarikā for help. Indîvarikā was at some distance away from her. So Vasantaka advises the King to run to her rescue. The King does so and gets an opportunity of embracing her. But Instead of remaining silent he addresses her in a flattering stanza. A'raṇyiká, who supposed that she had been helped by Indivariká, is startled to find that her rescuer is king Vatsa. She is, however, glad to find that it was he to whom her father had promised her in marriage. She, however, calls to Indîvarikā in alarm and when the latter comes the King has to go away and hide himself. Âranyikā departs with her companion, with a sad heart, smitten with love. The king too departs, full of deep longing and anxious to meet again the object of his new love.

Act III.—We learn from the monologue of a female attendant named Manoramā that a little play composed by Sâmkṛtyāyanî, a learned friend of Queen Vâsavadattâ, is to be performed for the amusement of the Queen. The play represented an episode in the courtship of Queen Vásavadattā and King Vatsarâja. A'raṇyikā is to play the part of Queen Vásavadattā and the Queen's attendant, Manoramā, is to appear in the role of King Vatsa. Manoramá while searching for A'raṇyîkā in the garden finds her in her love-sick condition. She overhears A'raṇyikā lamenting her hopeless passion for the King. Monoramá tries to cheer her up. At this very moment the Vidūshaka arrives there in search of A'raṇyikā by the King's command The two maidens overhear the King's confidant and learn of the King's passion for A'raṇyikā. In the conversation that follows between the Vidushaka and Manoramā, the latter whispers to him a device for bringing about the meeting of the lovers. Next comes the scene of the Mimic play. It is to be performed in the play-house attached to the palace. The Queen with her attendants and Sámkṛityáyanî comes to witness the play. A'raṇyikā appears in the role of the Queen. But Manoramā does not play the part of the King. For according to the device made known to the King through his companion, it is arranged that the King shall play his own part instead of Manoramā's playing it. The King then enters secretly and begins to act his part in the Mimic play. In playing his part he makes advances to

Araṇyikā in such a manner as to rouse the suspicion of the Queen. The Queen rises from her seat in a fit of displeasure unable any longer to witness acting of that kind and goes out. She finds Vasantaka who has been asleep in the adjoining room. Thinking that the King may also be there, she rouses him, when he reveals the truth in his drowsiness. The Queen thus comes to know the whole trick and in her anger breaks up the play. She then orders both A'raṇyikā and Vasantaka to be imprisoned and departs without listening to the apology of the King.

Act IV.—Manoramá enters and is sorely grieved to see that A'rṇyikâ has still been kept confined by the relentless Queen. The poor girls she says is in deep despair, not because of the hardships of the prison, but because she is not able to see the King. Just then Káuchanmālā, the Queen's attendant, enters and informs Manoramâ that the Queen has been in deep distress since she received a letter from her mother, Angáravatî, informing her that King Dṛdhavarman, husband of her mother's sister, has been held a captive for more than a year by the Kalinga King, and taunting her for King Vatsa's not having lifted a finger to rescue him. In the next scene Vâsavadattâ appears, seated in the ivory-tower of the palace, attended by Sâmkṛtyāyanî The latter tries to comfort the sorrowful Vâsavadattá, assuring her of the faithful affection of the king. At this time the King enters with the Vidûshaka, talking about the means of conciliating the Queen and setting A'raṇyikâ free from her captivity. He approaches Vásavadattá and tries to appease her. Being informed by Sámkṛtyáyanî of the real cause of the Queen's sorrow, the king informs her of the expedition sent by him against the Kalinga king and how the latter's armies have been defeated and how he expects shortly to hear of the complete overthrow and destruction of Kalinga. At this moment Vijayasena, the victorious general, and the chamberlain of Dṛdhavarman are announced. The chamberlain informs the king how Vijayasena defeated and slew the accursed king of Kalinga in battle and restored his master Dṛdhavasman to his kingdom. He then narrates how Dṛdhavarman's daughter Priyadarsiká is lost and no trace of her can be found. At this moment Manoramá hurriedlty enters with the sad news that A'raṇyikā has drunk poison. On hearing this Vásavadattá is smitten with penitence and at once orders her to be brought before the king who with his knowledge of magic spells, will save her life. A'ranyiká is then brought on the stage in a dying condition. The Chamberlain recognizes her and tells Vásavadattá that she is the lost Priyadarśikâ, the daughter of his master, king Dṛḍhavarman. King Vatsa repeats his magic formulas which counteract the effect of the poison and A'ranyiká is gradually restored to life. Vásavadattà is delighted to find that A'ranyikâ, who is no other than her cousin Priyadarśikā, also called Priyadarśaná is restored to life. She then places her cousin's hand in the hand of the King to indicate that she is his lawful wife, in accordance with the promise of Dṛḍhavarman. The play thus ends happily with the customary benedictory stanza, praying for universal peace, prosperity and contentment.

---

(2) The Sources of the Plot of the Play.

The plot of the Priyadarśiká, in its general outline, is derived from the semi-legandary life of King Udayana as given in the Bṛhatkathá of Gunâdhya. The story of the loves of Udayana, king of Kauśamî, also called Vatsarája, and Va'savadatta and of his romantic adventures, seems to have been exceedingly popular in ancient India, judging from the fact that it has been referred to and turned to literary account by many Sanskrit poets. It is referred to by Kâlidasa in his Meghaduta,—"प्राप्यावन्तीनुदयनकथाकोविदग्रामवृद्धान् and प्रद्योतस्य प्रियदुहितरं वत्सराजोऽत्र जह्रे; and by Śudraka in his Mrichchakatika, —यौगन्धरायण इवोदयनस्य राज्ञः. Bhása, one of the earlier poets, has taken the love intrigues of Udayana for the theme of two of his plays—स्वप्नवासवदत्त and प्रतिज्ञायौगंधरायण. Subandhu in his well-known Vásavadattā, deals with the adventures of Udayana in the acquisition of Vásavadattá. In the कथासरित्सागर of सोमदेवभट्ट, who lived in the 11th century, the story of उदयन is related at length. Udayana was the son of Sahasra'nîka (see note on Vatsara'ja p. 3). Sahasrânîka married Mṛgávatî, the daughter of Kṛtavarman, king of Ayodhyâ. When Mṛgávatî was pregnant, she had a desire to bathe in a pond of blood-water. While bathing she was snatched away by a bird of the race of Garuda and left on the Rising-mountain. A young sage saw her there lamenting and took her to the hermitage of the sage Ja'madagnya. There she gave birth to her son, Udayana, who was taken care of by Jámadagnya there. Udayana while still a boy, once rescued the serpent Vasunemi, the elder brother of Vāsuki, from a snake-charmer. The serpent, in gratitude, took Udayana to Pa'tala and bestowed upon him a lute and some unfading garlands and brought him back to Jámadagnya's hermitage. Udayana after his accession to the throne indulged too much in hunting, especially in taming wild elephants by the music of his lute Ghosavati. He set his heart upon marrying Vásavadattá, daughter of the powerful king चण्डमहासेन (also called प्रद्योत) of Ujjain and his queen Angáravatî. Chanda. also wished to bestow his daughter in marriage on Vatsa. But the enmity between the two kings prevented such a union, by negotiations. Afterwards चण्डमहासेन had Udayana seized and brought captive by a stratagem to Ujjain. He was kindly treated and ordered to teach music to Vàsavadattā. Thus Udayana had an opportunity of making love to Vásavadattá. But he was a prisoner all the same. His astute minister योगंधरायण contrived a plan of rescuing his royal master and one night Udayana fled away with Vásavadattá who had been won over to him without her father' knowledge, and safely came to Kaus'ambî. In the बृहत्कथामञ्जरी of Kshemedra, written also in the eleventh century, the story of Udayana occurs and differs little from that related in the Kathásaritságara. The only variation is that young Udayana was taken to Pa'tala by the serpent whom he had rescued and there he married a Na'ga-damsel (नागकन्या) and obtained the lute Ghoshavatî.

Now the episode in Udayana's courtship of Vásavadattá' which is dramatised in the Embryo—Act, agrees with what is related in the Kathá.; but the episode which forms the theme of the present play, *viz.* the love of Udayana and A'ranyiká, a captive princess, the daughter of the forest King Vindhyaketu, is not mentioned in the story of Udayana as related in the कथासरित्सागर. But the love intrigue of Udayana with a captive princess, Bandhumatî, which is briefly mentioned in the कथासरित्सागर, resembles the plot of the Priyadarsiká. We quote from the कथासारित्सागर the following passage relating to Bandhumatî :—

किंच बन्धुमतीं नाम राजपुत्रीं भुजार्जिताम् ।
गोपालकेन महितां कन्यां देव्या उपायनम् ॥

तथा मञ्जुलिकेत्येव नाम्नान्येनैव गोपिताम् ।
अपरामिव लावण्यजलवेरुद्धृतां श्रियम् ॥

वसन्तकसहायः सन्दृष्ट्वोद्याने लतागृहे ।
गान्धर्वविधिना गुप्तमुपयेमे स भूपतिः ॥

तच्च वासवदत्तास्य ददर्श निभृतस्थिता ।
प्रचुकोप च बद्धा च सा निनाय वसन्तकम् ॥

ततः प्रव्राजिकां तस्याः सखीं पितृकुलागताम् ।
स सांकृत्यायनीं नाम शरणं शिश्रिये नृपः ॥

सा तां प्रसाद्य महिषीं तया सैव कृताज्ञया ।
ददौ बन्धुमतीं राज्ञे पेशलं हि सतीमनः ॥

ततस्तं बन्धनाद्देवी सा मुमोच वसन्तकम् ।
स चागत्याग्रतो राज्ञीं हसन्निव जगाद ताम् ॥*

(Katháṣaritsāgara II. 6. 67-73.)

But neither the कथासरित्सागर nor the बृहत्कथामञ्जरी can be the source from which Harsha derived his plot of the *Priyadarsika*, since these two works, which are professedly abridgements of the बृहत्कथा, were written in the eleventh century, while our author lived in the 7th century. Moreover we know that the story of उदयन was known to old writers like कालिदास and सुबंधु and even to more ancient writers like Sudraka and Bhasa. The source from which all these authors derived their knowledge of the history of Udayana Vatsarája must, therefore, have been an ancient work, called बृहत्कथा, composed by गुणाढ्य who lived about the 1st century A. D. This बृहत्कथा or the large collection of stories was written in the पैशाची language (a low Prákrit dialect) and consisted of one *lakh* of verses. This great work was the inexhaustible storehouse of stories, from which many Sanskrit writers like Bhása, Kálidas, Bána, Shri-Harsha, Bhavabhûti, and others, derived the plots of their works. The original बृहत्कथा is not available at present but we have two excellent summaries of it, the बृहत्कथामञ्जरि by क्षेमेन्द्र and the कथासरित्सागर by सोमदेव, which we have mentioned

*The King in the passage is Udayana, the sovereign of the Vatsas, the Queen is his consort Vâsavadattâ, Gopâlaka is her brother, and Vasantaka is the King's merry companion.

above*. The story of Bandhumatî resembles that of Priya-dars'ikā, as the student can see from the passage from the कथासारित्सागर quoted above, the names उदयन, वत्सराज, वसन्तक, वासवदत्ता and साङ्कृत्यायनी, being common to both. Hence we conclude that Harsha took for his basis the meagre story of Bandhumatî, perhaps written in greater detail in the बृहत्कथा, and worked it up into the present charming play.

---

(3) Time Analysis of the play.

The action of the Priyadarśiká covers a period of a little over a year, from the autumn (शरद्) of one year to the autumn of another. For we are told in the *Vishkambhaka* of the first Act by the chamberlain of Dṛdhavarman, the king of the Anga country, that his master was already a captive of the king of Kalinga; and from the closing speech of the same chamberlain we learn that the season of the year is autumn; for he speaks of the uncommon severity of the autumnal heat and of the sun having passed from the zodiacal sign virgo to libra. From thiswe know that the month was A'svina, in which generally the sun is in libra. And we learn from the message sent by the Queen Angáravatî to her daughter Vâsavadattâ (see p. 46) some days after the events of the third act which happened on the full moon-day of Aśvina that it was more than a year since Dṛdhavarman was taken a captive. So the action of the play spreads over a period of a year and a few days more.

Act I. It is not possible exactly to fix the time of the action of the 1st Act. It begins in the forenoon of some day in the mouth of A'śvina some two hours before noon as the Act closes at mid-day (see Śl. 12). The King is introduced as holding conversation with his companion Vasantaka some day after his escape from prison and return

---

* There is also a third and a more faithful abridgement, which is also earlier, of the Bṛhatkathá, known as the Bṛhatkathá's'loka-sangraha, by one, Buddhasva'min. It is, however, incomplete, only 28 cantos being extant. In this also the events connected with the birth and early years of Udayana are narrated including his visits to the city of the Serpents and his acquisition there of the magic lute, Ghoshavatî and of the art of taming elephants. Col. U. Ed. Introd. pp. lxx, lxxi.

to Kausambî with Vásavadattâ. We learn from this conversation that Vatsarâja was incensed when he heard that Dṛdhavarman was taken prisoner and kept in custody by the King of Kalinga. So the news of Dṛhavarman's captivity must have reached Kaus'ambî by the time the Kaṇchuki in the Vishkambhaka reaches Vindhyaketu's capital. Again in the same scene when Vijayasena narrates the account of his conquest and utter destruction of Vindhyaketu, we are told that he reached the abode of Vindhyaketu after a forced march of three days and that the attack was made at day-break. And we know from the speech of the Kanchukî in the Vis'kambhaka that all was over by the time he returned to Vindyaketu's place from Agastya–tirtha where he had gone to bathe and that no trace of the attackers was found. So it follows that the battle was of short duration and Vijayasena, had left the place by or shortly after noon.; for when the Kanchukî arrived on the scene the sun was still very hot. Now Vijayasena must have taken at least three days to return to Kaus'ambî, so that he must have reched it on the seventh day from his starting from it. So the events mentioned in the Viskambhaka, *viz.* Vindhyaketu's destruction, the loss of the princess and the Chamberlain's resolve to go back to his captive master, must have taken place four days before the events of the first act.

Act II. An interval of at least one year (or more) separates the events of the first Act from those of the second; and for the following reasons. (1) It is clearly said in the Praves'aka of the fourth Act that Dṛdhavarman was in custody for more than one year; and this interval can only be placed between the first two Acts, as the third and the fourth Acts follow pretty closely upon the second. (2) From the conversation between Indîvarikâ and A'raṇyikâ we learn that a great intimacy had grown up between them. Again from the same conversation we further learn of the Queen's intention to inform the King that A'raṇyikâ had reached marriageable age, in accordance with his own bidding that he should be reminded when she reached that age. And in the same scene when the King sees A'raṇyikâ and discovers that she is Vindyaketu's daughter he exclaims—" Oh we have long been robbed." All this points to a long interval. (3) From the King's description of the beautiful scene presented by the garden attached to the Dhárágṛha and the tank in it, it is clear that autumn had just set in ; and that can be the autumn of the next year. The time of action of the second Act therefore, is some day in A'svina, as is evident also from the Queen's observing a fast in honour of the great sage Agastya and her intention to give a Svastiváyana on that occasion which is done after Bhâdrapada, (see p. 24 and com. thereon,) and the events mentioned therein take place late in the afternoon, as it is sunset when the King retires to his palace after his unexpected meeting with A'raṇyiká.

Act III—opens with the entrance of Manoramâ, rather late in the afternoon of the full-moon-day of A'svina. For in her speech Manoramâ tells us that the remaining portion of the play composed by Sâmkṛtyáyanî is to be acted before the Queen on the Kaumudi festival, which falls on the fifteenth day of A's'vina, and that her friend A'raṇyiká being absent-minded committed a mistake in her acting on the day. A'raṇyiká then enters and appears from her conversation with her confidante Mañoramaâ to have been deeply affected with love for the King and pining for his company day and night. And from the lips of the Vidúshaka who enters next we learn that the King also is love-sick, passes his nights sleeplessly and finds pleasure in nothing but devising means to obtain a sight of A'rnyika'. This shows that we must allow a period of five or six days at least to intervene between the second and the third Acts to account for the deep impression made on the minds of the lovers by each other's sight at their first meeting. When Manoramâ sees Vasantaka and learns from him how helpless his friend was on account of her friend A'ranyiká, she tells him how their meeting was to be brought about that very night when the acting was to be performed before the Queen. Vidûshaka then leaves her, and she starts to go to the play-house with A raṇyiká, and by the time they enter it, the twilight is already past (अतिक्रान्ता खलु सन्ध्या p. 31). So the action of the third Act begins late in the afternoon of the day and ends when it is bed time, after the breaking up of the Mimic play, by the Queen. See p. 44, King's speech.

Act IV. A few days' interval separates the fourth Act from the third. For in the opening speech of Manoramá she complains of the Queen's long continued anger and of the hardships of confinement to which her friend has been subjected.

This shows that A'ranyikâ was in prison for some days. Again from the conversation between Sâmkrityâyanî and Vâsavadattá we learn that the A'ranyiká-love affair was a recent event. And Vidūshaka's humorous suggestion to the King to observe a month's fast to gain the Queen's favour and his words further on इदानीमेव बन्धनात्कथमपि परिभ्रश्यागतोस्मि p. 40, show that not many days, even a week, could have elapsed after the events of the 3rd Act. So the interval separating the third from the fourth Act must be a very short one. But we have no means of determining the exact hour of the day when the action of the fourth Act begins. It lasts for a period of about three hours.

(4) Geography of the Play.

See Notes p. 49.

(5) Technical remarks.

It will be easily seen that the Priyadarsikà does not closely follow the various canons found in the Sans. treatises on dramaturgy, such as the Daśarupaka and the Sâhityādarpana, as the Ratnávalî does. The Sandhis are not elaborated and well proportioned. The Sringâraraso, the main sentiment of the play, is not well developed in its two parts विप्रलम्भ and संभोग. In this respect the Mâl. is far superior to it. In it the king's passion (अनुराग) which is compared to a plant is gradually developed as declared by the poet himself in the words बद्धमूलः, रूढरागप्रवालः, मुकुलितः (पुष्पित,) and फलितः; see IV. 1. A detailed description of the Sandhis and their *angas* is not attempted here as it is not of much use to the junior students. As a Nátiká the Priya. conforms to the rules of dramaturgy on broad lines. As regards the three chief requisites, the वस्तु is प्रख्यात as the story of Udayana and Vásavadattá was popular at the time the play was written. The Netá or hero is धीरललित (see *ante* p. 9). The Heroine belongs to the variety known as मुग्धा (defined as मुग्धा नववयःकामा रतौ वामा मृदुः क्रुधि। Das. R. II. 16). The chief sentiment is शृङ्गार or love. There is an occasional infusion of Karuṇa as in the lament of A'ranyiká (see pp. 15,24) and when she drinks poison, in order to put an end to her miserable existence (see p. 54). There is also a slight tinge of the हास्यरस as when the Vidu. says एते खलु राजानो

हास्यापि नर्त्यन्ते (p. 38), or advises the King saying मासोपवासं कृत्वा &c. (p. 48). As regards the *denouement* and the general setting the play opens with the usual नान्दी. The प्रस्तावना is not in its usual style but rather on the model of Bhása, as no other character than the Sûtradhára is introduced in it. In it the Sûtra. informs the audience of the name of the author, the title of the play and the occasion of its performance. Then there is a Viskambhaka in which the chamberlain of Dṛdhavarman, King of the Anga country, briefly narrates the part of the story, a knowledge of which is necessary for the understanding of the events related in the play. The Bîja or seed is also cast when the Kanch. says—येन सापि राजपुत्री यथा कथंचिद्वत्सराजायोपनीय &c. see p. 4). The Mukhasandhi begins where the King commits A'raṇyiká to the care of Vásavadattá and terminates with the close of the 2nd Act. The Bija germinates and sprouts up when the King sees A'raṇyiká (p. 18) and afterwards clasps her at the neck (p. 20). The प्रतिमुखसन्धि begins with the 3rd Act (see com.) wherein we have the गर्भसन्धि also. In the प्रति० there is यत्न for the attainment of the Phala or the final object; but to have it further postponed the poet has used the device of a गर्भनाटक,* which brings to light the King's intrigue and thus hinders the progress of love. In the fourth Act which is introduced by a Praveśaka, we have the अवमर्श and the निर्वहण Sandhis fused together, wherein the final object is attained; and the play closes with the usual Bharatavákya.

---

(6) Critical remarks on Harsha's three plays.

Of the three plays of Harsha, the Ratnâvalî and the Priyadars'ikâ have the same subject-matter, *i. e.*, the love intrigue of King Vatsa. Four characters are common to both of these plays, namely, King Vatsa, Queen Vāsavadattā, her attendant Kanchanamalá and the Vidushaka Vasantaka. Rumanvat, the usual general of the King's army is mentioned

---

*गर्भनाटक also called गर्भाङ्क (An act containing a play in it) is defined as—अङ्कोदरप्रविष्टो यो रङ्गद्वारा मुखादिमान् । अङ्कोऽपरः स गर्भाङ्कः सबीजफलवानपि॥ Sah. D. VI. 20 'A Secondary Act, incorporated into a principal Act and having the characteristics of a play in brief, such as its preliminaries, introduction, its Bîja and its final end, is called a गर्भाङ्क. This device has been used by Bhavabhúti in his Uttar., Act VII and by Rájas'ekhara in his Bâlarâmâyana.

in the Priyadarsikâ as a minister and Yaugandharâyaṇa mentioned but once in the Mimic play. Both are Nâtikās in four acts. Both contain several parallel situations. Hence they are called sister plays. The Priyadars'ikā is undoubtedly the earliest production of the author, judging from its simplicity and crudeness of construction as compared with the other two plays. The Ratnâvalî comes next, since it is more elaborate, and more polished. The Nágánanda, though not so elaborate and polished as the Ratnâvali, has to be put last, as it is Buddhistic in its tenor and sets forth the author's ideal of life in the last part of his life.

The *Ratnavali* is considered the best of the three plays of Harsha. It is pre-eminently a Sanskrit play which strictly conforms to the various canons of Sanskrit dramaturgy. It is for this reason that excerpts from this drama are frequently quoted by the later writers on dramaturgy. As we have pointed out, Damodargupta, a writer of the 8th century, in his Kuttanimata has highly eulogised this play. Dr. Macdonell, in his 'A History of Sanskrit Literature' writes "Altogether Ratnâvalî is an agreeable play with well drawn characters and many poetical beauties." See our Intro. to Ratnávalî, p. 30.

The Priyadarśiká, like the Rat., is a Nátiká named after the heroine Priya. who is known as A'raṇyiká up to the time of the *denouement*. This play is much inferior to the Ratnāvalî. The inventive genius and constructive skill of the poet do not shine out so pre-eminently in this play as they do in the other. But we must say to his credit that the actual development of the plot (the mere skeleton of which he got from the Bṛhatkathá) as it runs through all the four Acts to its finis is practically his own invention. The general simplicity of its style and form, the skill shown in the creation of the various incidents and situations which keep up the interest in the progress of plot and some striking descriptions in it make the play a pleasant reading. Some of the descriptions in the play are admirable—as the description of the palace-garden—'वृन्तैः क्षुद्रप्रवालस्थगितमिव तलं भाति शेफालिकानां &c.—Act II, 2, 3; the description of the beauty of A'raṇyikā—"पातालाद्भुवनावलोकाधिया किं नागकन्योत्थिता &c." Act II. 6; the description of the angry Queen—"स्निग्धं यद्यपि वीक्षितं &c.—Act. III, 13, 14, 15; &c. &c. The predominant sentiment in the *Priyadarsikâ* as in the *Ratnâvali* is love (शृंगार); but it has not been properly developed, as it has been in the Mâl, by his great predecessor, Kalidása. Harsha helps out his plot in both the plays by having recourse to superhuman agency. The King's restoring the dying A'ran. to life by means of magic formulas excites the sentiment of wonder (अद्भुत). The imprisonment of Priyadarsikā gives rise to the sentiment of pathos (करुण); while the sentiment of terror (भयानक) is roused when she is brought in a dying condition on the stage. The most striking feature of the drama, however, is the introduction of an Embryo—Act (गर्भाङ्क) in the third Act, forming an integral part of the drama. The whole scene is cleverly designed and skilfully managed. This गर्भाङ्क reminds us of a similar play within a play in Bhavabhuti's *Uttarráma-charita* and Shakespeare's *Hamlet*. Dr. A. B. Keith in his 'The Sanskrit Drama,' makes the following comments on the two sister plays—"The originality of his Nātikás is not perhaps great, but he has effectively devised the plot in both; the action moves smoothly and in either way there is ingenuity. The scene of the magician's activity in the *Ratnávalî* is depicted with humour and vivacity; the parrot's escape and its chatter are sketched with piquancy, and the exchange of costumes in the Ratnāvalî is natural and effective. The double comedy in the *Priyadars'iká* is a happy thought; the intrigue in Act IV is neatly conducted so as to show us Vásavadattá in the light of an affectionate niece, and the scene with the bee is attractive".

The Priyadarssikà bears a close resembleance to its sister play Ratnávali, both as regards the general conception of the theme and the method of its development, and so there are naturally many similar ideas and parallel situations in it. Some of these we note below—

In Act I of the Priyad., we have mention, made of the disappearance of the princess A'ianry., by her father's chamberlain and of her being subsequently brought to the king by his general Vijayasena; and we have in the introdctory scene of the Rat. Yaungandharàyaṇa, Vatsa's minister telling us of the rescue of Sâgariha from a ship-wreck. The scene in the garden in the second Act of Priy., wherein A'ráṇyikâ in the company of Indîvariká is seen by the king and his confidant has many points of resemblance to the scene in the 2nd Act of the Rat. In the third Act of the Priy, and also of the

Ratná. similar schemes are devised for the meeting of the lovers by Vasantaka and a maid-servant. Other similar episodes in the fourh Act of both the plays are the imprisonment of Vasantaka and of the princesses and their rescue by the king, in one case from poison and in the other from fire, and the final sanction of the Queen to the marriage of the Heroine of each play with the Hero. Other minor similarities are pointed out in the notes.

The Priyadarsikā, however, bears a closer resemblance to the Málavikâgnimitra of Kálidása in the general outline of its plot, both being based on the story of Bandhumatî (see *supra* p. xxv). Thus the hand of the Princess Priya. is promised to king Vatsa by her father while in the Mâl. an alliance is sought with king Agnimitra by Mâdhavasena by giving him in marriage his sister Mâlaviká. Both Mâdhav-sena and Dṛdhavarman, Priy.'s father, are taken prisoners by rival kings and both are finally rescued by the Heroes of the two dramas. Mâdhavasena's minister tries to bring Mâl. to king Agnimitra, while it is Dṛdh.'s chamberlain who tries to bring Priya. to king Vatsa. Both meet with accidents: the heroine of the Mâl. is brought by Vîrasena, the keeper of a border fort and given in charge of Dhárinî, Agnimitra's Queen, while Priya. is brought by Vijayasena, the victorious commander of the army of Vatsa, to his master, who in his turn orders her to be committed to the care of his queen Vâsavadattâ Both the Heroines are taught dancing, singing &c., and both are accidentally seen by the respective Kings, and love springs up between the heroes and the heroines of the two plays. To bring about the meeting of the two lovers the mimic play is arranged in the Priy., while a dancing exhibition is arranged in the Mâl. Mâlavikâ is seen with her attendent in a garden by the King and his confidant and so is A'raṇyiká in the Priyadarśiká. We have Kauśikî, the siser of Mádhavasena's minister, in the role of a religious lady, appearing as a friend of the Queen in the Mâl., and so we have Sâṃkṛtyáyanî in the third and fourth Acts of the Priy. The Vidû 's careless talk in sleep in the Mâl. betrays Mâlavika's meeting with the King, while Vasantaka's talk in sleep during the course of the Mimic play brings to light the ruse used for bringing about A'raṇyiká's meeting with the King in the Priy. The magic use of the ring bearing a snake's figure which counteracts the effect of poison in the case of the Vidu. who feigns to be bitten by a serpent in the fourth Act of the Mâl. has its reflex in the King's counteracting the effect of poison on A'raṇyiká by means of a charm. And finally we have the true identity of Mál. revealed in the Mál. in the last Act as that of A'raṇyiká in the present play. The similarities of ideas, expressions &c. found between the Priy. and the Nâgánanda we have pointed out in the notes.

The *Nágánanda* is a Nâtaka in five Acts and stands on a higher plane than the other two plays which are mere court-comedies. The play is of a unique type, since it depicts the grandeur of self-sacrifice in human life. As Dr. Keith remarks, " Harsha here rises to the task of depicting the emotions of self-sacrifice, charity, magnanimity, and resolution in the face of death." The Hero, Jimútaváhana, penetrated with the ideals of Buddhism, is convinced that to sacrifice oneself for the good of others is the highest duty. He has accepted the doctrine of non-violence and adheres to it so firmly that he will not make war even upon his enemy who has deprived him of his kingdom. When his friend and brother-in-law, Mitrāvasu, assures him of an easy victory over his enemy and the consequent restoration of his kingdom to him, Jimutavāhana replies :—

स्वशरीरमपि परार्थे यः खलु दद्यामयाचितः कृपया ।
राज्यस्य कृते स कथं प्राणिवधक्रौर्यमनुमन्ये ॥

' I will give my own life for the sake of another in compassion unasked; how then can I consent to the cruel slaughter of men merely for winning a kingdom. " Here Harsha reveals himself in uttering these sentiments Harsha who had been once the hero of hundred battles and who by his brilliant victories over his enemies had become the Paramount Lord in Hindustan, was in the last part of his life a staunch follower of the Buddhishtic doctrine of non-violence (अहिंसा).

(7) The principal characters on the play.

Vatsara''j (The Hero).

The Hero of the play Priyadarśiká, Vatsarája a king of Kauśámbî, has many charming legends and stories woven round his name. It seems that his life full of romantic adventures. made a deep impression on the popular mind in old days, as is clear from the remark in the प्रस्तावना of the play, "लोके हारि च वत्सराजचरितं." Hence there are no references to his great deeds in this play save one adventure, *viz.*, his escape from his captivity, in which he was kept by the powerful monarch, Mahasena Pradyota, of Avanti, and his carrying off the latter's daughter and making her his Queen. And since the poet chose to write a Nátiká it was not his object also to present his hero in any of the serious aspects of his charactor. Bound by the hard and fast rules of Sans. Dramaturgy he has cast his characters in the conventional mould He has taken care to show his hero in the enjoyment of courtly life, the stirring events of his public life having already won for him great popularity. We cannot, therefore, compare him with Agnimitra, the hero of the Mâlavikâgnimitra. But comparatively speaking the character of Vatsa is not so well developed in this play as it is in the Ratnāvali. He belongs to the class of heroes called धीरललित,—'Firm, gay, and tender-hearted.' He is courteous and affectionate to his Queen while engaged in a new love adventure. As soon as he sees a charming young maiden, he falls in love with her and thinks of nothing but meeting her again and making love to her. He is helped in his love intrigue by his companion, the Vidushaka, and Manoramā, an attendant of the Queen. In the Mimic play in which by a cunning device he is given an opportunity of meeting A'raṇyiká, he proceeds to act towards her in such an ardent manner that he rouses the suspicion of his queen Vâsavadattā. When the Queen knows the whole truth and breaks up the play in anger, he apologises to her in all humility and even falls at her feet. Though his Queen does not accept his apology or relent, he tries his utmost to conciliate her. And when the Queen knowing that A'raṇyikâ is her cousin Priyadarsika, places the latter's hand in the King's hand, he with delicacy withdraws his hand saying that he is satisfied that his Queen is reconciled. One noble trait of his character, however is brought out when he appreciates the valour of his fallen enemy and ungrudgingly bestows praise on him in the words—शोभितं विन्ध्यकेतुना। साधु विन्ध्यकेतो साधु। सत्पुरुषोचितं मार्गमनुगच्छतो यत्सत्यं व्रीडिता एव वयं विन्ध्यकेतोर्मरणेन. (Act I.).

A'RANYIKA OR PRIYADARS'IKA'.

Priyadarsikâ is the Heroïne of the play, as the very name of the play clearly shows it. She is called आरण्यिका up to the time of the *denouement*, because she was found in a forest: Priyadars'ikā is a colourless character, possessing no striking intellectual or moral qualities. She belongs to the variety of heroines known as मुग्धा, who is defined as—'मुग्धा नववयःकामा रतौ वामा मृदुः क्रुधि'। She is represented as a young maiden of rare beauty. As soon as the King catches sight of her he bursts into a panegyric of her beauty ' पातालाद्भुवनावलोकनधिया किं नागकन्योत्थिता। &c. (Act II. 6). When she sees the King she falls in love with him and remarks that her father was right in promising her to him, thus preferring him to other suitors (अयं स महाराजः। यस्याहं तातेन दत्ता। स्थाने खलु तातस्य पक्षपातः।). She is extremely timid and sensitive. She laments that her passion is hopeless and will never find its fulfilment. She therefore longs for death that would relieve her of her sorrow- सर्वथा मरणं वर्जयित्वा कुतः मे हृदयस्य अन्या निर्वृतिः। Fortunately she is cheered up and helped by her friend मनोरमा. But she gives way to sorrow and despondency to such an extent that she actually takes poison. Thus Priyadarśiká evinces none of those qualities which constitute a great character. There is, however, one admirable trait in her character also. She does not reveal her identity to the last, even to her confidante Manoramā and this speaks highly for her keen sense of family honour.

VA'SAVADATTA'.

Vāsavadattā is the chief Queen, elderly and majestic. Her love for her lord is sincere and deep and her jealousy proceeds from her true deep love. In the Mimic play, when the King makes love to A'raṇyikā, playing the part of the Queen, with great ardour, her suspicion is aroused. And when she learns the truth from the lips of the Vidushaka, who gave out the secret in his drowsiness, she breaks up the play in anger and orders both A'raṇyikā and the Vidûshaka to be imprisoned as being accomplices in the plot. She spurns the conilciation and prostration of the king. She is truly a मानिनी (a proud self-respecting woman). She keeps Araṇyikā for a pretty long time in prison. She is not easily appeased. When, however, she learns that A'raṇyikā has taken poison, she is at once struck with penitence and immediately orders her to be brought into the presence of the King, who is an expert in the treatment of poisons and magic formulas, for being restored to life. She is an affectionate niece, for we see her plunged in deep grief at the news of the long imprisonment of her aunt's husband (Act IV). The nobility of her mind is seen when she gladly bestows the hand of A'ranyikā, whom she now knows to be her cousin, Priyadarsikā, on the King, in fulfilment of her father's promise. In fact the picture of the Queen drawn here, though not so magnificent as that of Dhárinî in the Mál. (see V. 19) is quite in keeping with the requirements of a Nátiká.

The Vidûshaka.

The Vidûshaka is a boon companion of the King who amuses him in his lonely hours. He is a Bráhmaṇa but without learning, great wit or wisdom. He is greedy and ever eager to receive gifts. He excites laughter by his appearance, quaint remarks and movements. He helps the King in his love intrigue. When A'raṇyikā is attacked by bees and covering her face with a mantle calls to her friend for help, he cleverly advises the King to run to her rescue silently so that she may clasp him mistaking him for her friend. He is an accomplice in the scheme by which the King gets an opportunity of meeting and making love to Ar'aṇyikā in the Mimic play. But he is light-headed and gives out the truth of the whole plot in his drowsy condition. He, however, sometimes makes very clever and appropriate remarks. When the chamberlain of Dṛdhavarman informs the King that the Kaling king was killed and Dṛdhavarman restored to his throne, the Vidushaka says in the hearing of the queen, ईदृशे अभ्युदये अस्मिन् राजकुले एतद् करणीयम् । (राजानं निर्दिश्य वीणावादनं नाटयन्) गुरुपूजा (आत्मनो यज्ञोपवीतं दर्शयन्) ब्राह्मणस्य संत्कारः, (आरण्यिकां सूचयित्वा) सर्वबन्धनमोक्ष इति ।. When the King succeeds in restoring A'raṇyikā to consciousness, the Vidushaka again significantly reminds the Queen, "भवति......वैद्यस्य पारितोषिकं विस्मृतम् ।

DRAMATIS PERSONAE.

——:o:——

MALES.

सूत्रधारः—The stage-manager.
वत्सराजः (उदयनः)—The Hero, king of Kauśâmbî.
विदूषकः (वसन्तकः)—A Brâhmaṅa, the Hero's companion and confidant.
रुमण्वत्—Minister of Vatsarája.
विजयसेन :—The commander of the army of Vatsarája.
विनयवसु :—The chamberlain of Dṛdhavardman.

FEMALES.

आरण्यिका —(Whose real name is प्रियदार्शिका, also called प्रियदर्शना) The Heroine, daughter of king Dṛdhavarman.
वासवदत्ता—The Queen, wife of Vatsarâja and daughter of Mahâsena (also called Pradyota), king of Ujjain.
काञ्चनमाला—An attendant-maid of the Queen.
मनोरमा—A maid-servant, confidante of A'raṇyikâ.
इन्दीवरिका—A maid-servant of the Queen.
प्रतीहारी (यशोधरा)—The female door-keeper or portress of Vatsarâja
साङ्कृत्यायनी—An elderly holy lady, associate of Vásavadattâ.

PERSONS &c. MENTIONED.

योगन्धरायण :—The chief minister of Vatsarája.
दृढवर्मन्—King of the Anga country and father of the Heroine.
A bard, and Retinue of Vâsasvadattâ.

SCENE.

Praveśaka of Act I.—some part of the Vindhya forest.
Rest of the Play—Kaûśâmbî, the capital city of Udayana.

———

भूमिका ।

यस्याश्चोरश्चिकुरनिकुरः कर्णपूरो मयूरो
भासो हासः कविकुलगुरुः कालिदासो विलासः ।
हर्षो हर्षो हृदयवसतिः पञ्चबाणस्तु बाणः
केषां नैषा कथय कविताकामिनी कौतुकाय ॥

—जयदेवस्य ।

इह खलु सकलविद्याकलाकलापादिपीठेऽस्मिन्भारते वर्षे निजयशःसुरभीकृतदिगन्तरालाः प्रतिभाशालिनः परःशताः कवीश्वरा भासकालिदासादयः स्वकृत्याभरणैर्वाग्वधूं मण्डयन्ति स्म । तेषां च केचन प्रबन्धप्रमोदितरसिकमण्डलाः शब्दसर्गार्जितोर्जितयशस्का विदग्धधुरीणाः प्रतापसंतापितारिचक्रा वक्रेष्वप्यार्जवमुत्पादयन्तश्चक्रवर्तिनो राजानोऽभूवन्नित्यहो नवनवाश्चर्यनिर्माणचातुरी विधेः । श्रीसरस्वत्योः ख्यातनिसर्गभिन्नास्पदयोरप्येकसंस्थानं कस्य हि सहृदयस्य चेतः कुतूहलितं प्रमोदनिर्भरं च न कुर्यात् । एतेषु श्रीमच्छूद्रकयशोवर्मभीमटभोजादिषु कविनृपेष्वग्रेसरीभूतः **श्रीहर्षा**भिधः स्थानेश्वरेश्वरः **चक्रवर्तिश्रीहर्षवर्धना**ख्यया पुरावृत्तकोविदैरुद्घुष्यमाणकीर्तिर्नृपतिरितस्त्रयोदशशताद्वर्षेभ्यः प्राग्भारतभूमण्डलं प्रशशास । यस्य च **प्रियदर्शिका—रत्नावली—नागानन्द**समाख्यं रूपकत्रयमद्य यावद्रसिकान्तःकरणग्रहणेनात्मनो निर्मातुर्यथार्थनामत्वं प्रख्यापयद्रसिकानां हर्षं संवर्धयन्नाटकनिबन्धेषु गुणानुकूल्याद्धुरीवर्ति । यस्य चेभ्यस्य सभ्यो गद्यकविमूर्धन्यपदवीमारूढः कादम्बर्याः प्रणेता श्रीभट्टबाणः स्वस्वामिनः शूरस्य वदान्यस्य विक्रान्तस्योदारचरितस्य चरितमाख्यायिकारूपेण सुललितपदबन्धं निबबन्ध । सोऽयं चित्तचमत्कारी **हर्षचरिता**ख्यो गद्यप्रबन्ध एव श्रीहर्षनृपतेरितिवृत्तादिविज्ञाने प्रधानतया सहायतां समुपगच्छति प्राचीनवार्ताविविदिषूणामिति सुविदितमेव सुधियाम् । केचित्तु नव्यशिक्षिता नागानन्दादिरूपकप्रणेतृत्वं न श्रीहर्षवर्धननृपतेः किं तु कस्याप्यपरस्य तदनुजीविनः कवेरितिमन्यमानाः साग्रहं प्रत्यवतिष्ठन्ते । तेष्वपि भिन्नभिन्नमतप्रणाल्या महती विप्रतिपत्तिः । केचित्त्रयोविंशतिसंख्यकरूपककृतः श्रीमतो भासस्य, अन्ये हर्षवर्धनाश्रितपण्डितपारिषदानामेकतमस्य धावकस्य, अपरे चोपरिनिर्दिष्टगद्यगीर्वधूप्राणस्य श्रीबाणस्य न कथंचिदपि तावच्छ्रीहर्षस्य त्रितयमिदं रूपकाणामिति नानापरंपरानुसरणशीला बम्भ्रम्यमाणाः कष्टयन्ति चेतः शिष्टानाम् । सोऽयं सर्वोऽप्यूहसमूहो न विश्वसनीयत्वकक्षामवगाहत इति सविस्तरं विमर्शितमन्यत्रास्माभिरिति नात्र परतरं प्रस्तूयते ।

श्रीमान्हर्षः सर्वत्र भासकालिदासादिमहाकव्युपदिष्टपथानुसरणपरः स्वकृतिषु वैदर्भीमेव रीतिमवलम्बितवानिति स्फुटमेवावलोकयताम् । यां च रीतिं श्रीबिल्हण इत्थमुपवर्णयामास—“अनभ्रवृष्टिः श्रवणामृतस्य सरस्वतीविभ्रमजन्मभूमिः । वैदर्भ-

रीतिः कृतिनामुदेति सौभाग्यलाभप्रतिभूः पदानाम् ॥" इति । प्रसादश्लेषमाधुर्यादिकाव्यगुणैर्द्विगुणीकृतसरसत्वमस्य प्रबन्धत्रये सर्वतः समुल्लसतितराम् । पद्ये ह्यसमस्तपदप्रचुरप्रचाराद्गद्ये च सरलायाः सुस्पष्टया वाचो निबन्धनात्कविरयं भवभूत्यादिपश्चात्तनकव्यपक्षेया सुतरां संमानार्ह इति संमतमेव विपश्चिताम् ।

एतदीयप्रबन्धत्रये परस्परानुगुणगुणगणनक्रमेण **रत्नावली**समाख्या नाटिकैव शेखरीभूता यामुद्दिश्याह कुट्टनीमते श्रीदामोदरगुप्तः— "आश्लिष्टसंधिबन्धं सत्पात्रसुवर्णयोजितं सुतराम् । निपुणपरीक्षकदृष्टं राजति **रत्नावलीरत्नम्** ॥" इति । तदपेक्षया **प्रियदर्शिका** अतीव न्यूनगुणा । **नागानन्दं** तस्य कवेः चरमैव कृतिर्भवेदिति तस्य शान्तरसप्रधानाद्वस्तुस्वरूपात्सुव्यक्तमेव । नाट्यदृष्ट्या गुणपर्यालोचने मध्यस्थतामारूढं च । प्रियदर्शिकाया नाटिकात्वेन चत्वार एवाङ्काः । अत्र नायकः सुविख्यातचरितसौरभो बृहत्कथादिषु वर्णितहारिवृत्तान्तो वत्सराज उदयनो नाम धीरललितः । तस्य च उज्जयिनीनृपतेर्महासेनस्य प्रद्योतेत्यपरनामधेयस्यात्मजा वासवदत्ता पत्नी यात्र देवीति शब्देन व्यवहृता । नायिका च दृढवर्मनाम्नो राज्ञो दुहिता प्रियदर्शिका यस्या अत्र आरण्यिकेतिनाम्ना व्यवहारः । सा च मुग्धा । रसोऽत्र प्रधानः शृङ्गार एवाङ्गी । इतिवृत्तं चास्या बृहत्कथावर्तिवत्सराजचरितं बन्धुमतिचरितं चोपजीव्योपनिबद्धम् । अस्यां च नाटिकायामुपवर्णितं कथावस्त्वङ्कानुक्रमतो विभक्तं सारांशरूपेण अध्येतॄणां सुखावबोधायात्रोपनिबध्यते—

प्रथमाङ्के तावन्नान्दीपाठानन्तरं सूत्रधारभाषणे नाटिकाया अस्या कर्तुर्नामनिर्देशादेरुपन्यासः । ततो विष्कम्भके दृढवर्मनृपतेः कञ्चुकिनः प्रवेशस्तन्मुखेन पूर्ववृत्तस्य वस्तुनः किमपि निवेदनम् । तद्यथा—अङ्गाधिपतिर्दृढवर्मा मत्प्रार्थ्यमानापि स्वदुहिता कथमनेन वत्सराजाय दत्तेति बद्धानुशयेन वत्सराजो बन्धनान्न निवर्तते इति च लब्धरन्ध्रेण कलिङ्गराजेन सहसागत्य बलादवस्कन्द्य गाढप्रहारजर्जरीकृतो बन्धनं नीतः । ततश्च तस्मिन्नवस्कन्दसम्भ्रमे दिष्ट्या कथंचिद् दृष्टा तद्दुहिता प्रियदर्शिका 'अतःपरं नात्र स्थातुं युक्तं यथाकथंचिदेतां वत्सराजायोपनीय स्वामिनमनृणं करिष्यामीति मन्वानेन तत्कञ्चुकिनापवाह्य दृढवर्मणो मित्रभावान्वितस्याटविकस्य नृपस्य विन्ध्यकेतोर्गृहे स्थापिता । स च कञ्चुकी नातिदूरस्थमगस्त्यतीर्थं स्नानार्थं गतः । यदा स निवृत्तस्तदा तत्स्थानं कैरपि सह विन्ध्यकेतुना स्मर्तव्यतां नीतमपश्यत् । ततः स्वामिनमेव गत्वा तत्पादपरिचर्यया जीवितं सफलयिष्यामीति सोपि निर्गतः । तदनन्तरं वत्सराजविदूषकयोः प्रवेशो वत्सराजेन भृत्यादीनामात्मन्यविचला निष्ठा दृष्टा वासवदत्ता च स्त्रीरत्नमासादितमिति बन्धनप्रशंसा । ततो विन्ध्यकेतोरुपरि बहून्यहानि विजयसेनस्य प्रेषितस्य न चाद्यापि कोपि तत्सकाशादागत इति चिन्तापराय राज्ञे प्रतीहारी प्रविश्य देव विजयसेनोऽमात्यश्च रुमण्वान्प्रतीहारभूमिमुपस्थिताविति न्यवेदयत् । प्रवेष्टुं लब्धाज्ञौ च तौ प्रविश्योपाविशताम् । कुशलप्रश्नानंतरं विजयसेन कथय विन्ध्यकेतोर्वृत्तान्तं विस्तरतः श्रोतुमिच्छामीति राज्ञादिष्टो विजयसेनो यथाऽतर्कितं प्रातरेव निपतततो बलस्य तुमुलकलकलेन प्रतिबुद्धः विन्ध्यकेतुः केसरीव विन्ध्यकंदरान्निर्गत्य यथासंनिहितकतिपयसहायः सन् युयुधे यथा च निःशेषितसहाय

एक एव विमर्दिताधिकबलक्रोधवेगो दारुणतरं संप्रहारं कृत्वा शत्रुबलत्रितयमाकुलं कृत्वा शस्त्रप्रहारशतजर्जरितोरुवक्षा युधि निहतस्तथा सर्वमाख्यत् । व्यज्ञपयच्च देव सबन्धुपरिवारे हते विन्ध्यकेतौ शून्यीभूते तत्स्थाने हा तात हा मातः इति कृतकृपणप्रलपा विन्ध्यकेतोर्वेश्मन्युपलब्धाभिजात्यानुरूपा कन्यका तद्दुहितेत्यस्माभिरानीता द्वारि तिष्ठति । तां प्रति देवः प्रमाणमिति । तत एतां वासवदत्तायै समर्पय । वक्तव्या च देवी भगिनीबुध्या त्वयेयं सर्वदा द्रष्टव्या विशिष्टकन्यकोचितं नृत्यगीतादि सर्वं शिक्षयितव्या चेति प्रतीहारीमादिदेश । वासवदत्तापि तामरण्याल्लब्धेत्यारण्यिकाशब्देन व्यपदिष्टां स्वान्तःपुरेऽस्थापयत् । तदनन्तरं वैतालिकेनावेदितमध्याह्नसमयः स्नानार्थमुदतिष्ठन्नरपतिः । आह च रुमण्वन्तमभ्यन्तरं प्रविश्य कृतयथोचितक्रियाः सत्कृत्य विजयसेनं कलिङ्गोच्छित्तये प्रेषयाम इति ।

द्वितीयाङ्के तावत्प्रथमं राज्ञो विदूषकेण सह प्रवेशः । तत्र गृहीतव्रतामुपवासकृशां स्वप्रियां द्रष्टुं सोत्कण्ठो वत्सराजो वयस्येन वसन्तकेन सहोत्कण्ठाविनोदनार्थं धारागृहोद्यानं जगाम । अत्रान्तरे अगस्त्याय महर्षयेऽर्घ्यं दातुकामया देव्या शेफालिकाकुसुममालां लघु गृहीत्वागच्छेत्याज्ञप्ता इन्दीवरिका नाम चेटी धारागृहोद्यानदीर्घिकायाः कमलान्यवचित्य लघ्वागच्छेत्यादिष्टया आरण्यिकया सार्धं तदेवोद्यानमागतवती । यावच्च धारागृहोद्यानश्रिया स्फुटपङ्कजकान्तिहारिण्या हंसस्वनपुष्पसौगन्ध्यादिना रम्याया दीर्घिकाया दर्शनेन चाह्लादितचित्तो नृपो वसन्तकेन सह संभाषमाणस्तिष्ठति तावदारण्यिका तत्रागता प्रत्यक्षचरीवोद्यानदेवता विदूषकेण दृष्टा । राज्ञे निवेदिता च । किंन्वियं नागकन्या भवेदाहोस्विन्मूर्ता कौमुदीत्यादि वितर्कयन्नृप इन्दीवरिकारण्यकयोर्मिथआलापात्तां विन्ध्यकेतुदुहितेति ज्ञातवान् । अभवच्च तस्यामनुरक्तचितः । तदनन्तरं कमलान्यवचिन्वती मधुकरैरायास्यमानाऽरण्यिका तन्निवारणार्थं स्वसखीमाह्वयत् । तथा तां दृष्ट्वा विदूषकोपदेशाद्राजा तूष्णीमुपससार तमवालम्बत च सखीबुद्ध्याऽरण्यिका । वत्सराजोपि तां कण्ठे जग्राह स्वोत्तरीयेण भ्रमरान्निवारयितुमारेभे च । राजानं दृष्ट्वा ससाध्वसं दूरमपसृता आरण्यिका तं सस्पृहं पश्यन्ती स्वगतमाह अयं स महाराजो यस्याहं तातेन दत्ता । स्थाने खलु तातस्य पक्षपात इति । अत्रान्तरे सखीसाहाय्यार्थमागतामिन्दीवरिकां दृष्ट्वा राजा वसन्तकश्च कदलीगृहं प्रविश्य स्थितौ । निर्गते चेन्दीवरिकारण्यके । वत्सराजोप्यारण्यिकया हृतचित्तः क उपायः पुनरेतां द्रष्टुमिति चिन्तयन् परिणतप्रायं दिवसं दृष्ट्वा सवयस्यो गृहाभ्यन्तरं प्रविवेश ।

तृतीयाङ्के तावत्प्रथमं 'हञ्जे मनोरमे यः स साङ्कृत्यायन्यार्यपुत्रस्य मम च वृत्तान्तो नाटकोपनिबद्धस्तस्य नर्तितव्यशेषमद्य युष्माभिः कौमुदीमहोत्सवे नर्तितव्यमिति देव्या वासवदत्तयाज्ञप्ताया मनोरमायाः प्रवेशः । सा च ह्यः खलु आरण्यिकया प्रियसख्या शून्यहृदययान्यथैव नर्तितमद्य पुनर्वासवदत्ताभूमिकया तया यदि तथा क्रियते ततोवश्यं देवी कुप्यति । अतस्तामन्विष्योपालप्स्य इति मनसि कृत्वा धारागृहोद्यानदीर्घिकामागतवती । अपश्यच्च तां कदलीगृहं प्रविशन्तीम् । ततस्तस्या विश्रब्धभाषणाद्वत्सनृपेनुरक्तेयमिति ज्ञात्वा तामुपसृत्य समाश्वास्य मदनसन्तप्तगात्रायास्तस्याः शिशिरोपचारेण संतापं लघूकर्तुं प्रायतत । अत्रान्तर आरण्यिकायां दृढमनुरक्तेन वत्सराजेन प्रहितो

वसन्तकस्तत्रैवाजगाम। अवर्णयच्चात्मनः सुहृद आरण्यिकायाः कृते जातां दुरवस्थां सा चात्मनः सख्यास्तादृशीमवस्थां तस्मै। ततो वसन्तकेनातिलज्जालुका ते प्रियसखी तत्कथमेतयोः समागमो भविष्यतीत्युक्ता मनोरमा—अद्य रात्रावस्माभिर्भगवत्याः साङ्कृत्यायन्याः कृतिरुदयनचरितं नाम नाटकं देव्याः पुरतो नर्तितव्यम्। तत्रारण्यिका वासवदत्ता भविष्यति। अहमपि वत्सराजः। तच्चरितेनैव सर्वं शिक्षयितव्यम्। तदागत्य स्वयमेव स्वां भूमिकां कुर्वाणः समागमोत्सवमनुभवतु महाराजः। इति तस्य कर्णेऽकथयत्। वसन्तकोपि हृष्टो यावदेव युवां नेपथ्यग्रहणं कुरुथस्तावदेवाहं वयस्यं गृहीत्वागच्छामीत्युक्त्वा स्वभर्तुरन्तिकमयात्। मनोरमापि स्वसख्या सह प्रेक्षागृहमगात्। ततः प्रवृत्ते गर्भनाटके भर्तुरभिनयातिशयमसहमाना कुपिता वासवदत्ता भगवत्याधिकं कल्पितं काव्यमिति सरोषमुक्त्वा काञ्चनमालासहिता प्रेक्षागृहान्निर्गता। दृष्टश्च तया चित्रशालाद्वारे सुप्तो वसन्तकः। ततो राज्ञाप्यत्र भवितव्यमत एतं बोधयित्वा पृच्छामीति कांचमालामुक्त्वा तथा कृत्वा तमपृच्छत्। सोपि मूर्खोर्धसुप्तः सकलमेवं तन्त्रमाकुलीकृतवान्। वासवदत्तापि बध्यतामयं द्रक्ष्यामि तावदस्य प्रेक्षणीयमिति मनोरमामुक्त्वा नृत्यन्तं राजानं गत्वा आरण्यिकां च हस्तेनाकृष्य इन्दीवरिके गृहाणेमामिति दासीमादिश्य राज्ञा पादपतनेन प्रसाद्यमानापि अकृत्वैव प्रसादं गता। ततो वत्सराजोपि शयनीयं गत्वा देव्याः प्रसादनोपायं चिन्तयामीत्यभिधाय निष्क्रान्तः।

चतुर्थाङ्के प्रवेशके मनोरमा प्रथमं देव्या दीर्घरोषतां स्वसख्याया आरण्यिकायाश्च चिरबन्धनमधिकृत्यात्मन उद्वेगमाविष्करोति। ततस्तां मिलिता काञ्चनमालैवमकथमत्। अद्य देव्या स्वमात्राङ्गारवत्या प्रेषितो लेखोऽधिगतः। तस्मिंश्च लिखितमासीत्–तव मातृस्थाने स्थिताया मम भगिन्या भर्तुर्दृढवर्मणः समधिकं संवत्सरं कलिङ्गहतकेन बद्धस्य। तन्न युक्तमेतं वृत्तान्तं श्रुत्वापि समर्थस्य ते भर्तुरेवमौदासिन्यमवलम्बितुमिति। तद्वाचनात्प्रभृति दुर्मनायमानैव देवी तिष्ठतीति। तदनन्तरं देव्याः सह साङ्कृत्यायन्या प्रवेशः। तत्र यावत्साङ्कृत्यायनी नेदृशो वत्सराज इत्यादिवचनोपन्यासेन देवीं सान्त्वयति तावत्तस्या एव प्रसादनार्थं वत्सराजोपि तत्रोपस्थितः। ततः साङ्कृत्यायन्या अवगतदेवीवैमनस्यहेतुर्वत्सराज आह—देवि नाहमस्मिन्विषये उदासीन आसम्। अतिमहान्खलु कालः मम कलिङ्गोच्छित्तये विजयसेनं प्रेषितवतः। कतिपयान्यप्यहानि तस्माद्वार्ताया आगतायाः। अद्य श्वो वा कलिङ्गहतकं युद्धे बद्धं हतं वा श्रोष्यसीति। तच्छ्रुत्वा वासवदत्ता यावदेवात्मनः परितोषं दर्शयति तावदेव निहतकलिङ्गो दृढवर्मकञ्चुकिना विनयवसुना समेतो विजयसेनो लब्धप्रवेशानुज्ञ एत्य राजानं प्रणिपत्य स्थितः। निवेदितश्च कञ्चुकिना स्वराज्ये प्रतिष्ठापितस्य दृढवर्मणः कृतज्ञतादर्शनपूर्वः संदेशः। अत्रान्तरे मनोरमा ससंभ्रममेत्य भट्टिनि आरण्यिका कल्यमिषेणानीतं विषं पीत्वा प्राणसंशये वर्तते इति वासवदत्तायै न्यवेदयत्। ततो देव्याज्ञया तत्रानीतारण्यिका नागलोकाद् गृहीतविषविद्येन वत्सराजेन चिकित्सता लब्धासुर्बभूव। तां दृष्ट्वैयमेव सा चिरनष्टा मे राजपुत्री प्रियदर्शिका मे भगिनीति विनयवसुर्वासवदत्ताया आचष्ट। ततः स्वभगिनीलाभेन प्रीततरा देवी वासवदत्ता राज्ञो हस्ते प्रियदर्शिकामर्पितवती वत्सराजेन च प्रीतेन परिगृहीताम्। उपसंहृता चेदं नाटिका भरतवाक्येन कविना॥

श्रीहर्षदेवविरचिता ।

॥ प्रियदर्शिका ॥

॥ प्रथमोऽङ्कः ॥

धूमव्याकुलदृष्टिरिन्दुकिरणैराह्लादिताक्षी पुनः
पश्यन्ती वरमुत्सुकानतमुखी भूयो ह्रिया ब्रह्मणः ॥
सेर्ष्या पादनखेन्दुदर्पणगते गङ्गां दधाने हरे
स्पर्शादुत्पुलका करग्रहविधौ गौरी शिवायास्तु वः ॥ १ ॥

अपि च ।

कैलासाद्रावुदस्ते परिचलति गणेषूल्लसत्कौतुकेषु
क्रोडं मातुः कुमारे विशति विषमुचि प्रेक्षमाणे सरोषम् ।

मौलौ पुण्यप्रवाहा सुरसरिदमला राजते यस्य वाग्धौ
कालः कण्ठे तनौ वा त्रिभुवनभयहृद्यश्च भक्तार्तिहारी ।
पञ्चेषुर्यस्य शत्रुर्भवति भगवतो नंदनो वातिशस्त-
स्तस्मै सर्वेश्वराय प्रणतिरतिशयानंदकंदाय मेऽस्तु ॥ १ ॥

अथ तत्रभवान् महाकविः श्रीहर्षदेवः प्रियदर्शिकां नाम नाटिकां रिरचयिषुः प्रारिप्सितस्य ग्रन्थस्याविघ्नसमाप्त्यर्थं मङ्गलस्यावश्यकर्तव्यतया पूर्वरङ्गप्रधानाङ्गभूतामष्टपदां नान्दीं श्लोकद्वयेन तावदुपनिबध्नाति—**धूमेति** । गौरी पार्वती वः सामाजिकानां शिवाय कल्याणायास्तु । कीदृशीत्याह—करग्रहविधौ विवाहमङ्गले धूमेन हूयमानशमीपल्लवलाजादिसंपर्काद् वैवाहिकाग्निसमुत्थितेन व्याकुले दृष्टी नयने यस्याः सा तथोक्ता । पुनः इन्दुकिरणैः शिवशिरस्थचन्द्रमयूखैः आह्लादिते प्रमुदिते अक्षिणी यस्याः सा तथोक्ता । तथा च उत्सुकोत्कण्ठिता सती वरं पतिं पश्यन्ती । भूयः ब्रह्मणः पुरोधसश्चतुर्मुखात् ह्रिया लज्जया आनतमवनतं मुखं यस्यास्तादृशी । पुनश्च पादयोः नखाः पादनखा इन्दव इव पादनखेन्दवः । ते एव दर्पणानि तानि गते प्रतिफलिते गङ्गां दधाने हरे सेर्ष्या । सपत्नीदर्शनेन जातासूयेत्यर्थः । पुनश्च स्पर्शाद् हरकरस्पर्शादुत्पुलका जातरोमाञ्चा । शार्दूलविक्रीडितं वृत्तम् । तल्लक्षणं—सूर्याश्वैर्यदि मः सजौ सततगाः शार्दूलविक्रीडितम् ॥ इति ॥ १ ॥ विघ्नबाहुल्यशङ्कया पुनरपि मङ्गलमवतारयति—**अपि चेति** । **कैलासेति** । कैलासाद्रौ कैलासपर्वते उदस्ते रावणेनोत्क्षिप्ते परिचलति कम्पमाने सति । गणेषु प्रमथादिषु उल्लसदाविर्भवत्कौतुकं येषां तथा सत्सु । कुमारे कार्तिकेये मातुः क्रोडं भुजान्तरं विशति सति । विषमुचि शिवस्याभरणभूते सर्पे सरोषं किमिदमिति प्रेक्षमाणे ।

---

१ पश्यन्तीव समु०. २ नतमुखी. ३ भूयोह्रिया.

पादावष्टम्भसीदद्वपुषि दशमुखे याति पातालमूलं
क्रुद्धोऽप्याश्लिष्टमूर्तिर्भयघनमुमया पातु तुष्टः शिवो नः ॥ २ ॥

(नान्द्यन्ते)

सूत्रधारः—(परिक्रम्य ।) अद्याहं वसन्तोत्सवे सबहुमानमाहूय नानादिग्देशादागतेन राज्ञः श्रीहर्षदेवस्य पादपद्मोपजीविना राजसमूहेनोक्तः । यथास्मत्स्वामिना श्रीहर्षदेवेनापूर्ववस्तुरचनालंकृता प्रियदर्शिका नाम

तथा च पादस्य हरचरणस्य अवष्टम्भेन निर्भरनिवेशनेन सीदत् खिद्यमानं वपुर्यस्य तस्मिन् दशमुखे पातालमूलं याति सति । रावणचेष्टितेन क्रुद्धोपि भयेन घनं दृढं यथा तथा उमया आश्लिष्टमूर्तिरतः तुष्टः प्रीतः शिवः वः पातु ॥ स्रग्धरा वृत्तम् । तल्लक्षणं—म्रभ्नैर्यानां त्रयेण त्रिमुनियतियुता स्रग्धरा कीर्तितेयम् । इति ॥ २ ॥ श्लोकपादस्यापि पदत्वाभ्युपगमादष्टपदेयं नान्दी । तदुक्तं नाट्यप्रदीपे—श्लोकपादः पदं केचित्सुप्तिङन्तमथापरे । परेवान्तरवाक्यैकस्वरूपं पदमूचिरे ॥ इति ॥ नान्दीश्लोकत्वादुभयोरादौ भूदेवताको मगणः प्रयुक्तस्तेन गणशुद्धिः । उक्तं च भामहेन । क्षेमं सर्वगुर्दत्ते मगणो भूमिदैवतः । इति । नान्द्यां मनाक् काव्यार्थसूचनं कर्तव्यमित्युक्तत्वात्कविनापि तथा कृतम् । तथाहि प्रथमश्लोके तावत् गौरीशब्देन नायिकारण्यका धूमव्याकुलदृष्टिरित्यनेन तस्याः स्वपितुर्दृढवर्मणः कलिङ्गहतककृतविपत्तिजो विषादः इन्दुकिरणैरित्यनेन तस्याः कञ्चुकिना कृतमपवाहनं सुहृन्नृपस्य विन्ध्यकेतोराश्रयलाभाद्धर्षः पश्यन्ती वरमित्यनेन तस्याः यादृच्छिकं वत्सराजदर्शनं तदुत्पन्नं तत्समागमौत्सुक्यं ह्रिया प्रह्वाण इत्यनेन स्वानुरागस्य राज्ञ्याः परिजनज्ञानपरिजिहीर्षया गोपनं सेर्ष्येत्यादिना गर्भनाटके मनोरमायाः स्थाने देवीविप्रलम्भपूर्वं स्वयमेव नृत्यता राज्ञा संगतामारण्यकां दृष्ट्वा देव्या असूया स्पर्शादुत्पुलका इत्यनेन नायिकायाः द्वितीयाङ्के कण्टकितं कमलकाननमित्यत्र सूचितं सपुलकत्वमित्याद्यर्थजातं सूचितम् । द्वितीयश्लोकगतेन च कैलासाद्रावित्यादिना कलिङ्गराजकृते दृढवर्मणो राज्यपरिभ्रंशः पादावष्टम्भेत्यादिना कलिङ्गनृपस्य वत्सराजसैनिकाक्रान्तविषयस्य दुर्गप्रवेशस्तद्विनाशश्च आश्लिष्टमूर्तिरित्यनेन दृढवर्मणः पुनाराज्यप्राप्त्या परितुष्टया राज्ञ्या राज्ञो हस्ते प्रियदर्शिकासमर्पणमित्यादि प्रबन्धार्थः सूचितः ॥

नान्द्यन्त इति—नान्दीलक्षणमादिभरते—आशीर्नमस्क्रियारूपः श्लोकः काव्यार्थसूचकः । नान्दीति कथ्यते तस्यां पदादिनियमोपि वा । नान्दीपदैर्द्वादशभिरष्टाभिर्वाप्यलंकृता ॥ इति । एतन्निरुक्तिर्नाट्यप्रदीपे—नन्दन्ति काव्यानि कवीन्द्रवर्गाः कुशीलवाः पारिषदाश्च सन्तः । यस्मादलं सज्जनसिन्धुहंसी तस्मादियं सा कथितेह नान्दी ॥ इति । सूत्रं प्रयोजनानुष्ठानं धारयति सूत्रधारः । तल्लक्षणं—नाट्यस्य यदनुष्ठानं तत्सूत्रं स्यात्सबीजकम् । रङ्गदैवतपूजाकृत्सूत्रधार उदीरितः ॥ असूत्रयन्गुणान्नेतुः कवेरपि च वस्तुतः । रङ्गप्रसाधनप्रौढः सूत्रधार इहोच्यते ॥ इति । नाना दिशो येषां ते नानादिशः । ते च ते देशाश्च तेभ्य आगतेन । अविद्यमानं पूर्वं यस्याः सा अपूर्वा । अपूर्वा या वस्तु इतिवृत्तं तस्य रचना घटना तया अलंकृता । प्रियदर्शिका नामेति । नाटिका सट्टकादीनां

---

१ दृढः.

नाटिका कृतेत्यस्माभिः श्रोत्रपरंपरया श्रुतम्[1] । न तु प्रयोगतो[2] दृष्टा । तत्तस्यैव राज्ञः सर्वजनहृदयाह्लादिनो बहुमानादस्मासु चानुग्रहबुद्ध्या[3] यथावत्प्रयोगेण त्वया नाटयितव्येति । तद्यावन्नेपथ्यरचनां कृत्वा यथाभिलषितं संपादयामि । (परितोऽवलोक्य ।) आवर्जितानि सामाजिकै[4]र्मनांसीति मे निश्चयः[5] । कुतः ।

श्रीहर्षो निपुणः कविः परिषदप्येषा गुणग्राहिणी
लोके हारि च वत्सराजचरितं नाट्ये च दक्षा वयम् ।
वस्त्वेकैकमपीह वाञ्छितफलप्राप्तेः पदं किं पुन-
र्मद्भाग्योपचयादयं समुदितः सर्वो गुणानां गणः ॥ ३ ॥

(नेपथ्याभिमुखमवलोक्य ।) अये । कथं प्रस्तावनाभ्युद्यते मयि विदितास्मदभिप्रायोऽङ्गाधिपतेर्दृढवर्मणः कञ्चुकिनो[6] भूमिकां कृत्वास्मद्[7]भ्रातेत एवाभिवर्तते । तद्यावदहमप्यनन्तरभूमिकां[8] संपादयामि । (इति निष्क्रान्तः ।)

इति प्रस्तावना ।

नायिकाभिर्विशेषणम् । इत्युक्त्या नायिकाया नाम्ना नाटिकानिर्देशः । नेपथ्यं नाट्योचितवेषकल्पनं रङ्गभूमिर्वा तस्य रचना । नेपथ्यं स्याज्जवनिका रङ्गभूमिः प्रसाधनम् । इत्यजयः । आवर्जितानि अभिमुखीकृतानि वशीकृतानि वा । समजन्त्यस्मिञ्जना इति समाजः । अधिकरणे घञ् । समाजं समवयन्ति सामाजिकाः । 'समवायान्समवैति' इति ठक् ।

श्रीहर्षइति । श्रीहर्षः कविः निपुणः रमणीयकाव्यनिर्माणकुशलः । एषा परिषदपि गुणग्राहिणी । लोके वत्सराज उदयनः तस्य चरितं हारि मनोहरम् । वयं च नाट्ये अभिनयेनावस्थानुकृतौ दक्षा निष्णाताः । इह नाटिकाप्रयोगविषये उक्तेषु गुणेषु वा । एकैकमपि वस्तु वाञ्छितफलस्याभीष्टार्थसिद्धेः पदम् । किं पुनः मद्भाग्यस्योपचायत्प्रकर्षात्समुदितः अयं गुणानां गणः फलप्राप्तेः पदं स्यादिति वक्तव्यमित्यर्थः । शार्दूलविक्रीडितं वृत्तम् ॥ ३ ॥ अथाहमित्यारभ्य भारतीवृत्तिः । भारती संस्कृतप्रायो वाग्व्यापारो नटाश्रयः । इत्युक्तलक्षणा । तस्याश्चत्वारि अङ्गानि । प्ररोचना वीथी प्रहसनं प्रस्तावना चेति । तत्र प्ररोचनेयम् । काव्यार्थापत्तिरलंकारः । प्रस्तावनाभ्युद्यते प्रस्तावनां प्रयुञ्जाने । कञ्चुकिनः—अन्तःपुरचरो राज्ञां वृद्धो विप्रो गुणान्वितः । सर्वकार्यार्थकुशलः कञ्चुकीत्यभिधीयते ॥ मातृगुप्ताचार्या अपि आहुः—ये नित्यं सत्यसम्पन्ना कामदोषविवर्जिताः । ज्ञानविज्ञानकुशलाः कञ्चुकीयास्तु ते स्मृताः ॥ इति । भूमिका वेषग्रहणम् । **प्रस्तावना**—एतल्लक्षणं-नटी विदूषको वापि पारिपार्श्वक एव वा । सूत्रधारेणसहिताः संलापं यत्र कुर्वते । चित्रैर्वाक्यैः स्वकार्योत्थैः प्रस्तुताक्षेपिभिर्मिथः । आमुखं तत्तु विज्ञेयं नाम्ना प्रस्तावनापि सा ॥ इति ॥ अत्र कर्तुमिष्टापि प्रस्तावना न कृता ।

---

१ श्रुता. २ न प्रयो. ३ बुद्ध्या वा. ४ सामाजिकानां. ५ निश्चयः कृतः. ६ आन्तःपुरिककञ्चुकिभूमिकामादाय. ७ अस्मत्तातः. ८ अन्तरभू०, तदर्थभू०.

प्रथमोऽङ्कः ।

(ततः प्रविशति कञ्चुकी ।)

कञ्चुकी—(संशोकश्रमं[1] नाटयन् । निःश्वस्य ।) कष्टं भोः कष्टम् ।

राज्ञो विपद्बन्धुवियोगदुःखं देशाच्च्युतिर्दुर्गममार्गखेदः ।
आस्वाद्यतेऽस्याः कटुनिष्फलायाः फलं मयैतच्चिरजीवितायाः ॥४॥

(संशोकं[2] सविस्मयं च ।) तादृशस्यापि नामाप्रतिहतशक्तित्रयस्य रघुदिलीपनलै[3]स्तुल्यस्य देवस्य दृढवर्मणो मत्प्रार्थ्य[4]मानाप्यनेन स्वदुहिता वत्सराजायै[5] दत्तेति बद्धानुशयेन वत्सराजो[6] बन्धनान्न निवर्तत इति च लब्धरन्ध्रेण सहसागत्य कलिङ्गहतकेन विपत्तिरीदृशी क्रियत इति यत्सत्यमुपपन्नमपि न श्रद्दधे । कथमेकान्तनिष्ठुरमीदृशं च दैवमस्मासु । येन सापि राजपुत्री यथाकथंचिदेनां वत्सराजायोपनीय स्वामिनमनृणं करिष्यामीति मत्वा मया तादृशादपि प्रलयकालदारुणादवस्कन्दसंभ्रमादपवाह्य देवस्य दृढवर्मणो मित्रभावान्वितस्यैवाटविकस्य नृपतेर्विन्ध्यकेतोर्गृहे स्थापिता सती स्नानाय नातिदूरमित्यगस्त्यतीर्थे गते मयि क्षणात्कैरपि[7] निपत्य हते विन्ध्यकेतौ रक्षोभिरिव निर्मानुषीकृते दग्धे स्थाने नें[8] ज्ञायते कस्यामवस्थायां वर्तत इति । निपुणं च विचितमेतन्मया सर्वं स्थानम् । न च ज्ञातं किं तैरेव[9] दस्युभिर्नीताथवा दग्धेति । तत्किं करोमि मन्दभाग्यः । (विचिन्त्य ।) अये । श्रुतं[10] मया बन्धनात्परिभ्रष्टः प्रद्योततनयामपहृत्य वत्सराजः कौशाम्बीमागत इति ।

तामन्तरेणापि कञ्चुकिप्रवेशसूचनात् । अतः प्ररोचनैवेयमिति बोध्यम् । **राज्ञ** इति । राज्ञः मत्स्वामिनो दृढवर्मणः विपत् । बन्धूनां वियोगस्तेन दुःखम् । देशात् च्युतिः प्रभ्रंशः । दुर्गमे दुस्संचरे मार्गे मार्गगमनेनेत्यर्थः । खेदः श्रमः । कटुः दुर्विपाका रूक्षा वा निष्फला च या चिरजीविता दीर्घायुस्त्वं तस्या एतत्फलं मया आस्वाद्यते ॥ उपजातिर्वृत्तम् ॥ ४ ॥ अप्रतिहतमकुण्ठितं शक्तित्रयं यस्य तस्य । प्रभुशक्तिः उत्साहशक्तिः मन्त्रशक्तिश्चेति शक्तित्रयम् । बद्धः अनुशयः दीर्घद्वेषो येन । अनृणमविद्यमानं ऋणं यस्य तथाविधम् । तदिच्छामनुवर्त्येत्यर्थः । अवस्कंदोभियोगस्तस्य संभ्रमात्संरम्भात् । अटव्यां भव आटविकस्तस्य । विचितमन्विष्टम् । दस्युभिश्चौरैः । प्रद्योतः उज्जयिनीनायकः महासेनः । मगधेश्वर इति कथासरित्सागरे । कौशाम्बीमात्मनो

---

१ शोक०, सशोकं श्रमं. २ सशोकवि०. ३ नहुष. ४ मत्प्रार्थने. ५ वत्सराजस्य. ६ राजोपि दृढबन्धने वर्तते. ७ न्वितनया. ८ सापि न. ९ अथवा किमिहैव. १० एवं श्रुतं-

किं तत्रैव गच्छामि। (निःश्वस्यात्मनोऽवस्थां पश्यन्।) किमिवं हि राजपुत्र्या विना तत्र गत्वा कथयिष्यामि। अये। कथितं चाद्य मम विन्ध्यकेतुना— "मा भैषीः। जीवति तत्रभवान्महाराजो दृढवर्मा गाढप्रहारजर्जरीकृतो बद्धस्तिष्ठति।" इति। तदधुना स्वामिनमेव गत्वा पादपरिचर्यया जीवितशेषमात्मनः सफलयिष्यामि। (परिक्रम्योर्ध्वमवलोक्य।) अहो अतिदारुणता शरदातपस्य। यदेवमनेकदुःखसंतापितेनापि मया तीक्ष्णोऽवगम्यते।

घनबन्धनमुक्तोऽयं कन्याग्रहणात्परं तुलां प्राप्य।
रविरधिगतस्वधामा प्रतपति खलु वत्सराज इव॥ ५॥

(इति निष्क्रान्तः।)

इति विष्कम्भकः।

(ततः प्रविशति राजा विदूषकश्च।)

राजा—

भृत्यानामविकारिता परिगता दृष्टा मतिर्मन्त्रिणां
मित्राण्यप्युपलक्षितानि विदितः पौरानुरागोऽधिकम्।
निर्व्यूढा रणसाहसव्यसनिता स्त्रीरत्नमासादितं
निर्व्याजादिव धर्मतः किमिव न प्राप्तं मया बन्धनात्॥ ६॥

नगरीम्। कुशाम्बेन राज्ञा निर्मिता कौशाम्बी। जर्जरीकृतं विह्वलतामापादितम्। **घनबन्धनेति**। घनानां मेघानां बन्धनमुपरोधस्तस्मान्मुक्तः पक्षे घनं दृढं यत्प्रद्योतनृपकृतं बन्धनं तस्मान्मुक्तः कन्यायास्तदाख्यराशेः ग्रहणात्प्रवेशात्परमनन्तरं तुलां तुलराशिं प्राप्य। पक्षे कन्यायाः प्रद्योततनयाया वासवदत्ताया ग्रहणात्परमूर्ध्वं तुलामुत्कर्षं प्राप्य। अयं रविः। अधिगतं स्वधाम स्ववेश्म कौशाम्बीति यावत्। स वत्सराज इव प्रतपति नितरां दहति। पक्षे प्रतापवान्भवति। श्लिष्टोपमा। पथ्यार्यावृत्तम्॥ ५॥ **विष्कम्भकः**। वृत्तवर्तिष्यमाणानां कथांशानां निदर्शकः। संक्षेपार्थस्तुविष्कम्भो मध्यपात्रप्रयोजितः। एकानेककृतः शुद्धः संकीर्णो नीचमध्यमैः॥ इति तल्लक्षणं दशरूपके। शुद्धः केवलमध्यमैः। पात्रैः प्रयोगो भाषैक्यात्संकीर्णो नीचमध्यमैः॥ आदौ विष्कम्भकं कुर्यान्नाटकेषु महाकविः। अपेक्षितं परित्यज्य नीरसं वस्तुविस्तरम्। इत्याद्यन्यत्र च। **भृत्यानामिति**। भृत्यानामविकारिता विकृतत्वाभावः। स्वामिभक्तिरिति यावत्। परिगता ज्ञाता। मन्त्रिणां मतिः प्रज्ञा दृष्टा। मित्राणि उपलक्षितानि यथार्थतया ज्ञातानि। पौराणां मयि अनुरागोपि अधिकं यथा तथा विदितः। रणे साहसं तत्र व्यसनितासक्तिर्निर्व्यूढा अनुष्ठिता। स्त्रीरत्नं वासवदत्तारूपमासादितम्। निर्व्याजान्निष्कपटत्वेन फलाभिसन्धिराहित्येन वा अनुष्ठितात् धर्मत इव बन्धनान्मया किमिव न प्राप्तम्। सर्वमपि प्राप्तमित्यर्थः। शार्दूलविक्रीडितं वृत्तम्॥ लक्षणमुक्तम्॥ ६॥

---

१ अहह राज०; किं कथ०. २ परंतु गाढ०. ३–चर्यया. ४ एतत्तैक्ष्ण्यं. ५ परां.

विदूषकः—(सरोषम् ।) भो वयस्य । कथं तमेव दास्याः पुत्रं बन्धनहतकं प्रशंससि । तदिदानीं विस्मृतम् । यत्तथा नवग्रह इव गजपतिः खलखलायमानलोहशृङ्खलाबन्धप्रतिस्खलच्चरणः शून्यमुखपुष्करपिशुनितहृदयसंतापो रोषवशोत्तम्भितदृष्टिर्गुरुककरस्फोटितधरणिमार्गो रजनीष्वप्यनिद्रासुखमननुभूतोसि । (भो वअस्स । कहं तं एव्व दासीए उत्तं बन्धणहदअं पसंसेसि । तं दाणिं विसुमरिदं । जं तह णवग्गहो विअ गअवई खलखलाअमाणलोहसिङ्खलाबन्धपडिक्खलन्तचलणो सुण्णदुक्खरापिसुणिदहिअअसंदावो रोसवसुत्तम्भिददिठ्ठी गुरुअकरफोडिअधरणिमग्गो रअणीसु वि अणिद्दासुहं अणुहूदोसि ।)

राजा—वसन्तक दुर्जनः खल्वसि । पश्य ।

> **दृष्टं चारकमन्धकारगहनं नो तन्मुखेन्दुद्युतिः ।**
> **पीडा ते निगलस्वनेन मधुरास्तस्या गिरो न श्रुताः ।**
> **क्रूरा बन्धनरक्षिणोऽद्य मनसि स्निग्धाः कटाक्षा न ते**
> **दोषान्पश्यसि बन्धनस्य न पुनः प्रद्योतपुत्र्या गुणान् ॥ ७ ॥**

विदूषकः—(सगर्वम् ।) भोः । यदि तावद्बन्धनं सुखनिबन्धनं भवति

विदूषकः—नायकसहायान्यतमः । तल्लक्षणम्—कुसुमवसन्ताद्यभिधः कर्मवपुर्वेषभाषाद्यैः । हास्यकरः कलहरतिर्विदूषकः स्यात्स्वकर्मज्ञः ॥ इति । विस्मृतं किमिति काकुः । नैतद्विस्मर्तुं शक्यमिति भावः । खलखलायमानः तथाशब्दं कुर्वन् यः लोहशृङ्खलाबन्धस्तेन परिस्खलन्तौ चरणौ यस्य सः । उभयत्र समानम् । शून्यं यन्मुखपुष्करं मुखकमलं तेन पिशुनितः सूचितो हृदयसन्तापो येन । पक्षे मुखपुष्करं शुण्डाग्रम् । रोषवशेन क्रोधाधीनत्वात्क्रोधावेशेनेति यावत् । उत्तम्भिता दृष्टिर्येन सः । गुरुकः पृथुर्यः करो हस्तः शुण्डा च तेन स्फोटितो धरणिमार्गो येन । **दृष्टमिति** । अन्धकारेण गहनं निबिडं चारकं कारागृहं त्वया दृष्टम् । मनसिकृतमित्यर्थः । 'चारकं बन्धनालयः' इति वैजयन्ती । तस्याः वासवदत्तायाः मुखेन्दुद्युतिः वदनचन्द्रकान्तिः नो न दृष्टा । निगडस्वनेन शृङ्खलाशब्देन ते पीडा । मधुरास्तस्या गिरः भाषणानि न श्रुताः । अद्य क्रूरा बन्धनरक्षिणः कारागृहरक्षकाः तव मनसि स्थिताः । न ते तादृशाः स्निग्धाः स्नेहपूर्णाः कटाक्षा नयनप्रान्तविलोकितानि मनसि स्थिता गोचरीभूताः । एवं बन्धनस्य दोषान् पश्यसि न पुनः प्रद्योतपुत्र्याः वासवदत्तायाः गुणान् पश्यसि । अवधारयसीत्यर्थः । बहुगुणसमुदाये अल्पदोषा मज्जन्तीति भावः । शार्दूलविक्रीडितं वृत्तम् । लक्षणमुक्तपूर्वम् ॥७॥

---

१ सुतं (सुदं). २ (तामिदानीं) विस्मर (विंसुमेराहि). ३ यूथपतिः (जूहवई). ४ शून्यदुष्करपिशुनयद्धृ० (सुण्णदुक्खरापिसुणिज्जन्ताहि०) ५ स्थिराधिगतधरणिपृष्ठः (अहिगवधरणिपिट्ठो). ६ अनुवाचयसि (अणुवाचेसि); निद्रासुखं न प्राप्नोषि (निद्दासुहं ण पावेसि). ७ चारकं. ८ निगडबन्धनं सुखबन्धनं (निअल० सुहब०)

तत्कस्मात्त्वं दृढवमा बद्ध इति कलिङ्गराजस्योपरि रोषं बध्नासि ।
(भो । जइ दाव बन्धणं सुहणिबन्धणं होइ ता कीस तुमं दिढवम्मा बद्धोत्ति कलिङ्गरण्णो उवरि रोसं बन्धेसि ।)

राजा—(विहस्य ।) धिङ्मूर्ख । न खलु सर्वो वत्सराजो य एवं वासवदत्तामवाप्य बन्धनान्निर्यास्यति । तदास्तां तावदियं कथा । विन्ध्यकेतोरुपरि बहून्यहानि विजयसेनस्य प्रेषितस्य । न चाद्यापि तत्सकाशात्कश्चिदागतः । तदाहूयतां तावदमात्यो रुमण्वान् । तेन सह किंचिदालपितुमिच्छामि ।

(प्रविश्य ।)

प्रतीहारी—जयतु जयतु देवः । एष खलु विजयसेनोऽमात्यो रुमण्वानपि प्रतीहारभूमिमुपस्थितौ । (जेदु जेदु देव्वो । एसो क्खु विजअसेणो अमच्चो रुमण्णो वि पडिहारभूमिं उवट्ठिओ ।)

राजा—त्वरितं प्रवेशय तौ ।

प्रतीहारी—यद्देव आज्ञापयति । (जं देवो आणवेदि ।) (इतिनिष्क्रान्ता ।)

(ततः प्रविशति रुमण्वान्विजयसेनश्च)

रुमण्वान्—(विचिन्त्य ।)

तत्क्षणमपि निष्क्रान्ताः कृतदोषा इव विनापि दोषेण ।
प्रविशन्ति शङ्कमाना राजकुलं प्रायशो भृत्याः ॥ ८ ॥

(उपसृत्य ।) जयतु देवः ।

राजा—(आसनं निर्दिश्य ।) रुमण्वन् । इत आस्यताम् ।

रुमण्वान्—(सस्मितमुपविश्य ।) एष खलु जितविन्ध्यकेतुर्विजयसेनः प्रणमति ।

(विजयसेनस्तथा करोति ।)

राजा—(सादरं परिष्वज्य ।) अपि कुशली भवान् ।

विजयसेनः—अद्य स्वामिनः प्रसादात् ।

राजा—विजयसेन उपविश्यताम् ।

सुखनिबन्धनं सुखहेतु । **तत्क्षणमिति** । भृत्या राजसेवकाः तत्क्षणं तस्मिन्नेव क्षणे नृपतिपार्श्वान्निष्क्रान्ता निर्गता अपि दोषेण विनापि कृतदोषाः कृतापराधा इव शङ्कमाना सभयाः राजकुलं प्रविशन्ति । स्वभावोक्तिः । आर्या छन्दः ॥ ८ ॥

---

१ उद्वहसि (उन्नहासि). २ दिवसानि ३ आहूयताम०. ४ विन्ध्यकेतोर्विजेता. ५ स्थीयताम्.

(विजयसेन उपविशति ।)

राजा—विजयसेन कथय विन्ध्यकेतोर्वृत्तान्तम् ।

विजयसेनः—देव किमपरं कथयामि । यादृशः स्वामिनि कुपिते ।

राजा—तथापि विस्तरतः श्रोतुमिच्छामि ।

विजयसेनः—देव श्रूयताम् । इतो वयं देवपादादेशाद्यथादिष्टेन करितुरगपदातिसैन्येन महान्तमप्यध्वानं दिवसत्रयेणोल्लङ्घ्य प्रभातवेलायामतर्किता एव विन्ध्यकेतोरुपरि निपतिताः स्मः ।

राजा—ततस्ततः ।

विजयसेनः—ततः सोऽप्यस्मद्बल[1]तुमुलकलकलाकर्णनेन प्रतिबुद्धः केसरीव विन्ध्यकन्दरान्निर्गत्य विन्ध्यकेतुरनपेक्षितबलवाहनो यथासंनिहितकतिपयसहायः सहसा स्व[2]नामोद्घोषयन्नस्मानभि[3]योद्धुं प्रवृत्तः ।

राजा—(रुमण्वन्तमवलोक्य सस्मितम् ।) शोभितं विन्ध्यकेतुना । ततस्ततः ।

विजयसेनः—ततोऽस्माभिरयमसाविति द्विगुण[4]तरबद्धमत्सरोत्साहैर्महता विमर्देन निःशेषितसहाय एक एव विमर्दिताधिकबलक्रोधवेगो दारुणतरं संप्रहारमकरोत् ।

राजा—साधु विन्ध्यकेतो । साधु साधु ।

विजयसेनः—किं वा वर्ण्यते देव । संक्षेपतो विज्ञापयामि ।

पादातं पत्तिरेव प्रथमतरमुरःपेष[5]मात्रेण पिष्ट्वा
दूरा[6]न्नीत्वा शरौघैर्हरिणकुलमिव त्रस्तमश्वीयमाशाः ।

यादृश इति अतिदारुण इत्यर्थः । पादाभ्यां शत्रोः पुरो युद्धार्थमतति यातीति पदातिः । तुमुलः रणसंकुलः । कन्दरात् गुहायाः । अनवेक्षितं बलं सेना वाहनानि करितुरगरथादीनि येन । यथा संनिहिताः कतिपये सहाया यस्य सः । शोभितं शोभनं कृतमित्यर्थः । भावे क्तः । अतिशयेन द्वौ गुणौ यस्मिन्स द्विगुणतरः । यस्मिन्कर्मणि तद्यथा तथा इति वा । तथा बद्धो मत्सर उत्साहश्च यैस्ते तथोक्ताः तैः । विमर्दः कदनं नाशो वा । विमर्दितेन स्वसहायानां विमर्दनेन अधिको वृद्धिं गतो बलस्य क्रोधस्य च वेगो यस्य स तथा । संप्रहारं युद्धम् । **पादातमिति** । स विन्ध्यकेतुः पत्तिः पदातिः एव सन् प्रथमतरमुरसा स्ववक्षसा यः पेषः मर्दनं तन्मात्रेण एव पादातं पदातिसमूहम् । 'भिक्षादिभ्योऽण्' इत्यण् । पिष्ट्वा संचूर्ण्य । शरौघैः शरसमूहैः त्रस्तं हरिणकुलमिव अश्वीयमस्मदश्वसमूहम् । 'केशाश्वाभ्यां यञ्छावन्यतरस्याम्' इति छः । दूराद्दूरमाशा दिशो नीत्वा । दूरं विद्राव्येत्यर्थः । सर्वत्र

---

१ बलकलकला०. २ स्वमुद्घो०. ३ अभियोक्तुं. ४ द्विगुणबद्ध. ५ क्षेप. ६ दूर.

सर्वत्रोत्सृष्टसर्वप्रहरणनिवहस्तूर्णमुत्खाय खङ्गं
पश्चात्कर्तुं प्रवृत्तः करिकरकदलीकाननच्छेदलीलाम् ॥ ९ ॥

एवं बलत्रितयमाकुलमेक एव
कुर्वन्कृपाणकिरणच्छुरितांसकूटः।
शस्त्रप्रहारशतजर्जरितोरुवक्षाः
श्रान्तश्चिराद्विनिहतो युधि विन्ध्यकेतुः ॥ १० ॥

राजा—रुमण्वन्। सत्पुरुषोचितं मार्गमनुगच्छतो यत्सत्यं व्रीडिता ऐव वयं विन्ध्यकेतोर्मरणेन।

रुमण्वान्—देव त्वाद्विधानामेवं गुणैकपक्षपातिनां रिपोरपि गुणाः प्रीतिं जनयन्ति।

राजा—विजयसेन अप्यस्ति विन्ध्यकेतोरपत्यं यत्रास्य परितोषस्य फलं दर्शयामि।

विजयसेनः—देव इदमपि विज्ञापयामि। एवं सबन्धुपरिवारे हते विन्ध्यकेतौ तमनुसृतासु सहधर्मचारिणीषु विन्ध्याशिखराश्रितेषु जनपदेषु शून्यीभूते तत्स्थाने "हा तात हा मातः" इति कृतकृपणप्रलापा विन्ध्यकेतोर्वेश्मन्यभिजात्यानुरूपा कन्यका तद्दुहितेत्यस्माभिरानीता द्वारि तिष्ठति। तां प्रति देवः प्रमाणम्।

सर्वासु दिक्षु उत्सृष्टेः मुक्तः सर्वेषां प्रहरणानामायुधानां निवहः समूहो येन स तथोक्तः। तूर्णं शीघ्रं खङ्गमुत्खाय कोशादाकृष्य। उत्पूर्वात्खनतेर्ल्यप्। पश्चात्तदनन्तरं करिणां कराः शुण्डा एव कदल्यस्तासां काननं तस्य छेदस्य लीलां केलिम्। अनायासेन खण्डनमिति यावत्। कर्तुं प्रवृत्तः। स्रग्धरावृत्तम्। लक्षणमुक्तम् ॥ ९ ॥

एवमिति। एवमेक एव बलत्रितयं त्रिविधं करितुरगपदातिरूपं सैन्यमाकुलं व्याकुलं कुर्वन्। कृपाणस्य खङ्गस्य किरणैः छुरितो रूषितः अंसकूटोंऽसशिखरदेशो यस्य स तथोक्तः। शस्त्राणां प्रहारशतेन जर्जरितं विभिन्नमुरु विशालं वक्षो यस्य स तादृशः। चिराच्छ्रान्तः विन्ध्यकेतुः युधि विनिहतः। उदात्तालंकारः। वसन्ततिलका छन्दः। उक्ता वसन्ततिलका तभजा जगौगः। इति तल्लक्षणम् ॥ १० ॥ सत्पुरुषोचितां—तदुक्तं—द्वाविमौ पुरुषौ लोके स्वर्गमण्डलभेदिनौ। परिव्राड् योगयुक्तश्च रणे चाभिमुखो हतः ॥ इति। व्रीडिता लज्जां प्राप्ताः। एकस्य बहुभिर्घातादित्याशयः। बन्धवश्च परिवारश्च तैः सहितः सबन्धुपरिवारः तस्मिन्। सहधर्मचारिणीषु तत्पत्नीषु। कृतः कृपणः दीनः प्रलाप आर्तरवो यया सा। आभिजात्यं कुलीनता तस्यानुरूपा। देवः प्रमाणं

---

१ रुधिर. २ [illegible]रित. ३ इव. ४ पदेषु।विनष्टेषु. ५ तात. ६ आभिजातरूपा.

राजा—यशोधरे गच्छ[1]। त्वमेव वासवदत्तायाः समर्पय। वक्तव्या च देवी। भगिनीबुद्ध्या त्वयैव सर्वदा द्रष्टव्या। गीतनृत्तवाद्यादिषु विशिष्टकन्यकोचितं सर्वं शिक्षयितव्या। यदा वरयोग्या भविष्यति तदा मां[2] स्मारयेति।

प्रतीहारी—यद्देव आज्ञापयति। (जं देवो आणवेदि।) (इति निष्क्रान्ता।)

(नेपथ्ये वैतालिकः।)

लीलामज्जनमङ्गलोपकरणस्नानीयसम्पादिनः
सर्वान्तःपुरवारविभ्रमवतीलोकस्य ते संप्रति।
आयासस्खलदंशुका[3]व्यवहितच्छायावदातैः स्तनै-
रुत्क्षिप्तापरशातकुम्भकलशेवालंकृता स्नानभूः ॥ ११ ॥

राजा—(ऊर्ध्वमवलोक्य।) अये कथं नभोमध्यमध्यास्ते भगवान्सहस्रदीधितिः। संप्रति हि।

आभात्यर्कांशुतापक्वथदिव शफरोद्वर्तनैर्दीर्घिकाम्भ-
श्छत्राभं नृत्तलीलाशिथिलमपि शिखी बर्हभारं तनोति।

यथाकर्तव्यनिर्णये इत्यर्थः। विशिष्टकन्यकोत्तमकुलप्रसूता कन्या। **वैतालिक** इति। विविधेन तालेन चरतीति वैतालिकः बोधकरः। चरति इति ठक्। विविधतालः प्रयोजनमस्य इति वा ठञ्। एतल्लक्षणं भावप्रकाशे—तत्तत्प्रहरकयोग्यै रागैस्तत्कालवाचिकैः श्लोकैः। सरभसमेव वितालं गायन् वैतालिको भवति॥ इति। **लीलेति**। ते तव स्नानभूः लीलया सविलासं यन्मज्जनं स्नानं तदेव मङ्गलं तस्य उपकरणानि यानि स्नानीयानि स्नानोपयुक्तगन्धचूर्णादीनि तानि सम्पादयितुं शीलमस्येति तस्य। सर्वो योऽन्तःपुरसम्बन्धी वारविभ्रमवतीलोकः वाराङ्गनाजनस्तस्य। आयासेन श्रमेण स्खलद् यदंशुकं स्तनोत्तरीयं तेन अव्यवहिता अनाच्छन्ना या छाया कान्तिः तया अवदातैः गौरत्वेन भासमानैः। छाया येषां ते तथा अवदाताश्च तैरिति वा। स्तनैः। उत्क्षिप्ता अपरे शातकुम्भस्य सुवर्णस्य कलशा यस्यां सा तथेव। सम्प्रति अलंकृता। उत्प्रेक्षालंकारः। शार्दूलविक्रीडितं वृत्तम्। लक्षणमुक्तं प्राक्॥ ११॥

आभातीति। दीर्घिकाया उद्यानवाप्या जलं शफराणां मत्स्यविशेषाणामुद्वर्तनैरुत्प्लवनैः। अर्कांशुतापेन सूर्यकिरणोष्मणा क्वथदिवाभाति। शिखी मयूरः। नृत्तलीलया शिथिलं विस्रस्तं। नृत्तलीलायां सूर्यतापात् शिथिलमिति वा। बर्हभारं पिच्छसमूहं

---

[1] गच्छ गच्छ. [2] अस्मान्. [3] कव्यव०.

छायाचक्रं तरूणां हरिणशिशुरुपैत्यालवालाम्बुलुब्धः
सद्यस्त्यक्त्वा कपोलं विशति मधुकरः कर्णपालीं गजस्य ॥१२॥

रुमण्वन् । उत्तिष्ठोत्तिष्ठ । प्रविश्याभ्यन्तरमेव कृतयथोचितक्रियाः सत्कृत्य विजयसेनं कलिङ्गोच्छित्तये प्रेषयामः ।

(इति निष्क्रान्ताः सर्वे ।)

इति प्रथमोऽङ्कः ॥

॥ द्वितीयोऽङ्कः ॥

(ततः प्रविशति विदूषकः ।)

विदूषकः—ननु भणितोऽस्मीन्दीवरिकया यथा-आर्य उपवासनियमस्थिता देवी वासवदत्ता स्वस्तिवाचननिमित्तं शब्दायेतेति । तद्यावद्धारागृहोद्यानदीर्घिकायां स्नात्वा देवीपार्श्वं गत्वा कुक्कुटवादं करिष्यामि । अन्यथा कथमस्माभिः सदृशा ब्राह्मणा राजकुले प्रतिग्रहं कुर्वन्ति । (नेपथ्याभिमुखमवलोक्य) कथमेष प्रियवयस्योऽद्य देव्या विरहोत्कण्ठाविनोदननिमित्तं धारागृहोद्यानमेव प्रस्थितः । तद्यावद्वयस्येन सहैव गत्वा यथोदितमनुष्ठास्यामि । (णं भणिदोह्मि इन्दीवरिआए जह अज्ज उववासणिअमट्ठिआ देवी वासवदत्ता सोत्थिवाअणणिमित्तं सद्दावेदित्ति । ता जाव धाराघरुज्जाणदिग्घिआए ण्हाइअ देवीपासं गदुअ कुक्कुटवादं करिस्सं । अण्णहा कहं अह्माणं सरिसा ब्रह्मणा राअकुले पडिग्गहं करेन्ति । कहं एसो पिअवअस्सो अज्ज देवीए विरहुक्कण्ठविणोदणाणिमित्तं धाराघरुज्जाणं एव्व पत्थिदो । ता जाव वअस्सेण सह एव्व गदुअ जहोदिदं अणुचिट्ठिस्सं ।)

छत्राभमातपत्रवत् तनोति विस्तारयति । हरिणशिशुः आ समन्तात् लवान् जललवान् आलातीत्यालवालम् । तस्मिन् यदम्बु तत्र लुब्धः सन् तरूणां छायाचक्रमुपैति । मधुकरश्च गजस्य कपोलं सद्यः त्यक्त्वा कर्णपालीं श्रोत्रपुटं विशति । छायार्थमित्यर्थः । स्वभावोक्तिः । स्रग्धरा वृत्तम् ॥ १२ ॥

ततः प्रविशतीति । स्वस्तिवायनं स्वस्तिवाचनार्थं व्रतोपायनम् । शब्दायेत आह्वयेदित्यर्थः । कुक्कुटवादं दम्भार्थं वेदमजानन्नपि उच्चैः पठनम् । कुक्कुटोऽनृतवादः स्यात् इति मेदिनी । उत्कण्ठा अभिलाषपूर्वा स्मृतिः । सर्वेन्द्रियसुखास्वादो यत्रास्तीत्यभिमन्यते । तत्प्राप्तीच्छां ससङ्कल्पामुत्कण्ठां कवयो विदुः ॥ इति तल्लक्षणम् । तस्या विनोदनमपनयनम् । धारागृहं धारायन्त्रोपेतं गृहं धारागृहं धारागृहयुक्तमुद्यानं धारागृहोद्यानम् ।

---

१ कृतकोच्छि०. २ शब्दापयेत्. ३ यथोद्दिष्टं (जहोद्दिट्ठं.)

(ततः प्रविशति सोत्कण्ठो राजा ।)

राजा—

क्षामां मङ्गलमात्रमण्डनभृतं मन्दोद्यमालापिनी-
माापाण्डुच्छविना मुखेन विजितप्रातस्तनेन्दुद्युतिम् ।
सोत्कण्ठां नियमोपवासविधिना चेतो ममोत्कण्ठते
तां द्रष्टुं प्रथमानुरागजनितावस्थामिवाद्य प्रियाम् ॥१॥

विदूषकः—(उपसृत्य ।) स्वस्ति भवते । वर्धतां भगवान् । (सोत्थि होदे । वड्ढदु भवं ।)

राजा—(विलोक्य ।) वसन्तक । कस्मात्प्रहृष्ट इव लक्ष्यसे ।

विदूषकः—अर्चति खलु देवी ब्राह्मणम् । (अच्चदि क्खु देवी बह्मणं ।)

राजा—यद्येवं ततः किम् ।

विदूषकः—(सगर्वम् ।) भोः । ईदृशः खलु ब्राह्मणः । यश्चतुर्वेदपञ्चवेदषड्वेदब्राह्मणसहस्रपर्याकुले राजकुले प्रथमम्[3]हमेव देवीसकाशात्स्वस्तिवा[4]यनं लभे । (भो । ईरिसो क्खु बह्मणो । जो चउव्वेदपञ्चवेदछव्वेदबम्हणसहस्सपज्जाउले राअउले पुढमं अहं एव्व देवीसआसादो सोत्थिवाअणं लहेमि ।)

राजा—(विहस्य ।) वेदसंख्ययैवावेदितं ब्राह्मण्यम् । तदागच्छ महाब्राह्मण । धारा[5]गृहोद्यानमेव गच्छावः ।

विदूषकः—यद्देव आज्ञापयति । (जं देवो आणवेदि ।)

राजा—गच्छाग्रतः ।

क्षामामिति । नियमार्थे व्रतार्थमुपवासः तस्य विधिरनुष्ठानं तेन हेतुना क्षामां कृशाम् । मङ्गलानि कण्ठसूत्रनासामणिताटङ्कादीन्येव मङ्गलमात्राणि मण्डनानि बिभर्तीति ताम् । मन्दं यथा तथा उद्यमेन प्रयत्नेनाल्पतीति तथा ताम् । आपाण्डुः छविः कान्तिर्यस्य तेनापाण्डुना मुखेन विजिता प्रातस्तनस्येन्दोर्द्युतिर्यया ताम् । सोत्कण्ठां च । अत एव प्रथमानुरागेण जनिता अवस्था कृशत्वादिलक्षणा यस्यास्तामिव तां तथानुरागिणीं प्रियामद्य द्रष्टुं मम चेतः उत्कण्ठते उत्सुकं भवति । उपमास्वभावोक्त्योः संसृष्टिरलंकारः । शार्दूलविक्रीडितं वृत्तम् ॥ १ ॥ चत्वारो वेदा येषां ते चतुर्वेदाः । एवमन्यत्र । पञ्चवेदेत्यादिः परिहासार्थमुक्तिः । महाब्राह्मणेति उपहासार्थम् । अत्र महच्छब्दो निन्दापरः । तदुक्तं—शंखे तैले तथा मांसे वैद्ये ज्यौतिषके द्विजे । यात्रायां पथि निद्रायां महच्छब्दो न दीयते ॥ इति ।

---

१ मन्दोद्यता०. २ प्रचया०. ३ प्रथममेव लभते. ४ वाचनं. ५ धाराधरो.

विदूषकः—भो एहि गच्छावः । (परिक्रम्यावलोक्य च ।) भो वयस्य पश्य पश्य । अविरतपतद्विविधकुसुमसुकुमारशिलातलोत्सङ्गस्य परिमलनिलीनमधुकरभरभग्नबकुलमालतीलताजालकस्य कमलगन्धग्रहणोद्दाममारुतपर्यवबुद्धबन्धूकबन्धनस्याविरलतमालतरुपिहितातपप्रकाशस्यास्य धारागृहोद्यानस्य सश्रीकताम् । (भो एहि गच्छम्ह । भो वअस्स पेक्ख पेक्ख । अविरदपडन्तविविहकुसुमसुउमालसिलाअलुच्छङ्गस्स परिमलणिलीणमहुअरभरभग्गबउलमालदीलदाजालअस्स कमलगन्धगहणुद्दाममारुदपज्जवबुद्धबन्धूअबन्धणस्स अविरलतमालतरुपिहिदातपप्पआसस्स अस्स धाराघरुज्जाणस्स सस्सरीअअं ।)

राजा—वयस्य साध्वभिहितम् । अत्र हि ।

वृन्तैः क्षुद्रप्रवालस्थगितमिव तलं भाति शेफालिकानां
गन्धः सप्तच्छदानां सपदि गजमदामोदमोहं करोति ।
एते चोन्निद्रपद्मच्युतबहलैरजःपुञ्जपिङ्गाङ्गरागा
गायन्त्यव्यक्तवाचः किमपि मधुलिहो वारुणीपानमत्ताः ॥२॥

विदूषकः—भो वयस्य एतदपि तावत्पश्य पश्य । य एषोऽविरलपतत्कुसुमनिकरोऽद्यापि पत्रान्तरगलद्वर्षावसानसलिलबिन्दुरिव लक्ष्यते

अविरतं यथा तथा पतन्ति यानि विविधानि कुसुमानि तैः सुकुमारः मृदुस्पर्शः मनोहरो वा शिलातलस्य उत्सङ्गो मध्यप्रदेशो यत्र तत् ०त्सङ्गं तस्य । परिमलेन निलीनाश्च ते मधुकराश्च तेषां भरेण भग्नानि बकुलानां मालतीलतानां जातिलतानां जालकानि पुष्पगुच्छा यस्मिंस्तस्य । कमलानां गन्धस्य ग्रहणेन उद्दामा उत्कटो यो मारुतस्तेन पर्यवबुद्धानि विकसितानि बन्धूकानां बन्धूकपुष्पाणां बन्धनानि वृन्तानि यस्मिन् तस्य । अविरलाश्च ते तमालतरवश्च तैः पिहितो निवारित आतपप्रकाशः सूर्यालोको यस्मिन् तस्य । **वयस्य**—वयसा तुल्यः वयस्यः । 'नौवयोधर्म' इति यत् । **वृन्तैरिति** । शेफालिकानां निर्गुंडीकुसुमानां वृन्तैः बन्धनैः तलं भूमितलं क्षुद्रैः प्रवालैः अल्पैर्विद्रुमखण्डैः स्थगितमावृतमिव भाति । सप्तच्छदानां गन्धः सपदि तत्क्षणं गजमदस्य य आमोदः परिमलस्तस्य मोहं भ्रान्तिं तनोति जनयति । उन्निद्रेभ्यो विकसितेभ्यः पद्मेभ्यः च्युतः बहलः रजःपुञ्जः तेन पिङ्गः पीतवर्णः अङ्गरागः अङ्गवर्णो येषां ते । बहलरजःपुञ्ज एव पीतोङ्गरागो येषामिति वा । वारुणीपानेन पुष्परसमधुपानेन मत्ता अत एव अव्यक्तवाचः एते मधुलिहो मधुकराश्च किमपि गायन्ति । उत्प्रेक्षाभ्रान्तिमत्स्वभावोक्तीनां संसृष्टिः । स्रग्धरा वृत्तम् ॥ २ ॥ **अविरलेति** । अविरलं निरन्तरं यथा तथा पतन्कुसुमनिकरो यस्य सः । अद्यापि पत्रान्तरेभ्यो गलन्तः वर्षावसानसलिलबिन्दवो यस्य स इव लक्ष्यते । तं पश्येति सम्बन्धः ।

---

१ बहलो (बहणुद्दा०). २ प्रतिबुद्ध (पडिबु०). ३ बहुल. ४ काणपिङ्गा. ५ गेग्रपत्रा (णिअरो अग्गप). ६ वसानसमयसलि० (वसाणसमअ०).

सप्तपर्णपादपः। (भो वअस्स। एदं पि दाव पेक्ख पेक्ख। जो एसो अविरलपडन्तकुसुमणिअरो अज्ज वि पत्तन्तरगळन्तवरिसावसाणसलिलबिन्दू विअ लक्खीअदि सत्तवण्णपाअवो।)

राजा—वयस्य सम्यगुत्प्रेक्षितम्। बह्वेव सदृशं जलदसमयस्य। तथाहि।

बिभ्राणा मृदुतां शिरीषकुसुमश्रीहारिभिः शाद्वलैः
सद्यः कल्पितकुट्टिमा मरकतक्षोदैरिव क्षालितैः।
एषा संप्रति बन्धनाद्विगलितैर्बन्धूकपुष्पोत्करै-
रद्यापि क्षितिरिन्द्रगोपकशतैश्छन्नेव संलक्ष्यते ॥ ३ ॥

(ततः प्रविशति चेटी।)

चेटी—आज्ञप्तास्मि देव्या वासवदत्तया। हञ्जे इन्दीवरिके अद्य मयागस्त्यमहर्षयेऽर्घो दातव्यः। तद्गच्छ त्वम्। शेफालिकाकुसुममालां लघु गृहीत्वागच्छेति। एषाप्यारण्यिका धारागृहोद्यानदीर्घिकाया यावदेव विकसितानि कमलानि नास्ताभिलाषिणा सूर्येण मुकुलाय्यन्ते तावदेव लघ्ववचित्यागच्छत्विति। एषा तपस्विनी तां दीर्घिकां न जानाति। तद्गृहीत्वा तां गमिष्यामि। (नेपथ्याभिमुखमवलोक्य।) इत इत आरण्यिके एहि। (आणत्तह्मि देवीए वासवदत्ताए। हञ्जे इन्दीवरिए। अज्ज मए अगत्थिमहेसिणो अग्घो दादव्वो। ता गच्छ तुमं। सेहालिआकुसुममालं लहु गेण्हिअ आअच्छेत्ति। एसावि आरण्णिआ धाराघरुज्जाणदीहिआए जाव एव्व विआसिआइं कमलाइं ण अत्थाहिला-

---

बिभ्राणेति। शिरीषकुसुमानां श्रियं शोभां हरन्तीति तैः शाद्वलैः शादहरितप्रदेशैः मृदुतां कोमलतां बिभ्राणा। क्षालितैः निर्मृष्टैः मरकतक्षोदैः मरकतखण्डैः सद्यस्तत्क्षणं कल्पितकुट्टिमा इव स्थिता। एषा भूमिः सप्रति बन्धनाद्विगलितैः बन्धूकपुष्पाणामुत्करैः पुञ्जैः अद्यापि इन्द्रगोपकशतैः छन्ना इव लक्ष्यते। शार्दूलविक्रीडितं वृत्तम्॥ ३॥ हञ्जे इति चेटीं प्रति सम्बोधनम्। 'हण्डे हञ्जे हलाह्वाने नीचां चेटीं सखीं प्रति'। इत्यमरः। अगस्त्यमहर्षये। अत्र—अप्राप्ते भास्करे कन्यां शेषभूतैस्त्रिभिर्दिनैः। अर्घ्यं दद्युरगस्त्याय गौडदेशनिवासिनः॥ इति ब्रह्मवैवर्ते। भीमपराक्रमेऽपि—यस्तु भाद्रपदस्यान्त उदिते कलशोद्भवे। अर्घ्यं दद्यादगस्त्याय सर्वान्कामाँल्लभेत सः॥ इति। पद्यद्वयमुद्धृतं श्रीकृष्णसूरिभिः। अरण्ये भवा आरण्यिका। 'अरण्यान्मनुष्ये' इत्यनेनारण्यशब्दाद्वुञ्। 'प्रत्ययस्थात्कात्'० इति इत्वम्। मुकुलाय्यन्ते मुकुलवदाचरन्ति मुकुलायन्ते तथा क्रियन्ते। संकुच्यन्ते इत्यर्थः।

---

१ सम्यगुपलक्षितं वयस्येन। अत्र हि बह्वेव. २ अर्घ्यं दानव्यम्. ३ पुष्पाणि ल०. ४ यावदेव अस्ता० सूर्येण न मुकुल्यन्ते कमलानि (जाव एव्व अत्था० णमुउलाविज्जन्ति कमलाइं) तावदेवावचित्य. ५ तप. आरण्यि. ६ इत एहि आ.

सिणा सुज्जेण मउलाविज्जन्ति ताव एव्व लहुअं अवचिणुअ आअच्छदुत्ति । एसा तवस्सिणी तं दीहिअं ण जाणादि । ता गेण्हिअ तं गमिस्सं । इदो इदो आरण्णिए एहि ।)

(ततः प्रविशत्यारण्यिका ।)

आरण्यिका—(सबाष्पोद्वेगमात्मगतम् ।) तथा नाम तादृशे वंश उत्पन्नयान्यजनमाज्ञाप्य स्थितया सांप्रतं परस्य मयाज्ञप्तिः कर्तव्येति नास्ति खलु दुष्करं दैवस्य । अथवा ममैवैष दोषो येन जानत्यापि न व्यापादित आत्मा । तत्किं सांप्रतं करिष्यामि । अथवा दुष्करमिदानीं मया चिन्तितम् । वरमेवैतदपि । न पुनरात्मनो महार्घं वंशं प्रकाशयन्त्या मया लघूकृत आत्मा । तत्का गतिः । यथाभणितमनुष्ठास्यामि । (तह णाम तारिसे वंसे उप्पण्णाए अण्णजणं आण्णाविअ ठ्दिाए संपदं परस्स मए आणत्ती कादव्वेत्ति णात्थि क्खु दुक्खरं देव्वस्स । अहवा मह एव्व एसो दोसो जेण जाणन्तीए वि ण वावादिओ अप्पा । ता किं संपदं करिस्सं । अहवा दुक्खरं दाणिं मए चिन्तिदं । वरं एव्व एदं वि । ण उण अप्पणो महग्घं वंसं पआसअन्तीए मए लहूकिदो अप्पा । ता का गई । जहभणिदं अणुचिट्ठिस्सं ।)

चेटी—इत एह्यारण्यिके । (इदो एहि आरण्णिए ।)

आर०—इयमागच्छामि । (श्रमं नाटयन्ती ।) हञ्जे दूरे किमद्यापि दीर्घिका । (इअं आअच्छामि । हञ्जे दूरे किं अज्जवि दिग्घिआ ।)

चेटी—एषा शेफालिकागुल्मान्तरिता । तदेहि अवतरावः । (अवतरणं नाटयतः ।) (एसा सेहालिआगुम्मन्तरिआ । ता एहि ओदरह्म ।)

राजा—वयस्य किमन्यदिव चिन्तयसि । ननु ब्रवीमि बह्वेव सदृशं जलदसमयस्येति । (बिभ्राणा मृदुतामित्यादि पुनः पठति ।)

विदूषकः—(सक्रोधम् ।) भोः त्वं तावदेतदन्यच्च पश्यन्नुत्कण्ठानिर्भरं विनोदयस्यात्मानम् । मम पुनर्ब्राह्मणस्य स्वस्तिवाचनवेलातिक्रामति । तद्यावदहं त्वरितं दीर्घिकायां स्नात्वा देव्याः सकाशं गमिष्यामि । (भो तुमं दाव एदं अण्णं अ पेक्खन्तो उक्कण्ठाणिब्भरं विणोदेसि अप्पाणं । मम उण बह्मणस्स सोत्थिवाअणवेला अदिक्कमदि । ता जाव अहं तुवरिअं दीहिआए ण्हाइअ देवीए सआसं गमिस्सं ।)

तादृशे सुप्रसिद्धे । वरं मनाक्प्रियम् । महार्घमुदारम् । लघूकृतः लघुतां नीतः । गुल्मः स्तम्बः ।

---

१ सबाष्पमात्म०. २ उत्पन्ना दासजनमा० साम्प्रतं (उप्पण्णा दासजणं आणाविअ संपदं). ३ यंन्तिष्ठासि. ४ देवीसकाशं.

राजा—ननु मूर्ख पारंगता एव वयं दीर्घिकायाः । एवमनेकेन्द्रियसु[1]खातिशयमनुभवन्नपि नोपल[2]क्षयसि । पश्य ।

श्रोत्रं हंसस्वनोऽयं सुखयति दयितानूपुरै[3]र्ह्लादकारी
दृष्टिप्रीतिं विधत्ते तटतरुविवरालक्षिता सौधपाली ।
गन्धेनाम्भोरुहाणां परिम[4]लपटुना जायते घ्राणसौख्यं
गात्रा[5]णां ह्लादमेते विदधति मरुतो वारिसंप[6]र्कशीताः ॥ ४ ॥

तदेहि दीर्घिकातटमुपसर्पावः । (परिक्रम्यावलोक्य च ।) वयस्य पश्य पश्य ।

उद्यानदेवतायाः स्फुटपङ्कजकान्तिहारिणी स्वच्छा ।
दृष्टिरिव दीर्घिकेयं रमयति मां दर्शनेनैव ॥ ५ ॥

विदूषकः—(सकौतुकम् ।) भो वयस्य पश्य पश्य । कैषा[7] कुसुमपरिमलसुगन्धवेणिमधुकरावलिर्विद्रुमलतारुणहस्तपल्लवा उज्ज्वलत्तनुकोमलबाहुलता सत्यं प्रत्यक्षचरीवोद्यानदेवता स्त्री दृश्यते । (भो वअस्स पेक्ख पेक्ख । का एसा कुसुमपरिमलसुअन्धवेणीमहुअरावली विद्दुमलआरुणहत्थपल्लवा उज्जलन्ततणुकोमलबाहुलदा सच्चं पच्चक्खचरी विअ उज्जाणदेवदा इत्थिआ दीसइ ।)

राजा—(सकौतुकं विलोक्य ।) वयस्य निरतिशयस्वरूपशोभाजनितबहुविकल्पेयम् । यत्सत्यमहमपि नावगच्छामि । पश्य ।

पारंगतास्तीरं प्राप्ताः । अनेकानि च तानि इन्द्रियाणि तेषां सुखातिशयमतिशयितं सुखमित्यर्थः । तदेव दर्शयति—**श्रोत्रमिति** । दयितायाः प्रेयस्या नूपुरस्येव ह्लादं शब्दं करोतीति तथा । दयितामञ्जीरशिञ्जितसदृश इत्यर्थः। अयं हंसस्वनः श्रोत्रं कर्णौ इत्यर्थः। सुखयति । तटतरूणां विवरेभ्यो लक्षिता दृष्टा सौधपाली तटस्थिताट्टपंक्तिः दृष्टेः नयनयोः प्रीतिं मुदं विधत्ते । अम्भोरुहाणां परिमलेन पटुना स्फुटेन गन्धेन सौरभ्येण घ्राणस्य सौख्यं जायते । एते वारिसंपर्केण शीताः मरुतो वायवः गात्राणां ह्लादं विदधति च । स्वभावोक्तिः । स्रग्धरा छंदः ॥ ४ ॥ **उद्यानेति** । स्फुटानां विकसितानां पङ्कजानां कमलानां कान्त्या हरतीति हारिणी मनोहरा । दृष्टिपक्षे कान्तिवत् हारिणी । स्वच्छा उद्यानदेवताया दृष्टिः इव इयं दीर्घिका मां दर्शनेनैव रमयति । श्लिष्टोपमालंकारः । आर्योपगीतिः ॥ ५ ॥

कुसुमेति । कुसुमानां वेण्यां धृतानां परिमलेन सुगन्धा वेणिस्तत्र मधुकरावली यस्याः सा । पक्षे कुसुमानामुद्यानस्थानां । वेणिभूता मधुकरावली यस्याः सा । विद्रुमलतेव प्रवाललतेव अरुणः रक्तः हस्तपल्लवो यस्याः । पक्षे हस्त इव पल्लवो यस्याः । उज्ज्वलन्ती तनुः कोमला च बाहुलता यस्याः । निरतिशया चासौ स्वरूपशोभा च । तया । निरतिशये स्वरूपं च शोभा च ताभ्यामिति वा । जनिता बहवो विकल्पा कल्पना यया सा

---

१ सुखमनु०. २ लभसे. ३ राह्लाद. ४ माला. ५ गात्रस्या. ६ संस्पर्श. ७ का पुनरेषा (का उण.)

पातालाद्भुवनावलोकनपरा किं नागकन्योत्थिता
मिथ्या तत्खलु दृष्टमेव हि मया तस्मिन्कुतोऽस्तीदृशी।
मूर्ता स्यादिह कौमुदी न घटते तस्या दिवा दर्शनं
केयं हस्ततलस्थितेन कमलेनालोक्यते श्रीरिव ॥ ६ ॥

विदूषकः—(निरूप्य।) एषा खलु देव्याः परिचारिकेन्दीवरिका[3]। तद्गुल्मान्तारितौ भूत्वा पश्यावः। (एसा क्खु देवीए परिआरिआ इन्दीवरिआ। ता गुम्मन्तरिआ भविअ पेक्खह्म।)

(उभौ तथा कुरुतः।)

चेटी—(कमलिनीपत्रग्रहणं नाटयन्ती।) आरण्यिके अवचिनु त्वं पद्मानि। अहमप्येतस्मिन्नलिनीपत्रे शेफालिकाकुसुमान्यवचित्य देवीसकाशं गमिष्यामि। (आरण्णिए अवइणु तुमं पदुमाइं। अहं वि एदस्सिं णलिनीपत्तम्मि सेहालिआकुसुमाईं अवइणुअ देवीसआसं गमिस्सं।)

राजा—वयस्य संलाप इव वर्तते। तदवहिताः शृणुमः। कदाचिदित एव व्यक्तीभविष्यति।

(चेटी गमनं नाटयति।)

आर०—हला इन्दीवरिके। न शक्नोमि त्वया विना मुहूर्तमप्यत्रासितुम्। (हला इन्दीवरिए ण सक्कुणोमि तुए विणा मुहुत्तंवि एत्थ आसिदुं।)

चेटी—(विहस्य।) यादृशमद्य मया देव्या मन्त्रितं श्रुतं तादृशेन चिरमेव मया विना त्वयासितव्यम्। (जादिसं अज्ज मए देवीए मन्तिदं सुदं तारिसेण चिरं एव्व मए विणा तुए आसिदव्वं।)

तथोक्ता। **पातालेति**। भुवनस्य महीलोकस्यावलोकनपरा नागकन्यका पातालादुत्थिता किं स्यादिति विकल्पः। नैतत्स्यादित्याक्षिपति। तन्मिथ्या खलु। मया दृष्टमेव हि। तस्मिन्पाताले ईदृशी लावण्यसम्पन्ना कन्यका कुतः। इह मूर्ता मूर्तिमती कौमुदी स्यात्। एतदपि न। तस्याः कौमुद्या दिवादर्शनं न घटते संभवति। केयं तर्हि या हस्ततलस्थितेन कमलेन श्रीः इव आलोक्यते। सन्देहालंकारः। शार्दूलविक्रीडितं वृत्तम् ॥ ६ ॥

यादृशं यत्प्रकारकम्। त्वद्विवाहसम्बन्धीति गूढम्। मन्त्रितं भाषितम्। तादृशे न तदनु-

---

१ धिया. २ कुतस्त्री०. ३ रिका आगच्छति (आअच्छदि). ४ एतन्नास्ति बहुषु पुस्तकेषु. ५ नादृशं (नारिसं).

आर०—(सविषादम् ।) किं देव्या मन्त्रितम् । (देवीए मन्तिदं ।)

चेटी—एतत् । तदैषाहं महाराजेन भणिता यथा—यदैषा विन्ध्यकेतुदुहिता वरयोग्या भविष्यति तदाहं स्मारयितव्य इति । तत्सांप्रतं महाराजं स्मारयामि येनास्या वरचिन्तापर्याकुलो भविष्यति । (एवं । तदा एसा अहं महाराएण भणिदा जह जदा एसा विञ्झकेदुदुहिदा वरजोग्गा भविस्सदि तदा अहं सुमराइदव्वोत्ति । ता संपदं महाराअं सुमरावेमि जेण से वरचिन्तापज्जाउलो भविस्सदि ।)

राजा—(सहर्षम् ।) इयं सा विन्ध्यकेतोर्दुहिता । (सानुतापम् ।) चिरं मुषिताः स्मो वयम् । वयस्य निर्दोषदर्शना कन्यका खल्वियम् । विश्रब्धमिदानीं पश्यामः ।

आर०—(सरोषं कर्णौ पिधाय ।) तद्गच्छ त्वम् । न मम त्वयासंबद्धप्रलापिन्या प्रयोजनम् । (ता गच्छ तुमं । ण मह तुए असंबद्धप्पलाविणीए पओअणं ।)

(चेट्यपसृत्य पुष्पावचयं नाटयति ।)

राजा—अहो सुतरां प्रकटीकृतमाभिजात्यं धीरतया । वयस्य धन्यः खल्वसौ य एतदङ्गस्पर्शसुखभाजनं भविष्यति ।

(आरण्यिका कमलावचयं नाटयति ।)

विदूषकः—भो वयस्य पश्य पश्य । आश्चर्यमाश्चर्यम् । एषा सलिलचलत्करपल्लवप्रभाविस्तृतेनोपहसितशोभं करोति कमलवनमवचिन्वती । (भो वअस्स पेक्ख पेक्ख । अच्चरिअं अच्चरिअं । एसा सलिलचलन्तकरपल्लवप्पहाविच्छुरिदेण ओहसिअसोहं करेदि कमलवणं अवचिणन्ती ।)

राजा—वयस्य सत्यमेवैतत् । पश्य ।

रोषादित्यर्थः । सानुतापमनुतापेन पश्चात्तापेन सहितं यथा तथा । विस्रब्धं यथा तथा । असम्बद्धं संदर्भरहितमनर्थकमिति यावत् । यदा वरयोग्या भविष्यतीत्यादि जल्पतीति तथा । तया । एषा नर्मोक्तिः । एवं शाकुन्तलेपि इमामसम्बद्धप्रलापिनीं प्रियंवदामार्यायै गौतम्यै निवेदयिष्यामीति शकुन्तलावाक्यम् । एषा कमलानि अवचिन्वती सलिले जले चरन्ती । करपल्लवस्य प्रभा तस्या विस्तृतेन विस्तारेण प्रसरणेनेत्यर्थः ।

---

१ तदाहं म० । यथा–यैषा वि० यदा. २ त्वया प० (त्ताए प०). ३ चिरमु०. ४ एतन्नास्ति क्वचित्. ५ विच्छुरितेन (विच्छुरिदेण). ६ कमलं. ७ खल्वं.

अच्छिन्नामृतबिन्दु[1]वृष्टिसदृशीं प्रीतिं ददत्या दृशां[2]
याताया विगलत्पयोधरपटाद्द्रष्टव्यतां कामपि
अस्याश्चन्द्रमसस्तनोरिव करस्पर्शास्पदत्वं गता
नैते यन्मुकुलीभवन्ति सहसा पद्मास्तदेवाद्भुतम् ॥ ७ ॥

आर०—(भ्रमरबा[3]धां नाटयन्ती ।) हा धिक् हा धिक् । एते खल्वपरे परित्य[4]ज्य कमलिनीं नीलोत्पलवनानि समापतन्तो निपुणतरं बाधमाना आयासयन्ति मां दुष्टमधुकराः । (उत्तरीयेण मुखं पिधा[5]य सभयम् ।) हला इन्दीवरिके परित्रायस्व मां परित्रायस्व माम् । एते खलु दुष्टमधुकराः परिभविष्यन्ति । (हद्धि हद्धि । एदे क्खु अवरे परिच्चइअ कमलिणीं णीलुप्पलवणाइं समापडन्ता णिउणअरं बाधन्ता आआसअन्ति मं दुट्ठमहुअरा । हला इन्दीवरिए परित्ताएहि मं परित्ताएहि मं । एदे क्खु दुट्ठमहुअरा परिभविस्सन्ति ।)

विदूषकः—भो वयस्य पूर्णास्ते मनोरथाः । यावदेव ग[6]र्भदास्याः सुता नागच्छति तावदेव त्वमपि तूष्णीको भूत्वोपसर्प । एषापि सलिलशब्दसू[7]चितेन पदसंचारेणेन्दीवरिकागच्छतीति ज्ञात्वा त्वा[8]मेवावलम्बिष्यते । (भो वअस्स पुण्णा दे मणोरहा । जाव एव्व गब्भदासीए सुदा ण आअच्छदि दाव एव्व तुमं वि तुण्हीको भविअ उवसप्प । एसा वि सलिलसद्दसूइदेण पअसंचारेण इन्दीवरिआ आअच्छदित्ति जाणिअ तुमं एव्व ओलम्बिस्सदि ।)

राजा—साधु वयस्य साधु । कालानुरूपमुपदिष्टम् । (इत्यारण्यिका समीपमुपसर्पति ।)

अच्छिन्नेति । दृशां नयनानां पश्यतामितिशेषः । दृशेति पाठे अवलोकनेनेत्यर्थः । अच्छिन्ना अनवरता या अमृतबिन्दूनां वृष्टिस्तस्याः सदृशीं प्रीतिमानन्दं ददत्याः । विगलन्यः पयोधरपटः स्तनांशुकं तस्मात्कामपि अनिर्वचनीयां द्रष्टव्यतां दर्शनीयतां यातायाः । चन्द्रमसः पक्षे विगलन्नपसृतः य पयोधरो मेघः स एव पटस्तस्मात् । अतश्चन्द्रमस्तनोरिव अस्याः करस्पर्शास्पदत्वं हस्तसंपर्कस्य पक्षे किरणसंसर्गस्य आस्पदत्वं स्थानतां गता एते पद्माः कमलानि । वा पुंसि पद्ममिति पुल्लिंगता । सहसा न मुकुलीभवन्ति इति यत्तदेवाद्भुतम् । विशेषोक्तिः । शार्दूलविक्रीडितं वृत्तम् ॥ ७ ॥ अपरे कुसुमसनाथवण्याकृष्टाः प्रथमे । एते अन्ये इत्यर्थः । समापतन्तः संभूयाभिगच्छन्तः । निपुणतरं समधिकम् । द्विगुणतरमिति साधीयान्पाठः । परिभविष्यन्ति मामाक्राम्येयुरित्यर्थः । एवं शाकुन्तलेपि—हला परित्रायेथां मामनेन दुर्विनीतेन मधुकरे-

---

१ वृष्टिपात. २ दृशा. ३ संबाधं, नाटयति. ४ परिवर्ज्य कमलनीलोत्पलवनं समाप० द्विगुणतरमाया० (परिवज्जिअ कमलणीउप्पलवणं समा० दिउणदरं आ०). ५ पिदधाति. ६ एषा दासी (एसा दासी). ७ श्रुतेन (सुणिदेण). ८ स्वयमेव त्वामव० (सअं एव्व तुमं).

आर०—(पदशब्दाकर्णनं नाटयन्ती ।) इन्दीवरिके लघूपसर्प लघूपसर्प । आकुलीकृतास्मि दुष्टमधुकरैः । (इन्दीवरिए । लहु उवसप्प लहु उवसप्प । आउलीकिदह्मि दुट्ठमहुअरेहिं । (राजानमवलम्बते ।)

(राजा कण्ठे गृह्णाति । आरण्यिकोत्तरीयं मुखादपनीय राजानमपश्यन्ती भ्रमरावलोकनं नाटयति ।)

राजा—(स्वोत्तरीयेण भ्रमरान्निवारयन् ।)

अयि विसृज विषादं भीरु भृङ्गास्तवैते
परिमलरसलुब्धा वक्त्रपद्मे पतन्ति ।
विकिरसि यदि भूयस्त्रासलोलायताक्षी
कुवलयवनलक्ष्मीं तत्कुतस्त्वां त्यजन्ति ॥ ८ ॥

आर०—(राजानं दृष्ट्वा साध्वसं नाटयन्ती ।) कथं नैषेन्दीवरिका । (सभयं राजानं त्यक्त्वापसरन्ती ।) इन्दीवरिके । लघ्वागच्छ लघ्वागच्छ । परित्रायस्व माम् । (कहं ण एसा इन्दीवरिआ । इन्दीवरिए । लहु आअच्छ लहु आअच्छ । परित्ताएहि मं ।)

विदूषकः—भवति सकलपृथ्वीपरित्राणसमर्थेन वत्सराजेन परित्रायमाणा चेटीमिन्दीवरिकामाक्रन्दसि । (होदि सअलपुढवीपरित्ताणसमत्थेण वच्छराएण परित्ताअन्ती चेडिं इन्दीवरिअं अक्कन्दसि ।

(राजा "अयि विसृज–" इत्यादि पुनः पठति ।)

आर०—(राजानमवलोक्य सस्पृहं सलज्जं चात्मगतम् ।) अयं खलु स महाराजो यस्याहं तातेन दत्ता । स्थाने खलु तातस्य पक्षपातः । (आकुलतां नाटयति ।) (अअं क्खु सो महाराओ जस्स अहं तादेण दिण्णा ठाणे क्खु तादस्स पक्खवादो ।)

णायास्यमानामिति । गर्भादारभ्य दासी गर्भदासी । तूष्णीकः मौनी । लघु शीघ्रम् । **अयीति** । अयि भीरु विषादं मुञ्च । एते परिमलरसे सौगन्ध्यास्वादे लुब्धा भृङ्गाः तव वक्त्रपद्मे पतन्ति । त्रासेन भयेन लोले चञ्चले आयते दीर्घे अक्षिणी यस्याः सा त्वं यदि भूयः कुवलयवनलक्ष्मीं इतस्ततो दृष्टिपातेन विकिरसि तर्हि त्वां कुतः परित्यजन्ति । न त्यजेयुरेव । मालिनी वृत्तम् । ननमयययुतेयं मालिनी भोगिलोकैः । इति तल्लक्षणम् ॥ ८ ॥ स्थाने युक्तः । पक्षपातः अतिशयितं प्रेम ।

---

१ इति रा०. २ वसन्ति. ३ लघ्वेवागच्छागच्छ. ४ भुवन०...माणापि किं चेटीमा०

चेटी—आयासिता खल्वारण्यिका दुष्टमधुकरैः। तद्यावदुपसर्प्य समाश्वासयामि। आरण्यिके मा बिभिहि। एषोपगतास्मि। (आआसिआ क्खु आरण्णिआ दुट्ठमहुअरेहिं। ता जाव उवसप्पिअ समस्सासेमि। आरण्णिए मा भआहि। एसा उवअदम्हि।)

विदूषकः—भोः अपसरापसर। एषा खल्विन्दीवरिकागता। एतं वृत्तान्तं प्रेक्ष्य देव्यै निवेदयिष्यति। (अङ्गुल्या निर्दिश्य।) तदिदमेव कदलीगृहं प्रविश्य मुहूर्तं तिष्ठावः। (भो ओसर ओसर। एसा क्खु इन्दीवरिआ आअदा। एदं उत्तन्तं पेक्खिअ देवीए णिवेदइस्सदि। ता इमं एव्व कदलीघरं पविसिअ मुहुत्तं चिट्ठह्म।)

(उभौ तथा कुरुतः।)

चेटी—(उपसृत्य कपोलौ स्पृशन्ती।) हञ्जे आरण्यिके। कमलसदृशस्य तव वदनस्यायं दोषो यन्मधुकरा एवमपराध्यन्ति। (हस्ते गृहीत्वा।) तदेहि गच्छावः। परिणतो दिवसः। (हञ्जे आरण्णिए कमलसरिसस्स तुह वअणस्स अअं दोसो जं महुअरा एव्वं अवरज्झन्ति। ता एहि गच्छह्म। परिणदो दिअहो।)

(गमनं नाटयतः।)

आर०—(कदलीगृहाभिमुखमवलोक्य।) हञ्जे इन्दीवरिके अतिशिशिरतया सलिलस्योरुस्तम्भ इव समुत्पन्नः। तच्छनैः शनैर्गच्छावः। (हञ्जे इन्दीवरिए अदिसिसिरदाए सलिलस्स ऊरुत्थम्भो विअ समुप्पण्णो। ता सणिअं सणिअं गच्छह्म।)

चेटी—तथा। (तह।)

(इति निष्क्रान्ते।)

विदूषकः—भोः एहि निष्क्रामावः। तां गृहीत्वैषा दास्याः सुतेन्दीवरिका गता। (भो एहि णिक्कमह्म। तं गेण्हिअ एसा दासीए सुदा इन्दीवरिआ गदा।)

राजा—(निःश्वस्य।) कथं गता। सखे वसन्तक। न खल्वविघ्नमभिलषितमधन्यैः प्राप्यते। (विलोक्य।) सखे पश्य पश्य।

ऊरुस्तम्भ ऊर्वोर्जडिमा। वस्तुतस्तु प्रियस्पर्शादयम्। अविघ्नमभिलषितमि०—एवं शाकुन्तलेपि—अहो विघ्नवत्यः प्रार्थितार्थसिद्धयः। इति।

---

१ मा भैषीः मा भैषीः। एषागतास्मि (मा आहि एसा आअदह्मि). २ तदेतं (ता एदं). ३ कम्पः. ४ अस्मात्परं—तथा कुरुतः। इत्यधिकं बहुषु पुस्तकेषु.

आबद्धमुखमपीदं कण्टाकितं कमलकाननं तस्याः ।
सुकुमारपाणिपल्लवसंस्पर्शसुखं कथयतीव ॥ ९ ॥

(निःश्वस्य ।) सखे । क इदानीमुपायः पुनस्तां द्रष्टुम् ।

विदूषकः—भोः त्वमेव पुत्तलिकां भङ्क्त्वेदानीं रोदिषि । न मम खलु ब्राह्मणस्य वचनं करोषि । (भो तुमे एव्व पुत्तलिअं भञ्जिअ दाणिं रोदिसि । ण मह क्खु बह्मणस्स वअणं करेसि ।)

राजा—किं मया न कृतम् ।

विदूषकः—तदिदानीं विस्मृतम् । यथा तूष्णीको भूत्वोपसर्पेति मया भणितम् । अतिसंकटे यद्भवान्प्रविश्यालीकपाण्डित्यदुर्विदग्धतया " अयि विसृज विषादम् " इत्येतैरन्यैश्च कटुवचनैर्निर्भर्त्स्य सांप्रतं किं रोदिषि । पुनरप्युपायं पृच्छसि । (तं दाणिं विसुमरिदं । जह तुण्हीको भविअ उवसप्पेत्ति मए भणिदं । आदिसंकडे जं भवं पविसिअ अलिअपंडिच्चदुव्विदद्धदाए अइ विसिज विसादेत्ति एदेहिं अण्णेहिं अ कडुअवअणेहिं णिब्भच्छिअ संपदं किं रोदिसि । पुणो वि उवाअं पुच्छसि ।)

राजा— कथं समाश्वासनमपि निर्भर्त्सितमिति भणितं मूर्खेण ।

विदूषकः—ज्ञातमेव कोऽत्र मूर्ख इति । तत्किमेतेन । अस्तमयाभिलाषी भगवान्सहस्त्ररश्मिः । तदेह्यभ्यन्तरमेव प्रविशावः । (जाणिदं एव्व को एत्थ मुक्खोत्ति । ता किं एदेण । अत्थमआहिलासी भअवं सहस्सरस्सी । ता एहि अब्भन्तरं एव्व पविसह्म ।)

राजा—(विलोक्य ।) अये परिणतप्रायो दिवसः । अहह । संप्रति हि—

हृत्वा पद्मवनद्युतिं प्रियतमेवेयं दिनश्रीर्गता
रागोऽस्मिन्मम चेतसीव सवितुर्बिम्बेऽधिकं लक्ष्यते ।

आबद्धेति । इदं कमलकाननं पद्मवनं आबद्धं मुकुलितं मुखं यस्य तदाबद्धमुखमपि । कण्टकितं सञ्जातकण्टकं सरोमाञ्चं च सत् । तस्या आरण्यिकायाः यः सुकुमारः पाणिपल्लवः तस्य संस्पर्शेन जातं सुखं कथयतीव । उत्प्रेक्षालंकारः । पथ्यार्यावृत्तम् ॥ ९ ॥ पुत्तलिकां पाञ्चालिकाम् । अतिसंकटे इति सोपहासम् । अलीकपाण्डित्यं मिथ्यावैदग्ध्यं तेन दुर्विदग्धः साभिमानः पण्डितंमन्य इत्यर्थः । तस्य भावस्तत्ता तया । अस्तमयमभिलषतेऽसावस्तमयाभिलाषी आसन्नास्तमय इत्यर्थः । **हृत्वेति** । इयं दिनश्रीः पद्मवनस्य कान्तिं शोभां हृत्वा प्रिया आरण्यिका इव गता । अस्मिन्पुरोदृश्यमाने सवितुर्बिम्बे मम चेतसि इव रागो रक्तिमा अनुरागश्च अधिकं

---

१ अभ्युपायः. २ मे मूर्खस्य (मे मुक्खस्स). ३ तदा भणितः...विहृत्य 'अपि... कटुवचनैः भङ्क्त्वा साम्प्रतं. ४ गृहीतं. ५ दिवसा...रः (दिवसअरो).

चक्राह्वोऽहमिव स्थितः सहचरीं ध्यायन्नलिन्यास्तटे
संजाता सहसा ममेव भुवनस्याप्यन्धकारा दिशः ॥ १० ॥

(इति निष्क्रान्ताः सर्वे ।)

इति द्वितीयोऽङ्कः ।

तृतीयोऽङ्कः ।

(ततः प्रविशति मनोरमा ।)

मनोरमा—आज्ञप्तास्मि देव्या वासवदत्तया हञ्जे मनोरमे यः स साङ्कृत्यायन्यार्यपुत्रस्य मम च वृत्तान्तो नाटकोपनिबद्धस्तस्य नर्तितव्यशेषमद्य युष्माभिः कौमुदीमहोत्सवे नर्तितव्यमिति । ह्यः खल्वारण्यिकया प्रियसख्या शून्यहृदययान्यथैव नर्तितम् । अद्य पुनर्वासवदत्ताभूमिकया तया यदि तथा क्रियते ततोऽवश्यं देवी कुप्यति । तत्कुत्र तावत्तां प्रेक्ष्योपालप्स्ये । (विलोक्य ।) एषारण्यिकात्मनैव किमपि किमपि मन्त्रयमाणा दीर्घिकातीरे कदलीगृहं प्रविशति । तद्गुल्मान्तरिता भूत्वा श्रोष्यामि तावदस्या विश्रब्धजल्पितानि । (आणत्तह्मि देवीए वासवदत्ताए हञ्जे मणोरमे जं तं संकिच्चायणीए अज्जउत्तस्स मम अ उत्तन्तं णाडओवणिबद्धं तस्स णच्चिदव्वसेसं

दृश्यते । चक्राह्वः चक्रवाकः अहमिव सहचरीं ध्यायन् नलिन्याः तटे स्थितः । दिशः मम इव भुवनस्यापि सहसा अन्धकाराः अन्धकारवत्यः । अनाह्लादकरा इत्यर्थः । जाताः । 'अर्श आदिभ्योऽच्' इति मत्वर्थीयः अच् । उपमा । शार्दूलविक्रीडितं वृत्तम् ॥ १० ॥

इत आरभ्याङ्कसमाप्तिं यावत्प्रतिमुखगर्भसन्धी । तत्रादौ वत्सराजारण्यिकासमागमहेतोरनुरागबीजस्य द्वितीयाङ्कोपक्षिप्तस्य मनोरमाविदूषकाभ्यां ज्ञायमानतया किंचिल्लक्ष्यस्य वासवदत्तयाऽज्ञाततया चालक्ष्यस्य दृश्यादृश्यरूपतयोद्भेदः प्रतिमुखसन्धिः । सांकृत्यायनी नाम काचित्परिव्राजिका ग्रन्थनिर्माणकुशला वासवदत्ताया विनोदयित्री । नर्तितव्यशेषं नाटयितव्यशेषम् । कौमुदीमहोत्सवे आश्विनस्य पूर्णिमायां क्रियमाणोत्सवे । शून्यमन्यविषयगतं हृदयं यस्य सा । हृदयेनासंनिहितेत्यर्थः । तया । भूमिका वेषः । उपालप्स्ये दोषं दास्यामि । मन्त्रयमाणा आत्मना व्याहरन्ती । गुल्मः लतागहनं तेनान्तरिता पिहिता । विस्रब्धजल्पितानि स्वैरभाषितानि ।

---

१ यत्सा० च चरितं (चरिदं). २ वासवदत्ताया वेषं कृत्वा तथा नर्तिते देव्याः कोपो भविष्यति (०दत्ताए वेसं करुअ तह णच्चिदे देवीए कोवो हुविस्सदि).

अज्ज तुझेहिं कोमदीमहूसवे णच्चिदव्वंति । हिओ क्खु आरण्णिआए पिअसहीए सुण्ण-हिअआए अण्णहा एव्व णच्चिदं । अज्ज उण वासवदत्ताभूमिआए ताए जइ तह करीअदि तदो अवस्सं देवी कुप्पदि । ता कहिं दाव तां पेक्खिस्सं उवालम्भिस्सं । एसा आरण्णिआ अप्पणा एव्व किं वि किं वि मन्तअन्ती दिग्घिआतीले कदलीघरअं पविसदि । ता गुम्मन्तरिआ भविअ सुणिस्सं दाव से विसद्धजप्पिदाणिं ।)

(ततः प्रविशत्यासनस्था कामावस्थां नाटयन्त्यारण्यिका ।)

आर०—(निःश्वस्य ।) हृदय दुर्लभजनं प्रार्थयमानं त्वं कस्मान्मां दुःखितां करोषि । (हिअअ दुल्लहजणं पत्थअन्तो तुमं कीस मं दुक्खिदं करेसि ।)

मनो०—तदेतदस्याः शून्यहृदयत्वस्य कारणम् । किं पुनरेषा प्रार्थयते । अवहिता तावच्छ्रोष्यामि । (तं एदं एदस्य सुण्णहिअअत्तणस्स कारणं । किं उण एसा पत्थेदि । अवहिदा दाव सुणिस्सं ।)

आर०—(सास्रम् ।) कथं तथा नाम सौम्यदर्शनो भूत्वा महाराज एवं संतापयति माम् । आश्चर्यमाश्चर्यम् । (निःश्वस्य ।) अथवा ममैवैषाऽभागधेयता । न पुनर्महाराजस्य दोषः । (कहं तह णाम सोम्मदंसणो भविअ महाराओ एव्वं संदावेदि मं । अच्चरिअं अच्चरिअं । अहवा मह एव्व एसा अभाअहेअदा । ण उण महाराअस्स दोसो ।)

मनो०—(सबाष्पम् ।) कथं महाराज एवास्याः प्रार्थनीयः । साधु प्रियसखि साधु । आभिजात्यसदृशस्तेऽभिलाषः । (कहं महाराओ एव्व से पत्थणिज्जो । साहु पिअसही साहु । अभिजाअसरिसो दे अहिलासो ।)

आर०—कस्मै तावदेतं वृत्तान्तं निवेद्य सह्यवेदनमिव दुःखं करिष्यामि । (विचिन्त्य ।) अथवा अस्ति मे हृदयानिर्विशेषा प्रियसखी मनोरमा । तस्या अप्येतल्लज्जया न पारयामि कथयितुम् । सर्वथा मरणं वर्जयित्वा कुतो मे हृदयस्यान्या निर्वृतिः । (कस्स दाव एदं उत्तन्तं णिवेदिअ सज्झवेअणं विअ दुक्खं काराइस्सं । अहवा अत्थि मे हिअअणिव्विसेसा पिअसही मणोरमा । ताए वि एदं लज्जाए ण पारेमि कहिदुं । सव्वहा मरणं वज्जिअ कुदो मे हिअअस्स अण्णा णिव्वुदी ।)

दुर्लभजनं वत्सराजमित्यर्थः । प्रार्थयमानमभिलषत् । अवहिता सावधाना । अभागधेयता मन्दभाग्यत्वम् । हृदयान्निर्गतो विशेषो यस्याः सा । पारयामि शक्नोमि । निर्वृतिः सुखम् ।

---

१ त्यारण्यिका । (आ०–कामावस्थां नाटयन्ती निःश्वस्य ।). २ शोभन (शोहण०). ३ साधु प्रियसखि. ४ इदानीं (दाणिं).

मनोरमा—(सास्रम् ।) हा धिक् हा धिक् । अतिभूमिं गतोऽस्यास्तपस्विन्या अनुरागः । तत्किमिदानीमत्र करिष्यामि । (हद्धि हद्धि । अदिभूमिं गदो से तवस्सिणीए अणुराओ । ता किं दाणिं एत्थ करिस्सं ।)

आर०—(साभिलाषम् ।) अयं स उद्देशो यस्मिन्मधुकरैरायास्यमानावलम्ब्य महाराजेन समाश्वासितास्मि भीरु मा बिभीहीति । (अअं सो उद्देसो जस्सिं महुअरेहिं आआसिज्जन्ती ओलम्बिअ महाराएण समस्सासिदह्मि भीरु मा भआहित्ति ।)

मनोरमा—(सहर्षम् ।) कथमेषापि दृष्टा महाराजेन । सर्वथास्त्यस्या जीवितस्योपायः । यावदुपसृत्य समाश्वासयाम्येनाम् । (सहसोपसृत्य ।) युक्तं नाम हृदयस्यापि लज्जितुम् । (कहं एसा वि दिट्ठा महाराएण । सव्वहा अत्थि से जीविदस्स उवाओ । जाव उवसप्पिअ समस्सासेमि णं । जुत्तं णाम हिअअस्स वि लज्जिदुं ।)

आर०—(सलज्जमात्मगतम् ।) हा धिक् हा धिक् । सर्वं श्रुतमेतया । तदत्र युक्तमेव प्रकाशयितुम् । (प्रकाशं हस्ते गृहीत्वा ।) प्रियसखि मा कुप्य मा कुप्य । लज्जैवात्रापराध्यति । (हद्धि हद्धि । सव्वं सुदं एदाए । ता एत्थ जुत्तं एव्व पआसइदुं । पिअसहि मा कुप्प मा कुप्प । लज्जा एव्व एत्थ अवरज्झदि ।)

मनो०—(सहर्षम् ।) सखि अलं शङ्कया । एतन्म आचक्ष्व । सत्यमेव त्वं महाराजेन दृष्टा न वेति । (सहि अलं संकाए । एदं मे आअक्ख । सच्चं एव्व तुमं महाराएण दिट्ठा ण वेत्ति ।)

आर०—(सलज्जमधोमुखी) श्रुतमेव प्रियसख्या सर्वम् । (सुदं एव्व पिअसहीए सव्वं ।)

मनोरमा—यदि दृष्टा महाराजेन त्वं तदलं संतापितेन । स एवेदानीं दर्शनोपायपर्याकुलो भविष्यति । (जइ दिट्ठा महाराएण तुमं ता अलं संतप्पिदेण । सो एव्व दाणिं दंसणोवाअपज्जाउलो भविस्सदि ।)

अतिभूमिं परां कोटिम् । तपस्विन्याः अनुकम्प्यायाः । वराक्या इत्यर्थः । हृदयस्यापि स्वहृदयादव्यतिरिक्ताया ममेत्यर्थः । आत्मगतं, प्रकाशं—सर्वश्राव्यं प्रकाशं स्यादश्राव्यं स्वगतं मतम् । इति दशरूपके । दर्शनोपायपर्याकुलः दर्शनोपायचिन्ताव्यग्रः ।

---

१ नाम किं, हृदयस्य—सखीजनस्य. २ लज्जां नाटयन्ती आ०. ३ तव दर्श०.

आर०—अयं सखीजनः पक्षपातेन मन्त्रयते। अयि सखि-पक्षपातिनि। देवीगुणनिगडनिबद्धे खलु तस्मिञ्जने कुत एतत्। (अअं सहीअणो पक्खवादेण मन्तेदि। अइ सहिपक्खवादिणि। देवीगुणणिअलणिबद्धे क्खु तस्सिं जणे कुदो एदं।)

मनोरमा—(विहस्य।) हला अपण्डिते कमलिनीबद्धानुरागोऽपि मधुकरो मालतीं प्रेक्ष्याभिनवरसास्वादलम्पटः कुतस्तामनासाद्य स्थितिं करोति। (हला अपण्डिदे कमलिणीबद्धाणुराओ वि महुअरो मालदीं पेक्खिअ अहिणवरसास्सादलम्पडो कुदो तं अणासादिअ ठ्ठिदिं करेदि।)

आर०—किमेतेनासंभावितेन। तदेहि। अधिकं खलु शरदातपेन संतप्तान्यद्यापि न मेऽङ्गानि संतापं मुञ्चन्ति। (किं एदिणा असंभाविदेण। ता एहि। अहिअं क्खु सरदादवेण संतप्पाइं अज्ज वि ण मे अङ्गाइं संदावं मुञ्चन्दि।)

मनोरमा—अयि लज्जालुके न युक्तमेतदवस्थां गतयापि त आत्मा प्रच्छादयितुम्। (अइ लज्जालुए ण जुत्तं एदावत्थं गदाए वि दे अप्पा पच्छादिदुं।)

(आरण्यिका मुखमवनमयति।)

मनोरमा—अयि अविश्रम्भशीले किमिदानीं प्रच्छादयसि। निश्वासनिभाविनिर्गतो दिवसं रात्रिमपि तवानुरागोऽविरतपतत्कुसुमशरशरनिवहप्रवृत्तहुङ्कारशब्द इव न भणति। (आत्मगतम्।) अथवा न खल्वयं काल उपालम्भस्य। तद्यावन्नलिनीपत्राण्यस्या हृदये दास्यामि। (उत्थाय

देवीगुणा एव निगडः लोहबन्धस्तेन निबद्धे। मालतीं जातिपुष्पम्। लम्पटो लोलुपः। स्थितिं करोति स्वास्थ्यमेति। लज्जां लाति इति लज्जालुः। 'मितद्र्वादिभ्य उपसंख्यानम्' इति वार्त्तिकेन डुः। सैव लज्जालुका। अविश्रम्भशीले प्रकृत्यात्मन्यविश्वासिनि। निश्वासनिभविनिर्गतः निश्वासच्छलेन विनिर्गतः। अविरतं पतन्त्यः कुसुमशरस्य मदनस्य शरनिवहो बाणसमूहस्तस्मात्प्रवृत्तः हुंकारशब्द इव। न भणति न तवावस्थां कथयति किम्।

---

१ एतद्वाक्यं नास्ति पुस्तकान्तरे. २ सखीजनपक्षपातेन मन्त्रयसे (सखीअणपक्खवादेन मन्तेसि). ३ एतन्नास्ति क्वचित्.

४ अस्य स्थाने—श्वासनिभान्निर्गतो दिवसं रात्रिमपि तवानुरागः।
अविरतपतन्मन्मथशरशतहुङ्कारशब्द इव॥
(सासणिहा णिग्गमिओ दिअहं रत्तिंपि तुज्झ अणुराओ।
अविरअपडंतमम्महसरसअहुंकार सद्दोव्व॥) इति पद्यं क्वचित्.

५ तत्तावत्.

दीर्घिकाया नलिनीपत्राणि गृहीत्वारण्यिकाया हृदये ददती।) [1]समाश्वसितु सखी समाश्वसितु सखी। (अइ अविसम्भसीले किं दाणिं पच्छादेसि। णीसासणिद्दविणिम्गओ दिअहं रत्तिं वि तुज्झ अणुराओ अविरदपडन्तकुसुमसरसरणिवहपउत्तहुंकारसद्दो विअ ण भणइ। अहवा ण हु अअं कालो उवालम्भस्स। ता जाव णलिणीपत्ताई से हिअए दाइस्सं। समस्ससदु सही समस्ससदु सही।)

(ततः प्रविशति विदूषकः।)

विदूषकः—अतिमहान् खलु प्रियवयस्यस्यारण्यिकाया उपर्यनुरागः। येन परित्यक्तराजकार्यस्तस्या एव दर्शनोपायं चिन्तयन्नात्मानं विनोदयति। (विचिन्त्य।) [2]कुत्रेदानीं तां प्रेक्षे। अथवा तत्रैव तावद् दीर्घिकायामन्विष्यामि। ([3]परिक्रामति।) (अदिमहन्तो क्खु पिअवअस्सस्स आरण्णिआए उवरिं अणुराओ। जेण परिच्चत्तराअकज्जो ताए एव्व दंसणोवाअं चिन्तअन्तो अप्पाणं विणोदेइ। कहिं दाणिं तं पेक्खे। अहवा तहिं एव्व दाव दिग्घिआए अण्णेसामि।)

मनोरमा—(आकर्ण्य।) पदशब्द इव श्रूयते। तत्कदलीगुल्मान्तरिते भूत्वा प्रेक्षावहे तावत्क एष इति। (पदसद्दो विअ सुणीअदि। ता कदलीगुम्मन्तरिदा भविअ पेक्खह्म दाव को एसोत्ति।)

(उभे तथा कृत्वा पश्यतः।)

आर०—कथं स एव महाराजस्य पार्श्वपरिवर्ती ब्राह्मणः। (कहं सो एव्व महाराअस्स पस्सपरिवट्टी बह्मणो।)

मनोरमा—कथं वसन्तक एव। ([4]सहर्षमात्मगतम्।) अपि नाम तथा भवेत्। (कहं वसन्तओ एव्व। अवि णाम तह हवे।)

विदूषकः—(दिशोऽवलोक्य।) किमिदानीमारण्यिका सत्यमेवे[5] संवृत्ता। (किं दाणिं आरण्णिआ सच्चं एव्व संवुत्ता।)

मनोरमा—(सस्मितम्।) सखि राजवयस्यः खलु ब्राह्मणस्त्वामुद्दिश्य मन्त्रयते। तत्तावदवहिते शृणुवः। (सहि राअवअस्सो क्खु बह्मणो तुमं उद्दिसिअ मन्तेदि। ता दाव अवहिदा सुणह्म।)

(आरण्यिका सस्पृहं सलज्जं च शृणोति।)

विदूषकः—(सोद्वेगम्।) यदा[6] तावन्मया गुरुमदनसंतापानिस्सह-

तथा भवेत् राजाज्ञयारण्यिकान्वेषणार्थमागतो भवेदित्याशयः। गुरुर्दुर्भरः मदनसंतापस्तेन

---

१ सखि समाश्वसिहि समा०. २ तत्कु०. ३ इति प०. ४ स्वग०. ५ एवारण्यिका. ६ यदा तावन्मया इति नास्तिपुस्तकान्तरे।

शरीरस्य प्रियवयस्यस्य वचनेन देव्योर्वासवदत्तापद्मावत्योरन्यासां च देवीनां भवनान्यन्विष्यता न सा दृष्टा तदा यत्र दीर्घिकायां दृष्टेदमपि तावत्प्रेक्षिष्य इत्यागतोऽस्मि । तद्यावदिहापि नास्ति । किमिदानीं करिष्ये । (जदा दाव मए गुरुमअणसंदावणीसहसरीरस्स पिअवअस्सस्स वअणेण देवीणं वासवदत्तापदुमावदीणं अण्णाणं अ देवीणं भवणाइं अण्णेसन्तेण ण सा दिट्ठा तदा जहिं दिग्घिआए दिट्ठा इदं वि दाव पेक्खिस्सं ति आअदोह्मि । ता जाव इह वि णत्थि । किं दाणिं करिस्सं ।)

मनोरमा—श्रुतं प्रियसख्या । (सुदं पिअसहीए ।)

विदूषकः—(विचिन्त्य ।) अथवा भणित एवाहं वयस्येन । यदि तामन्विष्यन्न प्रेक्षसे तत्ततोऽपि तावद्दीर्घिकातस्तस्याः करतलस्पर्शद्विगुणितसुखशीतलानि नलिनीपत्राणि गृहीत्वागच्छेति । तत्कथमेतानि ज्ञातव्यानि । (अहवा भणिदो एव्व अहं वअस्सेण । जइ तं अण्णेसन्तो ण पेक्खसि ता तदो वि दाव दिग्घिआदो ताए करअलप्परिसदिउणिअसुहसीअलाइं णलिणीपत्ताइं गोण्हिअ आअच्छेति । ता कहं एदाइं जाणिदव्वाइं ।)

मनोरमा—अयं ममावसरः । (उपसृत्य विदूषकं हस्ते गृहीत्वा ।) वसन्तक एहि । अहं ते ज्ञापयामि । (अअं मे अवसरो । वसन्तअ एहि । अहं दे जाणावेमि ।)

विदूषकः—(सभयम् ।) कस्य त्वं ज्ञापयासि । किं देव्याः । न खलु मया किमपि मन्त्रितम् । (कस्स तुमं जाणावेसि । किं देवीए । ण हु मए किं वि मन्तिदं ।)

मनोरमा—वसन्तक अलं शङ्कया । यादृश्यारण्यिकायाः कृत आत्मनः प्रियवयस्यस्यावस्था त्वया वर्णिता ततो द्विगुणतरा भर्तुरपि कृते मम प्रियसख्या अवस्था । तत्पश्य पश्य । (उपसृत्यारण्यिकां दर्शयति ।) (वसन्तअ अलं संकाए । जादिसी आरण्णिआए किदे अत्तणो पिअवअस्सस्स अवत्था तुए वण्णिदा तदो दिउणदरा भट्टिणो वि किदे मम पिअसहीए अवत्था । ता पेक्ख पेक्ख ।)

निस्सहं दुर्बलं शरीरं यस्य तस्य । अस्वस्थवचनेन इति पाठे पर्याकुलवचनेन अस्वस्थ इति वचनेन वा । इदमपि दीर्घिकास्थानमपि । तस्याः करतलस्य स्पर्शेन द्विगुणितसुखानि च तानि शीतलानि च ।

---

१ अस्वस्थव०. २ देव्या वासवदत्तायाः प्रेमावत्याश्च. ३ तदा यत्र दीर्घिकायां दृष्टा इति नास्ति क०. ४ अन्वेषयन्, ५ स्पर्शसुख. ६ ० दरं उण (०तरं पुनः).

विदूषकः—(दृष्ट्वा सहर्षम् ।) सफलो मे परिश्रमः । स्वस्ति भवत्यै । (सफलो मे परिस्समो । सोत्थि होदीए ।)

(आरण्यिका सलज्जं कमलिनीपत्राण्यपनीयोत्तिष्ठति ।

मनोरमा—आर्य वसन्तक । तव दर्शनेनैवापगतः प्रियसख्याः संतापो येन स्वयमेव नलिनीपत्राण्यपनयति । तदनुगृह्णात्वार्य इमानि । (अज्ज वसन्तअ तुह दंसणेण एव्व अवंगदो पिअसहीए संदावो जेण सअं एव्व णलिणीपत्ताइं अवणेइ । ता अणुगण्हादु अज्जो इमाइं ।)

आरण्यका—(सावेगम् ।) अयि परिहासशीले । कस्मान्मां लज्जयसि । (किंचित्पराङ्मुखी तिष्ठति ।) (अइ परिहाससीले । कीस मं लज्जावेसि ।)

विदूषकः—(सविषादम् ।) तिष्ठन्तु तावन्नलिनीपत्राणि । अतिलज्जालुका ते प्रियसखी । तत्कथमेतयोः समागमो भविष्यति । (चिट्ठदु दाव णलिणीपत्ताइं । अदिलज्जालुआ दे पिअसही । ता कहं एदाणं समाअमो भविस्सदि ।

मनोरमा—(क्षणं विचिन्त्य सहर्षम् ।) वसन्तक एवमिव । (कर्णे कथयति ।) (वसन्तअ एव्वं विअ ।)

विदूषकः—साधु प्रियसखि साधु । (अपवार्य ।) यावदेव युवां नेपथ्यग्रहणं कुरुथस्तावदेवाहमपि वयस्यं गृहीत्वागच्छामि । (इति निष्क्रान्तः ।) साहु पिअसहि साहु । जाव एव्व तुह्मे णेवच्छग्गहणं करेत्थ दाव एव्व अहं वि वअस्सं गेण्हिअ आअच्छामि ।)

मनोरमा—अतिकोपने उत्तिष्ठोत्तिष्ठ । नर्तितव्यमस्माभिस्तस्यैव नाटकस्य नर्तितशेषम् । तदेहि । प्रेक्षागृहमेव गच्छावः । (परिक्रम्यावलोक्य ।) इदं प्रेक्षागारम् । यावदेहि प्रविशावः । (प्रविष्टकेनावलोक्य ।) साधु साधु सर्वं सज्जीकृतम् । देव्यागन्तव्यम् । (अदिकोवणे । उट्ठेहि उट्ठेहि । णच्चिदव्वं अह्मेहिं तस्स एव्व णाडअस्स णच्चिदसेसं । ता एहि । पेक्खाघरं एव्व गच्छह्म । इदं पेक्खागारं । जाव एहि पविसह्म । साहु साहु । सव्वं सज्जीकिदं । देवीए आअन्तव्वं ।

(ततः प्रविशति देवी साङ्कृत्यायनी विभवतश्च परिवारः ।)

नेपथ्यग्रहणं वासवदत्तावत्सराजयोः वेषग्रहणमिति यावत् ।

---

१ ओगदो. २ लज्जापयसि. ३ साहु पिअसहि. ४ णच्चिदव्व (नर्तितव्य०). ५ ०घरं. ६ साधु एवं सज्जी०.

वासवदत्ता—भगवति अहो ते कवित्वम् । येनैतद्गूढवृत्तान्तं नाटकोपनिबद्धं सानुभवमप्यस्माकमार्यपुत्रचरितमदृष्टपूर्वमिव दृश्यमानमधिकतरं कौतूहलं वर्धयति । (भवअदि अहो दे कवित्तणं । जेण एदं गूढउत्तन्तं णाडओवणिबद्धं साणुभवं वि अह्माणं अज्जउत्तचरिदं अदिट्ठपुव्वं विअ दिसन्तं अहिअअरं कोदूहलं वड्ढअदि ।

साङ्कृत्यायनी—आयुष्मति आश्रयगुण एवायमीदृशो यदसारमपि काव्यमवश्यमेव शृण्वतां श्रवणसुखमुत्पादयति । पश्य ।

प्रायो यत्किंचिदपि प्राप्नोत्युत्कर्षमाश्रयान्महतः ।
मत्तेभकुम्भतटगतमेति हि शृङ्गारतां भस्म ॥ १ ॥

वासवदत्ता—(सस्मितम्) भगवति सर्वस्य वल्लभो जामाता भवतीति ज्ञायत एवैतत्[2] । तत्किमेतेन कथानुबन्धेन । वरं तदेव नर्तितव्यं द्रष्टुम् । (भअवदि सव्वस्स वल्लहो जामादो होदित्ति जाणिअदि एव्व एदं । ता किं एदिणा कहाणुबन्धेण । वरं तं एव्व णच्चिदव्वं[3] दट्ठुं ।)

साङ्कृत्यायनी—एवम् । इन्दीवरिके प्रेक्षागृहमादेशय ।

चेटी—एतु एतु भट्टिनी । (एदु एदु भट्टिणी ।)(सर्वाः परिक्रामन्ति ।)

साङ्कृत्यायनी—(विलोक्य ।) अहो प्रेक्षणीयता प्रेक्षागृहस्य ।

आभाति रत्नशतशोभितशातकुम्भ-
स्तम्भावसक्तपृथुमौक्तिकदामरम्यम् ।
अध्यासितं युवतिभिर्विजिताप्सरोभिः
प्रेक्षागृहं सुरविमानसमानमेतत् ॥ २ ॥

कवित्वं काव्यनिर्माणनैपुण्यम् । गूढः वृत्तान्तः यस्य तत् । नाटकोपनिबद्धं प्रयोगार्हं कृतम् । प्रेक्षागृहं नाट्यशाला । **प्राय इति** । यत्किंचिन्निःसारं माहात्म्यरहितं वापि वस्तु महत आश्रयात्सम्बन्धात्प्रायः उत्कर्षमौत्कृष्ट्यं प्राप्नोति । अत्र दृष्टान्तमाह—भस्म असारत्वेन प्रसिद्धं मत्तेभस्य मत्तगजस्य कुम्भतटगतं सत् शृङ्गारतां शृङ्गारः भूषणं गजमण्डनविशेषो वा तत्तां प्राप्नोति हि ध्रुवम् ॥ १ ॥ **आभातीति** । रत्नानां शतानि रत्नशतानि तैः शोभिताः शातकुम्भस्य सुवर्णस्य स्तम्भास्तेषु अवसक्तानि पृथूनि मौक्तिकदामानि मुक्तामालास्तै रम्यम् । विजिताः स्वस्वरूपतिरस्कृता इत्यर्थः । अप्सरसो याभिस्ताभिः युवतिभिः अध्यासितमेतत्प्रेक्षागृहं सुरविमानसमानमाभाति । वसन्ततिलकं वृत्तम् । लक्षणमुक्तम् ॥ २ ॥

---

१ यतीति. २ एव. ३ णच्चिदं.

मनोरमारण्यिके—(उपसृत्य।) जयतु जयतु भट्टिनी। (जेदु जेदु भट्टिणी।)

वासवदत्ता—मनोरमे अतिक्रान्ता खलु संध्या। तद्गच्छतम्। लघु गृह्णीतं नेपथ्यम्। (मणोरमे अदिक्कन्दा क्खु संज्झा ता गच्छह। लहु गण्हह णेवच्छं।)

उभे—यद्देव्याज्ञापयति। (इति प्रस्थिते।) (जं देवी आणवेदि।)

वासवदत्ता—आरण्यिके एतैरेव मदङ्गपिनद्धैराभरणैर्नेपथ्यभूमिं गत्वात्मानं प्रसाधय। (आभरणान्यङ्गादवतार्यारण्यिकायाः समर्पयति) मनोरमे त्वमपि नलगिरिग्रहणपरितुष्टेन तातेनार्यपुत्रस्य दत्तान्याभरणानी-न्दीवरिकासकाशाद्गृहीत्वा नेपथ्यभूमिं गत्वात्मानं मण्डय येन सुसदृशी दृश्यसे महाराजस्य। (आरण्णिए एदेहिं एव्व मदङ्गपिणद्धेहिं आभरणेहिं णेवच्छभूमिं गदुअ अप्पाणं पसाहेहि। मणोरमे तुमं वि णलगिरिग्गहणपरितुट्ठेण तादेण अज्जउत्तस्स दिण्णाइं आभरणाइं इन्दीवरिआसआसादो गेण्हिअ णेवच्छभूमिअं गदुअ अप्पाणं मण्डेहि जेण सुसदिसी दीससि महाराअस्स।)

(मनोरमा इन्दीवरिकासकाशादाभरणानि गृहीत्वा सहारण्यिकया निष्क्रान्ता।)

इन्दीवरिका—इदमासनम्। उपविशतु भट्टिनी। (एदं आसणं। उवविसदु भट्टिणी।)

वासवदत्ता—(आसनं निर्दिश्य।) उपविशतु भगवती। (उवविसदु भअवदी।) (उभे उपविशतः[3]।)

(ततः प्रविशति गृहीतनेपथ्यः कञ्चुकी।)

कञ्चुकी—

अन्तःपुराणां विहितव्यवस्थः
पदे पदेऽहं स्खलितानि रक्षन्।

मदङ्गपिनद्धैर्मदङ्गे बद्धैः। धारितैरित्यर्थः। प्रसाधय मण्डय। नलगिरिर्नाम इन्द्रदत्तः प्रद्योतस्य गजः तस्य आलानमुत्पाट्य प्रभ्रष्टस्य ग्रहणं तेन परितुष्टस्तेन। **अन्तःपुराणामिति**। अन्तःपुराणामवरोधस्त्रीणां विहिता व्यवस्था व्यवस्थापनं येन सः। पदे पदे प्रतिपदं स्खलितानि प्रमादान् रक्षन् परिहरन्। राजदारान् प्रमादेभ्यो रक्षन्नित्यर्थः। संप्रति जरातुरः दण्डनीत्यां दण्डेन नीतिस्तमवलम्ब्य गमनं तेन नृपस्य सर्वचरितमनुकरोमि विडम्बयामि। नृपो पुराणामन्तःप्रजानां स्थितिपालनादिरूपां व्यवस्थां करोति। प्रजाः

१ एतन्नास्ति पुस्तकान्तरे. २ इदं. ३ आसनग्रहणं नाटयतः.

जरातुरः संप्रति दण्डनीत्या
सर्वं नृपस्यानुकरोमि वृत्तम् ॥ ३ ॥

भोः आज्ञापितोऽस्मि विमानिताशेषशत्रुसैन्येन यथार्थनाम्ना महासेनेन समादिश्यतामन्तःपुरेषु यथा—श्वो वयमुदयनोत्सवमनुभवामः । अतो युष्माभिरुत्सवानुरूपवेषोज्ज्वलेन परिजनेन सह मन्मथोद्यानं गन्तव्यमिति ।

साङ्कृत्यायनी—(कञ्चुकिनं निर्दिश्य ।) राजपुत्रि प्रवृत्ता प्रेक्षा । दृश्यताम् ।

कञ्चुकी—तदेतदादेष्टव्यं[1] परिजनेन सह गन्तव्यमिति । न[2] गृहीतनेपथ्येनेति । कुतः ।

पादैर्नूपुरिभिर्नितम्बफलकैः शिञ्जानकाञ्चीगुणै-
र्हारापादितकान्तिभिः स्तनतटैः केयूरिभिर्बाहुभिः ।
कर्णैः कुण्डलिभीः करैः सवलयैः सस्वस्तिकैर्मूर्धजै-
र्देवीनां परिचारिकापरिजनोऽप्येतेषु संदृश्यते ॥ ४ ॥

न खलु किंचिदत्रापूर्वमनुष्ठेयम् । केवलं स्वाम्यादेश इति मत्वाहं समा[3]दिष्टस्तदाज्ञाशेषं राजपुत्र्यै निवेदयामि । (परिक्रम्यावलोक्य च ।) इयं

प्रमादेभ्यो निवारयति । दण्डनीत्या अर्थशास्त्रानुसारेण प्रजा रक्षति च । दण्डनीतिनिरुक्तिस्तु-दण्डेन नीयते चेदं दण्डं नयति वा पुनः । दण्डनीतिरिति ख्याता त्रीन् लोकानतिवर्तते ॥ इति । श्लिष्टोपमालंकारः । वृत्तमुपजातिः । स्यादिन्द्रवज्रा यदि तौ जगौ गः । उपेन्द्रवज्रा जतजास्ततो गौ । अनन्तरोदीरितलक्ष्मभाजौ पादौ यदीयावुपजातयस्ताः ॥ इति तल्लक्षणम् ॥ ३ ॥ विमानितानि तिरस्कृतान्यशेषाणां शत्रूणां सैन्यानि येन । महासेनश्चण्डमहासेन इत्यपराभिध उज्जयिनीनृपः । प्रेक्षा नृत्तम् । प्रेक्षाधीरीक्षणं नृत्तम् । इति हैमः । **पादैरिति** । नूपुराणि मञ्जीरा एषां विद्यन्ते इति नूपुरिणस्तैः पादैः । शिञ्जानाः शब्दायमानाः काञ्चीगुणा मेखलादामानि येषां येषु वा तैस्तथोक्तैः नितम्बफलकैः प्रशस्तनितम्बैः । हारैः मुक्तासरैः आपादिता निर्मिता कान्तिर्येषां तादृशैः स्तनतटैः । केयूरिभिः अङ्गदसहितैः बाहुभिः । कुण्डलिभिः कुण्डलधारिभिः कर्णैः । सवलयैः कङ्कणयुक्तैः करैः सस्वस्तिकैः स्वस्तिकाख्यालङ्कारधरैः । स्वस्तिकं मङ्गलः द्रव्यविशेषो वा तद्युक्तैः । मूर्धजैः केशपाशैः उपलक्षितः । देवीनां पूज्याया देव्याः । पूजार्थे बहुवचनम् । परिचारिकापरिजनः सेवकवर्गोऽपि एतेषु अन्तःपुरेषु दृश्यते । पूर्वमेव कृतनेपथ्यो वर्तते इत्यर्थः । शार्दूलविक्रीडतं वृत्तम् ॥ ४ ॥

१ एतावदेव. २ गृहीत० नादेष्टव्यम् ; न वेषोज्ज्वलेनेति. ३ समादिष्टं.

सा वासवदत्ता वीणाहस्तया काञ्चनमाल्यानुगम्यमाना गन्धर्वशालां प्रविष्टा । यावदस्याः कथयामि । (परिक्रामति ।)

(ततः प्रविशति गृहीतवासवदत्तानेपथ्यासनस्थारण्यिका वीणाहस्ता काञ्चनमाला च ।)

आर०—हला काञ्चनमाले कस्मात्पुनश्चिरयत्यद्यापि वीणाचार्यः । (हला कञ्चणमाले कीस उण चिराअदि अज्ज वि वीणाआरिओ ।)

काञ्च०—भर्तृदारिके दृष्टस्तेनैक उन्मत्तः । तस्य वचनं श्रुत्वा चित्रेण भावितोऽपहसंस्तिष्ठति । (भट्टिदारिए दिट्ठो देण एक्को उम्मत्तो । तस्स वअणं सुणिअ चित्तेण भाविदो ओहसन्तो चिट्ठइ ।)

आर०—(सहस्ततालं विहस्य ।) हञ्जे सुष्ठुतं पृच्छति । सदृशाः सदृशे रजन्त इति द्वावत्रोन्मत्तौ । (हञ्जे सुठु एदं पुच्छदि । सरिसा सरिसे रज्जन्तित्ति दुवे एत्थ उम्मत्ता ।)

साङ्कृत्यायनी—राजपुत्र्याः सदृशमाकारं पश्याम्यस्यास्तादृशेनाकारेणावश्यं त्वदीयां भूमिकां संभावयिष्यति ।

कञ्चुकी—(उपसृत्य ।) राजपुत्रि देवस्त्वामाज्ञापयति । श्वोऽवश्यमस्माभिर्वीणां वादयन्ती श्रोतव्या । तत्त्वया नवतन्त्रीसज्जया घोषवत्या स्थेयमिति ।

आर०—आर्य यद्येवं लघु वीणाचार्यं विसर्जय । (अय्य जइ एव्वं लहु वीणाआरिअं विसज्जेहि ।

कञ्चुकी—एष वत्सराजं प्रेषयामि । (इति निष्क्रान्तः ।)

आर०—काञ्चनमाले उपनय मे घोषवतीं यावदस्यास्तन्त्रीः परीक्षे । (कञ्चणमाले उवणेहि मे घोसवदीं जाव से तंतीओ परिक्खेमि ।)

(काञ्चनमाला वीणामर्पयति । आरण्यिकोत्सङ्गे वीणां कृत्वा सारयति ।)

(ततः प्रविशति गृहीतवत्सराजनेपथ्या मनोरमा ।)

वासवदत्तात्र वासवदत्तावेषधारिणी आरण्यिका ज्ञेया । गंधर्वशाला प्रेक्षागृहम् । चित्रेण भावितो वैचित्र्यहृतचित्तः । सहस्ततालं हस्तौ प्रताड्य । सदृशाः सदृशे इ०—सर्वः सगन्धेषु विश्वसिति । द्वावप्यत्रारण्यकौ । इति समानार्थं वचनं शाकुन्तले । तादृशेन राजपुत्र्युचितेन । घोषवत्या वीणया सहितया । लघु शीघ्रम् । समदनावस्थो राजा स्वमनोवस्थामाह-

---

१ चिरयतेऽय. २ सुणिअ तेण माविदत्थो हसन्तो (भावितार्थो हसन्). ३ सुष्ठ्वेतद्गण्यते (मणीअदि)..रज्जन्तीति. ४ राजपुत्रि यादृशमाका०.

मनोरमा—(स्वगतम्।) चिरयति खलु महाराजः। किं न कथितं वसन्तकेन। अथवा देव्या बिभेति। यदीदानीमागच्छेत्ततो रमणीयं भवेत्। (चिराअदि क्खु महाराओ किं ण कहिदं वसन्तएण। अहवा देवीए भाअदि। जइं दाणिं आअच्छे तदो रमणिज्जं हवे।)

(ततः प्रविशति राजावगुण्ठितशरीरो विदूषकश्च।)

राजा—

संतापं प्रथमं तथा न कुरुते शीतांशुरद्यैव मे
निश्वासा ग्लपयन्त्यजस्रमधुनैवोष्णास्तथा नाधरम्।
संप्रत्येव मनो न शून्यमलसान्यङ्गानि नो पूर्वव-
द्दुःखं याति मनोरथेषु तनुतां संचिन्त्यमानेष्वपि॥ ५॥

वयस्य सत्यमेवोक्तं मनोरमया। यथैषा मम प्रियसखी महाराजस्य देव्या दर्शनपथादपि रक्ष्यते तदयं समागमोपायः। अद्य रात्रावस्माभिरुदयनचरितं नाम नाटकं देव्याः पुरतो नर्तितव्यम्। तत्रारण्यिका वासवदत्ता भविष्यति। अहमपि वत्सराजः। तच्चरितेनैव सर्वं शिक्षितव्यम्। तदागत्य स्वयमेव स्वां भूमिकां कुर्वाणः समागमोत्सवमनुभवत्विति।

विदूषकः–यदि मां न प्रत्यायस्येषा मनोरमा तव वेषं धारयन्ती तिष्ठति। तदुपसृत्य स्वयमेव पृच्छ। (जइ मं ण पत्तिआअसि एसा मणोरमा तुह वेसं धारअन्ती चिट्ठइ। ता उवसप्पिअ सअं एव पुच्छ।)

राजा—(मनोरमामुपसृत्य।) मनोरमे सत्यमिदं यद्वसन्तकोऽभिधत्ते।

मनोरमा—भर्तः सत्यमेव। मण्डयैतैराभरणैरात्मानम्। (इत्याभरणान्यङ्गादवतार्य राज्ञे समर्पयति।) (भट्टा सच्चं एव्व। मण्डअ एदेहिं आभरणेहिं अप्पाणं)

(राजा परिदधाति।)

संतापमिति। शितांशुः चन्द्रमा मे मम प्रथमं पूर्वं यथा संतापमकरोत् तथा अद्यैव न कुरुते। तथा उष्णा निश्वासाः अधुनैव प्राग्यथा तथा अजस्रमनवरतमधरं न ग्लपयन्ति। सम्प्रत्येव पूर्ववत् मनः न शून्यमङ्गानि च नो नालसानि। तथाहि मनोरथेषु संचिन्त्यमानेषु सम्पन्नप्राया इति चिन्त्यमानेष्वपि दुःखं मनस्तापः तनुतां याति ह्रस्वीभवति॥ शार्दूलविक्रीडितं छन्दः॥ ५॥ निभृतेन निगूढम्। उद्देशः कथासंदर्भः। वीणां वादयन् वीणावादनशिक्षणप्रसङ्गेन। मय्यनुरागं जनयित्वेत्यर्थः। पटाक्षेपेण जवनिकामाक्षिप्य। आकस्मिकप्रवेशसूचनार्थमिदम्।

विदूषकः—एते खलु राजानो दास्यौपि एवं नर्त्यन्ते। अहो कार्यस्य गुरुता। (एदे क्खु राणाओ दासीए वि एव्वं णच्चाविअन्ति। अहो कज्जस्स गरुअदा।)

राजा—(विहस्य।) मूर्ख नैष कालः परिहासस्य। निभृतेन चित्रशालां प्रविश्य मनोरमया सहास्मन्नृत्तं पश्यता स्थीयताम्।

(उभौ तथा कुरुतः।)

आरण्यिका—काञ्चनमाले तिष्ठतु वीणा। प्रक्ष्यामि तावत्किमपि। (कञ्चणमाले चिट्ठदु वीणा। पुच्छिस्सं दाव किं वि।)

राजा—शृणोमि तावत्कतमोऽयमुद्देशो वर्तते। (इत्यवहितः शृणोति।)

काञ्चनमाला—पृच्छतु भर्तृदारिका। (पुच्छदु भट्टिदारिआ।)

आर०—सत्यमेव तातो मन्त्रयते एवं यथा—यदि वीणां वादयन्नपहरति मां वत्सराजोऽवश्यं बन्धनान्मुञ्चामीति। (सच्चं एव तादो मन्तेदि एव्वं जह जइ वीणं वादअन्तो अवहरेदि मं वच्छराओ अवस्सं बन्धणादो मुञ्चेमित्ति।)

राजा—(प्रविश्य पटाक्षेपेण सहर्षं वस्त्रान्ते ग्रथितं बध्नाति।) एवमेतत्। कः संदेहः।

सपरिजनं प्रद्योतं विस्मयमुपनीय वादयन्वीणाम्।
वासवदत्तामपहरामि न चिरादेवेति पश्यामि॥ ६॥

यतः सुसंविहितं सर्वं यौगन्धरायणेन।

वासवदत्ता—(सहसोत्थाय।) जयतु जयत्वार्यपुत्रः। (जेदु जेदु अज्जउत्तो।)

राजा—(स्वगतम्।) कथं प्रत्यभिज्ञातोऽस्मि देव्या।

साङ्कृत्यायनी—(सस्मितम्।) राजपुत्रि अलमलं संभ्रमेण। प्रेक्षणीयकमेतत्।

ग्रथितं बध्नाति शुभशकुनं दृष्ट्वाऽभिमतसिद्धिसूचनार्थं वस्त्रपल्लवग्रन्थिबन्धनं लोकरीतिः। **सपरिजनमिति**। वीणां वादयन् मनोहारिणा वीणावादनेनेत्यर्थः। प्रद्योतं महासेनं सपरिजनं विस्मयमुपनीय प्रापय्य। वासवदत्तां न चिरादेवापहरामि अपहरिष्यामीति पश्यामि मन्ये। एतदुत्तरार्धं वृत्तलक्षणाननुसारि नातिमनोहरं चेति व्यक्तम्॥ ६॥ सुसंनिहितमिति पाठे सम्यक्संनिधौ स्थापितम्। यौगन्धरायण उदयनस्य प्रधानामात्यः।

---

१ दासीव्व (दास्य इव). २ ग्रन्थिं. ३ ०दत्तापहरणमपि; दत्ताहरणं; पश्याम्यहं. ४ सुसंनिहितं.

राजा—(आत्मगतं सहर्षम्) इदानीमुच्छ्वसितोऽस्मि ।

वासवदत्ता—(सविलक्षस्मितमुपविश्य ।) कथं मनोरमैषा । मया पुनर्ज्ञातमार्यपुत्र एष इति । साधु मनोरमे साधु । शोभनं नर्तितम् । (कहं मणोरमा एसा । मए उण जाणिदं अज्जउत्तो एसोत्ति । साहु मणोरमे सहु । सोहणं णच्चिदं ।)

साङ्कृत्या०—राजपुत्रि स्थान एव कृता भ्रान्तिस्ते मनोरमया । पश्य ।

रूपं तन्नयनोत्सवास्पदमिदं वेषः स एवोज्ज्वलः
सा मत्तद्विरदोचिता गतिरियं तत्सत्त्वमत्यूर्जितम् ।
लीला सैव स एव सान्द्रजलदह्लादानुकारी स्वरः
साक्षाद्दर्शित एष नः कुशलया वत्सेश एवानया ॥ ७ ॥

वासवदत्ता—हञ्जे इन्दीवरिके बद्धेनार्यपुत्रेणाहं वीणां शिक्षिता । तदस्य कुरु नीलोत्पलदामकेन निगडनम् । (शिरसोऽपनीय नीलोत्पलदामार्पयति ।) (हञ्जे इन्दीवरिए । बद्धेण अज्जउत्तेण अहं वीणं सिक्खाविदा । ता से करेहि णीलुप्पलदामएण णिअलणम् ।)

(इन्दीवरिका तथा कृत्वा पुनस्तत्रैवोपविशति ।)

आरण्यिका—काञ्चनमाले कथय कथय । ननु सत्यमेव मन्त्रयते तातो यदि वीणां वादयन्नपहरति मां वत्सराजस्ततोऽवश्यं बन्धनान्मुञ्चामीति । (कञ्चणमाले कहेहि कहेहि । णं सच्चं एव्व मन्तेदि तादो जइ वीणं वादअन्तो अवहरेदि मं वच्छराओ तदो अवस्सं बन्धणादो मुञ्चेमित्ति ।)

काञ्चनमाला—भर्तृदारिके सत्यम् । तथा कुरु यथा वत्सराजस्यावश्यं बहुमता भवसि । (भट्टिदारिए सच्चं । तह करेहि जह वच्छराअस्स अवस्सं बहुमदा होसि ।)

रूपमिति । इदं दृश्यमानं गृहीतवत्सराज भूमिकाया मनोरमायाः नयनानन्दकरं रूपं तद्वत्सराजस्यैव । तदभिन्नमेव । उज्ज्वलः वेषः स एव । इयमनया प्रकटीकृता मत्तद्विरदस्य मत्तगजस्योचिता तत्सदृशी गतिः सैव । उदयनस्यैव । अत्यूर्जितं अतिमहत् सत्त्वं मनोगाम्भीर्यं पौरुषं वा तदेव । लीला सैव । सान्द्रः सजलः यः जलदस्तस्य ह्रादः स्वनस्तमनुकरोतीति तथा । तत्सदृशः । स्वरः स एव । एवं कुशलया नाट्यचतुरया अनया एष वत्सेश एव नः दर्शितः । शार्दूलविक्रीडितं वृत्तम् ॥ ७ ॥

---

१ उच्छ्वसि० . २ रमा खलु. ३ कारिता भ्रान्तिर्मनो०. ४ णिअलं. ५ तथैव. ६ सत्यमेव.

राजा—निष्पादितमेव काञ्चनमालया यत्तदास्माभिरभिलषितम्।

आरण्यिका—यद्येवं तदादरेण वादयिष्यामि। (गायन्ती वादयति) (जइ एव्वं ता आदरेण वादइस्सं।)

घनबन्धनसंरुद्धं गगनं दृष्ट्वा मानसमेतुम्॥
अभिलषति राजहंसो दयितां गृहीत्वात्मनो वसतिम्॥ ८॥

घणबन्धणसंरुद्धं गअणं दट्ठूण माणसं एेदुं॥
अहिलसइ राअहंसो दइअं घेऊणं अप्पणो वसइं॥

(विदूषको निद्रां नाटयति।)

मनोरमा—(हस्तेन चालयन्ती।) वसन्तक पश्य पश्य। प्रियसखी मे नृत्यति (वसन्तअ पेक्ख पेक्ख पिअसही मे णच्चइ।)

विदूषकः—(सरोषम्।) दास्याः सुते त्वमपि न ददासि स्वप्तुम्। यदाप्रभृति प्रियवयस्येनारण्यिका दृष्टा तदाप्रभृति तेन सह मया रात्रिंदिवं निद्रा न दृष्टा। तदन्यतो निष्क्रम्य स्वप्स्यामि। (निष्क्रम्य शेते) (दासीए सुदे तुमं वि ण देसि सुविदुं। जदप्पहुदि पिअवअस्सेण आरण्णिआ दिट्ठा तदप्पहुदि तेण सह मए रत्तंदिवं णिद्दा ण दिट्ठा। ता अण्णदो णिक्कमिअ सुविस्सं।)

(आरण्यिका पुनर्गायति।)

अभिनवरागक्षिप्ता मधुकरिका वामकेन कामेन॥
उत्ताम्यति प्रार्थयमाना द्रष्टुं प्रियदर्शनं दयितम्॥ ९॥

अहिणवराआक्खित्ता महुअरिआ वामएण कामेण।
उत्तम्मइ पत्थन्ती दट्ठुं पिअदंसणं दइअं॥

राजा—(तदाकर्ण्य श्रुत्वा सहसोपसृत्य।) साधु राजपुत्रि साधु। अहो गीतमहो वादित्रम्। तथाहि।

निगडनं पदबन्धनम्। **घनबन्धनेति**। राजहंसः मरालः घनानां मेघानां बन्धनेन संहत्या संरुद्धं व्याप्तं गगनं दृष्ट्वा दयितां गृहीत्वा आत्मनो वसतिं मानसं सर एतुमभिलषति। गूढार्थस्तु राजहंसो नृपश्रेष्ठो वत्सराजः गगनं तत्सदृशं कारागृहं घनबन्धनेन संरुद्धं निरुद्धं दृष्ट्वा दयितां वासवदत्तां गृहीत्वा शिष्यात्वेन स्वीकृत्य तस्या मानसमेतुं तस्मिन्ननुरागं जनयितुमिति यावत्। तत्र आत्मनो वसतिं निवासमभिलषति। अप्रस्तुतप्रशंसालंकारः॥ ८॥ रात्रिंदिवं रात्रौ दिवा च। अचतुरेत्यादिना निपातः। **अभिनवेति**। वामकेन कुटिलेन दुर्लभवस्तुनि प्रवर्तकेनेत्यर्थः। कामेन अभिनवरागे क्षिप्ता मधुकरिका प्रियदर्शनं दयितं द्रष्टुं प्रार्थयमाना उत्कटतया वाञ्छन्ती उत्ताम्यति पर्याकुला भवति। अत्राप्रस्तुतभृङ्गीवर्णनेन नायिकाप्रतीतेरप्रस्तुतप्रशंसालंकारः॥ ९॥

---

१ आलपितव्य न. २ णेदुं (नेतुं). ३ घेत्तूण. ४ दिवारत्तं (दिवारात्रिं). ५ इति नि०. ६ एतन्नास्ति पुस्तकान्तरे.

व्यक्तिर्व्यञ्जनधातुना दशविधेनाप्यत्र लब्धाधुना
विस्पष्टो द्रुतमध्यलम्बितपरिच्छिन्नस्त्रिधायं लयः ।
गोपुच्छप्रमुखाः क्रमेण यतयस्तिस्रोऽपि संपादिता-
स्तत्वौघानुगताश्च वाद्यविधयः सम्यक्त्रयो दर्शिताः ॥ १० ॥

आरण्यका—(वीणां परित्यज्यासनादुत्थाय राजानं साभिलाषं पश्यन्ती ।) उपाध्याय प्रणमामि । (उवज्झाअ पणमामि ।)

राजा—(सस्मितम् ।) यदहमिच्छामि तत्ते भूयात् ।

वादित्रं वादनकौशलमित्यर्थः । **व्यक्तिरिति** । अधुना अत्र श्रवणपथमापतिते वाद्यानुगते गीते । व्यञ्जनधातुना व्यज्यन्ते विशेषा अनेनेति व्यञ्जनः स चासौ धातुश्च व्यञ्जनधातुः । वाद्यवादनोत्थस्वरो धातुः । तदुक्तं-ये प्रहारविशेषोत्थाः स्वरास्ते धातवो मताः । विस्तारकरणा विद्धव्यञ्जनाश्चेति धातवः ॥ व्यञ्जनधातुर्वीणावादनप्रकारः । दशविधेन दशप्रकारेण । तदुक्तं मुनिना-इति दशविधः प्रयोज्यो वीणायां व्यञ्जनो धातुः । दाशविध्यं चोक्तं-व्यञ्जनधातोर्ह्येयं कलतलनिष्कोटितं तथोन्मृष्टम् । रेफोवमृष्टपुष्पावनुस्वनो बिन्दुरधरश्च ॥ एतेषां लक्षणानि विस्तरभिया नोच्यन्ते । व्यक्तिर्लब्धा । वृत्तिर्लब्धेतिपाठे वृत्तिः गीतवाद्ययोर्गुणप्रधानत्वरूपा व्यवहृतिः । तदुक्तं वृत्तिर्गुणप्रधानत्वरूपा व्यवहृतिर्मता । चित्रा वृत्तिर्दक्षिणा च तिस्रः स्युरिति वृत्तयः ॥ यत्र वाद्यप्रधानत्वं गीतस्य गुणता सा चित्रावृत्तिः । यत्र उभयोः समता सा वृत्तिवृत्तिः । यत्र गीतप्रधानता वाद्यस्य गुणता सा दक्षिणा वृत्तिः । अयं श्रूयमाणः लयः गीतवाद्यादीनां कालक्रियासाम्यं द्रुतः मध्यः लम्बितः इत्येवं परिच्छिन्नः त्रिधा त्रिप्रकारेण विस्पष्टः । क्रियानन्तरविश्रान्तिर्लयः स त्रिविधो मतः । द्रुतो मध्यो विलम्बश्च द्रुतः शीघ्रतमो मतः । द्विगुणाद्विगुणौ ज्ञेयौ तस्मान्मध्यविलम्बितौ ॥ गोपुच्छा पूर्वं लघुः मध्ये दीर्घा पुनः क्रमेण लघुतां प्राप्ता इत्येवं गोपुच्छस्वरूपा गोपुच्छा । तत्प्रमुखाः तिस्रोः यतयः समास्रोतोगतागोपुच्छासंज्ञाः यतयोपि संपादिताः निर्वाहिताः । तत्वं औघः अनुगतं च येषु ते तत्त्वौघानुगताः त्रयः वाद्यविधयः सम्यग्यथाशास्त्रं दर्शिताः । "एतेषां नियमनं चैवम्—चित्रवृत्त्यां लयो द्रुतं यतिः समा वाद्यमोघमिति । वृत्तिवृत्त्यां लयो मध्यं यतिः स्रोतोगता वाद्यमनुगतमिति । दक्षिणवृत्त्यां लयो विलम्बितं यतिर्गोपुच्छा ॥ वाद्यं तत्वमिति च ।" इति श्रीनिवासाचार्याः । उक्तं च—त्रिविधं गीते कार्यं वादित्रं वैणमेव वाद्यज्ञैः । तत्त्वं तथाप्यनुगतमोघो वा नैककरणं तु । लयतालवर्णपदयतिगीत्यक्षरवादकं भवेत्तत्वम् । गीतं तु यदनुगच्छत्यनुगतमिति तद्भवेद्वाद्यम् । अविद्धकरणबहुलं ह्युपर्युपरिपाणिकं द्रुतलयं च । अनपेक्षितगीतार्थं वाद्यमयौघो विधातव्यम् ॥ इति । लयादीनामन्यान्यपि लक्षणान्युपलभ्यमानानीह विस्तरभिया नोक्तानि ॥ शार्दूल० वृत्तम् ॥ १० ॥ उपेत्याधीयते

---

१ वृत्तिः. २ अमुना. ३ परित्यज्य.

काञ्चनमाला—(आरण्यिकाया आसनं निर्दिश्य ।) इहैवोपविशतु उपाध्यायः । (इह एव्व उववसिदु उवज्झाओ ।)

राजा—(उपविश्य ।) राजपुत्री क्वेदानीमुपविशतु ।

काञ्चनमाला—(सस्मितम् ।) इदानीमेव भर्तृदारिका विद्यमानेन परितोषिता युष्माभिः । तदर्हत्येवैषोपाध्यायपीठिकायाः । (दाणिं एव्व भट्टिदारिआ विज्जामाणेन परितोसिदा तुह्मेहिं । ता अरुहदि एव्व एसा उवज्झाअपीठिआए।)

राजा—उपविशत्वर्हेयमर्धासनस्य । राजपुत्रि स्थीयताम् ।

(आरण्यिका काञ्चममालां पश्यति ।)

काञ्चनमाला—(सस्मितम् ।) भर्तृदारिके उपविश । कोऽत्र दोषः । शिष्यविशेषा खलु त्वम् । (भट्टिदारिए उववस । को एत्थ दोसो । सिस्सविसेसा क्खु तुमं ।)

(आरण्यिका सलज्जमुपविशति ।)

वासवदत्ता—(सलज्जम् ।) भगवत्याधिकं कल्पितं काव्यम् । न खल्वहं तस्मिन्काल एकासने आर्यपुत्रेण सहोपविष्टा । (भअवदीये अहिअं कप्पिदं कव्वं । ण हु अहं तस्सिं काले एक्कासणे अज्जउत्तेण सह उवविट्ठा ।)

राजा—राजपुत्रि पुनः श्रोतुमिच्छामि । वादय वीणाम् ।

आरण्यिका—(सस्मितम् ।) काञ्चनमाले चिरं खलु मम वादयन्त्याः परिश्रमो जातः । इदानीं निःसहान्यङ्गानि । तन्न शक्नोमि वादयितुम् । (कञ्चणमाले चिरं क्खु मम वादअन्तीए परिस्समो जादो । दाणिं णिस्सहाइं अङ्गाइं । ता ण सक्कुणोमि वादइदुं ।)

काञ्चनमाला—उपाध्याय सुष्ठु परिश्रान्ता भर्तृदारिका । कपोलतलबद्धस्वेद[3]लवाथाः पश्यास्या वेपेते अग्रहस्तौ । तत्समाश्वस्ता भवतु मुहूर्तम् । (उवज्झाअ सुट्ठु परिस्सन्ता भट्टिदारिआ । कवोलतलबद्धसेअलवाए पेक्ख से वेवन्ति अग्गहत्था । ता समस्सत्ता होतु मुहुत्तअं ।)

राजा—काञ्चनमाले युक्तमभिहितम् । (हस्ते[4] ग्रहीतुमिच्छति ।)

(आरण्यिका हस्तमपसारयति ।)

अस्मादित्युपाध्यायः । विद्यामानेन गानविद्याप्रावीण्यप्रशंसयेत्यर्थः । कपोलतले बद्धा स्वेदलवा यस्याः । अग्रौ च तौ हस्तौ च इति कर्मधारयः । हस्ताग्रहस्तयोर्गुणगुणिनोर्भेदाभेदादिति वामनः ।

---

१ विद्यागुणपरि०-ध्यायपीठिकायै. २ उवट्ठिदा (उपस्थिता). ३ स्वेदकणजालका । ४ हस्ते.

वासवदत्ता—(सासूयम् ।) भगवति आधिकमेतदपि त्वया कृतम् । न खल्वहं काञ्चनमाला काव्येन वञ्चयितव्या । (भअवदि अहिअं एदं वि तुए किदं । ण हु अअं कञ्चणमाला कव्वेण वञ्चइदव्वा ।)

साङ्कृत्यायनी—(विहस्य ।) आयुष्मति ईदृशमेव काव्यं भविष्यति ।

आर०—(सरोषमिव ।) अपेहि काञ्चनमाले अपेहि । न मे बहुमतासि । (अवेहि कञ्चणमाले अवेहि । ण मे बहुमदासि ।)

काञ्चन०—(सस्मितम् ।) यद्यहं तिष्ठन्ती न बहुमता तदेषा गच्छामि । (इति निष्क्रान्ता ।) (जइ अहं चिठ्ठन्ती ण बहुमदा ता एसा गच्छाम्हि)

आर०—(ससंभ्रमम् ।) काञ्चनमाले तिष्ठ तिष्ठ । अयमस्याग्रहस्तः समर्पितः । (कञ्चणमाले चिठ्ठ चिठ्ठ । अहं से अग्गहत्थो समप्पिदो ।)

राजा—(आरण्यिकाया हस्तं गृहीत्वा ।)

सद्योऽवश्यायबिन्दुव्यतिकरशिशिरः किं भवेत्पद्मकोशो
ह्लादित्वं नास्य मन्ये सदृशमिदमुषस्येव वीतातपस्य ।
मुञ्चन्त्येते हिमौघं नखरजनिकराः पञ्च किं सोऽपि दाही
ज्ञातं स्वेदापदेशादविरतममृतं स्यन्दते व्यक्तमेतत् ॥ ११ ॥

अपि च ।

एतेन बालविद्रुमपल्लवशोभापहारदक्षेण ।
हृदये मम त्वयायं न्यस्तो रागः स्वहस्तेन ॥ १२ ॥

सद्य इति । अयं मया गृहीतः करः सद्यस्तत्कालं य अवश्यायबिन्दूनां नीहारकणानां व्यतिकरः सम्बन्धस्तेन शिशिरः शीतलः पद्मकोश कमलमुकुलः भवेत्किम् । नैतत्संभवतीत्याह । अस्य नीहारकणसनाथस्य पद्ममुकुलस्य अधुनाह्लादित्वमानन्दकारित्वं न मन्ये । यतः वीतातपस्य आतपरहितस्य । पीतातपस्येति पाठे गृहीतबालातपस्य । अस्य उषस्येव सदृशं योग्यम् । उषस्येव पद्मकोशः आह्लादको भवेदिति भावः । वितर्कान्तरमाह एते पञ्च नखरजनिकराः नखचन्द्राः हिमौघं नीहारसंदोहं मुञ्चन्ति किम् । नैतदपि । यतः सोपि रजनिकरः दाही विरहिणां दहनशीलः । न तु सर्वदानन्दकरो यथायम् । तत्किमेतत्स्यादित्यत्र निर्णयमाह—ज्ञातं मया सम्यगवगतम् । एतद् स्वेदापदेशात्स्वेदव्याजेन अमृतमविरतं स्यन्दते स्रवति । एतत् व्यक्तं स्पष्टमेव । संदेहापह्नुतिसंकीर्णोत्प्रेक्षा । शार्दूलवि० वृत्तम् । **एतेनेति** । एतेन बालः यः विद्रुमपल्लवः प्रवालाङ्कुरस्तस्य शोभाया अपहारे मोषणे दक्षेण । अत्यन्तं तत्सदृशेन स्वहस्तेन त्वया मम हृदये अयं रागः रक्तिमा अनुरागश्च न्यस्तोऽर्पितः ॥ १२ ॥

---

१ अहं. २ पीता०.

आर०—(स्पर्शविशेषं नाटयन्ती।) हा धिक् हा धिक्। एतां मनोरमां स्पृशन्त्या अनर्थमेव मेऽङ्गानि कुर्वन्ति। (हद्धि हद्धि। एदं मणोरमं परिसन्तीए अणत्थं एव्व मे अङ्गाइं करेन्ति।)

वासवदत्ता—(सहसोत्थाय।) भगवति पश्य त्वम्। अहं पुनरलीकं न पारयामि प्रेक्षितुम्। (भअवदि पेक्ख तुमं। अहं उण अलिअं ण पारेमि पेक्खिदुं।)

साङ्कृत्यायनी—राजपुत्रि धर्मशास्त्रविहित एष गान्धर्वो विवाहः। किमत्र लज्जास्थानम्। प्रेक्षणीयकमिदम्। तन्न युक्तमस्थाने रसभङ्गं कृत्वा गन्तुम्।

(वासवदत्ता परिक्रामति।)

इन्दीवरिका—(विलोक्य।) भट्टिनि वसन्तकश्चित्रशालाद्वारे प्रसुप्तस्तिष्ठति। (भट्टिणि वसन्तओ चित्तसालादुवारे पसुत्तो चिट्ठइ।)

वासवदत्ता—(निरूप्य।) वसन्तक एवैषः। (विचिन्त्य।) राज्ञाप्यत्र भवितव्यम्। तद्बोधयित्वा प्रक्ष्यामि तावदेनम्। (प्रबोधयति।) (वसन्तओ एव्व एसो। रण्णा वि एत्थ होदव्वं। ता बोधिअ पुच्छिस्सं दाव णं।)

विदूषकः—(निद्राजडमुत्थाय सहसा विलोक्य।) मनोरमे किं नर्तित्वागतः प्रियवयस्यः। अथवा नृत्यत्येव। (मणोरमे किं णच्चिअ आअदो पिअवअस्सो। आदु णच्चदि एव्व।)

वासवदत्ता—(सविषादम्।) कथमार्यपुत्रो नृत्यति। मनोरमेदानीं कुत्र। (कहं अज्जउत्तो णच्चदि। मणोरमा दाणिं कहिं।)

विदूषकः—एषा चित्रशालायां तिष्ठति। (एसा चित्तसालाए चिट्ठइ।)

मनो०—(सभयमात्मगतम्।) कथमन्यथैव हृदये कृत्वा देव्या मन्त्रितम्। एतेनापि मूर्खबटुकेनान्यथैव बुद्ध्वा सर्वमाकुलीकृतम्। (कहं अण्णहा एव्व

अनर्थमिव मेऽङ्गानि कुर्वन्ति कोपि दुःसहो मनोविकारो मेऽङ्गानि प्रज्वलयतीत्यर्थः। विकुर्वत इति पाठे मदनविकारवशानि भवन्तीत्यर्थः। अलीकमवास्तवम्। गान्धर्वः—तदुक्तं—क्षत्रियस्य तु गान्धर्वो विवाहः श्रेष्ठ उच्यते। इति। अत्र मनुः—इच्छयान्योन्यसंयोगः कन्यायाश्च वरस्य च। गान्धर्वः स तु विज्ञेयो मैथुन्यः कामसंभवः॥ इति। अस्थाने अकारणे अनुचिते काले वा। कुत्सितः बटुः बटुकः। कुत्सायां कन्।

---

१० न्तीए अग्गहत्थेण एव्व विकेरन्ति (न्त्या अग्रहस्तेनैव विकुर्वते).

ट्ठिअए करिअ देवीए मन्तिदं । एदेण वि मुक्खबडुएण अण्णहा एव्व बुद्धिअ सव्वं आउलीकिदं ।)

वासवदत्ता—(सरोषं हसन्ती ।) साधु मनोरमे साधु । शोभनं त्वया नर्तितम् । (साहु मणोरमे साहु । सोहणं तुए णच्चिदं ।)

मनो०—(सभयं कम्पमाना पादयोर्निपत्य ।) भट्टिनि न खल्वहमत्रापराध्यामि । एतेन खलु हताशेन बलादलंकरणानि गृहीत्वा द्वारस्थितेनेह निरुद्धा । न पुनर्ममाक्रन्दन्त्याः शब्दो मुरजानिर्घोषान्तरितः केनापि श्रुतः । (भट्टिणि ण हु अहं एत्थ अवरज्झामि । एदेण खु हदासेण बलादो अलंकरणाइं गेण्हिअ दुवारट्ठिदेण इह णिरुद्धा । ण उण मह अक्कन्दन्तीए सद्दो मुरअणिग्घोसन्तरिओ केण वि सुदो ।)

वासवदत्ता—हञ्जे उत्तिष्ठ । ज्ञातं सर्वम् । वसन्तकः खल्वारण्यिकावृत्तान्तनाटके सूत्रधारः । (हञ्जे उट्ठेहि । जाणिदं सव्वं । वसन्तओ क्खु आरण्णिआउत्तन्तणाडए सुत्तधारो ।)

विदूषकः—स्वयमेव चिन्तय । कुत्रारण्यिका कुत्र वसन्तक इति । (सअं एव्व चिन्तेहि । कहिं आरण्णिआ कहिं वसन्तओत्ति ।)

वासवदत्ता—मनोरमे सुगृहीतं कृत्वैनमागच्छ तावत् । प्रेक्षणीयमस्य पश्यामि । (मणोरमे सुग्गहीदं करिअ णं आअच्छ दाव । पेक्खणीअं से पेक्खाह्मि ।)

मनो०—(स्वगतम् ।) इदानीं समाश्वसितास्मि (विदूषकं करे बध्नाति । प्रकाशम् ।) हताश इदानीमनुभवात्मनो दुर्नयस्य फलम् । (दाणिं समस्ससिदह्मि । हदास दाणिं अणुभव अत्तणो दुण्णअस्स फलं ।)

वासवदत्ता—(ससंभ्रममुपसृत्य ।) आर्यपुत्र प्रतिहतमेतदमङ्गलम् । (इति पादयोर्नीलोत्पलदामापनयन्ती सोत्प्रासम् ।) मर्षत्वार्यपुत्रो यन्मनोरमेति कृत्वा नीलोत्पलदामकेन बन्धितोऽसि । (अज्जउत्त पडिहदं एदं अमङ्गलं । मरिसदु अज्जउत्तो जं मणोरमेत्ति करिअ णीलुप्पलदामएण बन्धाविदोसि ।)

(आरण्यिका सभयमपसृत्य तिष्ठति ।)

आरण्यिकायाः वृत्तान्तो नृपेण समागम इत्यर्थः । स एव नाटकं तत्र सूत्रधारो योजकः । सुगृहीतं सुबद्धम् । दुर्नयस्याकुटिलनीतेः । असमीक्ष्यकारिताया इत्यर्थः । अन्यदन्यथापरिणामि ।

---

१ मुक्ख(मूर्खनि०); मए आक्कन्दिदेवि...वरिदो (वान्तरितो) न केण वि सद्दो. २ आअच्छ । ०पेक्ख से पेक्खह्म. ३ अपनयति । ४ (सोत्प्रासं) मर्षयतु इत्यादि राजा वैलक्ष्यं नाटयति ' इत्येतस्य परस्तात्पठ्यते पुस्तकान्तरे । जं इत्यत्र तुमं इ. पा. च.

राजा—(सहसोत्थाय विदूषकं मनोरमां च दृष्ट्वात्मगतम् ।) कथं विज्ञातोऽस्मि देव्या । (वैलक्ष्यं नाटयति ।)

साङ्कृत्यायनी—(सर्वानवलोक्य सस्मितम् ।) कथमन्यदेवेदं प्रेक्षणीयकं संवृत्तम् । अभूमिरियमस्माद्विधानाम् । (इति निष्कान्ता ।)

राजा—(स्वगतम् ।) अपूर्वोऽयं कोपप्रकारः । दुर्लभमत्रानुनयं पश्यामि । (विचिन्त्य ।) एवं तावत्करिष्ये । (प्रकाशम् ।) देवि त्यज्यतां कोपः ।

वासवदत्ता—आर्यपुत्र कोऽत्र कुपितः । (अज्जउत्त को एत्थ कुविदो)

राजा—कथं न कुपितासि ।

स्निग्धं यद्यपि वीक्षितं नयनयोस्ताम्रा तथापि द्युति-
र्माधुर्येऽपि सति स्खलत्यनुपदं ते गद्गदा वागियम् ।
निश्वासा नियता अपि स्तनभरोत्कम्पेन संलक्षिताः
कोपस्ते प्रकटप्रयत्नविधृतोऽप्येष स्फुटं लक्ष्यते ॥ १३ ॥

(पादयोर्निपत्य ।) प्रसीद प्रिये प्रसीद ।

वासवदत्ता—आरण्यिके त्वं कुपितेति संभावयन्नार्यपुत्रः प्रिये प्रसीदेति प्रसादयति । तदुपसर्प । (इति हस्तेनाकर्षति ।) (आरण्णिए तुमं कुविदत्ति संभावअन्तो अज्जउत्तो पिए पसीदत्ति पसादअदि । ता उवसप्प ।)

आर०—(सभयम् ।) भट्टिनि न खल्वहं किमपि जानामि । (भट्टिणि ण हु अहं किं वि जाणामि ।)

वासवदत्ता—आरण्यिके त्वं कथं न जानासि । इदानीं ते शिक्षयामि । इन्दीवरिके गृहाणैनाम् । (आरण्णिए तुमं कहं ण आणासि । दाणिं दे सिक्खावेमि । इन्दीवरिए गेण्ह एदं ।)

विदूषकः—भवति अद्य कौमुदीमहोत्सवे तव चित्तमपहर्तुं वयस्येन प्रेक्षणीयमनुष्ठितम् । (होदि अज्ज कोमुदीमहूसवे तुह चित्तं अवहरिदुं वअस्सेण पेक्खणीअं अणुचिट्ठिदं ।)

स्निग्धमिति । यद्यपि स्निग्धं स्नेहपूर्णं वीक्षितमीक्षणं तथापि नयनयोः द्युतिः ताम्रा । ताम्रत्वं कोपात् । माधुर्ये सत्यपि । बाह्यतो मधुरं भाषमाणाया अपीत्यर्थः । ते तव गद्गदा अस्फुटं प्रवर्तमाना वागनुपदं पदे पदे स्खलति । निश्वासाः नियता निरुद्धा अपि स्तनयोः उत्कम्पेन संलक्षिताः स्फुटं दृष्टाः । एवमेष ते कोपः प्रकटेन स्फुटेन प्रयत्नेन विधृतोऽन्तःसरुद्धोपि स्फुटं प्रकटं लक्ष्यते । शार्दूल० वृत्तम् ॥ १३ ॥ तव चित्तमपहर्तुमाक्रष्टुं तव रञ्जनार्थमित्यर्थः ।

---

१ एतन्नास्ति क्वचित्. २ प्रसाद.

वासवदत्ता—एतं युष्माकं दुर्नयं प्रेक्ष्य हासो मे जायते । (एदं तुह्माणं दुण्णअं पेक्खिअ हासो मे जाअदि ।)

राजा—देवि अलमन्यथा विकल्पितेन[1] । पश्य ।

भ्रूभङ्गैः क्रियते ललाटशशिनः कस्मात्कलङ्को मुधा
वाताकम्पितबन्धुजीवसमतां नीतोऽधरः किं स्फुरन् ।
मध्यश्चाधिककम्पितस्तनभरेणायं पुनः खिद्यते
कोपं मुञ्च तवैव चित्तहरणायैतन्मया क्रीडितम् ॥ १४ ॥

देवि प्रसीद प्रसीद । (इति पादयोः[4] पतति ।)

वासवदत्ता—हञ्जे निवृत्तं प्रेक्षणकम् । तदेहि । अभ्यन्तरमेव प्रविशावः । (इति निष्क्रान्ता[5] ।) (हञ्जे णिवुत्तं पेक्खणअं । ता एहि । अब्भन्तरं एव्व पविसह्म ।)

इति गर्भनाटकम् ।

राजा—(विलोक्य ।) कथमकृत्वैव प्रसादं गता देवी ।

स्वेदाम्भःकणभिन्नभीषणतरभ्रूभङ्गमेकं रुषा
त्रासेनापरमुत्प्लुतोत्प्लुतमृगव्यालोलनेत्रोत्पलम् ।
उत्पश्यन्नहमग्रतो मुखमिदं देव्याः प्रियायास्तथा
भीतश्चोत्सुकमानसश्च महति क्षिप्तोऽस्म्यहं संकटे ॥ १५ ॥

तद्यावदिदानीं शयनीयं गत्वा देव्याः प्रसादनोपायं चिन्तयामि ।

(इति निष्क्रान्ताः सर्वे ।)

इति तृतीयोऽङ्कः ।

अन्यथाविकल्पितेन अहमारण्यिकायामासक्त इत्यादिसंशयेन । **भ्रूभङ्गैरिति** । कस्मात्केन हेतुना ललाटमेव शशी तस्य भ्रूभङ्गैः कोपजनितभ्रूविकारैः मुधा व्यर्थमकारणमिति यावत् । कलङ्कः क्रियते । ललाटशशी मलिनीक्रियते इत्यर्थः । किं किमर्थं स्फुरन् कोपात्कम्पमानः अधरः वातेनाकम्पितं यद्बन्धुजीवकुसुमं तस्य समतां तुल्यतां नीतः । कस्मात्पुनः अयं मध्यः अधिकं बलवत्कम्पितौ यौ स्तनौ तयोः भरेण खिद्यते खेदं प्राप्यते । कोपं मुञ्च यतो मया तव चित्तहरणायैवैतत् क्रीडितम् । शार्दूलविक्रीडितं वृत्तम् ॥ १४ ॥

स्वेदाम्भः इति । रुषा क्रोधेन हेतुभूतेन उत्पन्ना ये स्वेदाम्भःकणा घर्मजलविन्दवस्तैः भिन्नं चितं च तत् भीषणतरा अतिशयेन भीषणा तथा भ्रूभङ्गा यत्र तादृक् च इदं पुरोदृश्यमानं देव्या मुखमेकम् । त्रासेन भयेन उत्प्लुतोत्प्लुतो वेगादग्रं धावन्यो मृगस्तस्येव व्यालोले अतिचञ्चले नेत्रोत्पले नेत्रकमले यस्य तादृक् प्रियाया आरण्यिकाया इदमपरं मुखमग्रत उत्पश्यन् विभावयन् अहं भीतश्च उत्सुकमानसश्च सन्महति संकटे क्षिप्तोस्मि । शार्दूल० वृत्तम् ॥ १५ ॥ इति तृतीयोङ्कः ।

---

१ विकल्पनेन. २ अधुना. ३ येवं. ४ पुन पा. ५ निष्क्रान्तः स्त्रीवर्गो विदूषकश्च. ६ मृगी.

॥ चतुर्थोऽङ्कः ॥

(ततः प्रविशति मनोरमा)

मनोरमा—(सोद्वेगम् ।) अहो दीर्घरोषता देव्याः । एतावन्तं कालं बद्धाया अपि प्रियसख्या आरण्यिकाया उपर्यनुकम्पां न गृह्णाति । सा तपस्विन्यात्मनो बन्धनस्य क्लेशेन तथा न संतप्यते यथा भर्तुर्दर्शननिराशतया । ईदृशं चास्या दुःखं येनाद्यैवात्मानं व्यापादयन्ती मया कथमपि निवारिता । एतं वृत्तान्तं भर्त्रे निवेदयेति वसन्तकं भणित्वागतास्मि । (अहो दिग्घरोसदा देवीए । एत्तिअं[1] कालं बद्धाए पिअसहीए आरण्णिआए उवरि अणुकम्पं ण गेण्हइ । सा तवस्सिणी अत्तणो बन्धणस्स किलेसेण तह ण संतप्पदि जह भट्टिणो दंसणणिरासदाए । ईरिसं च से दुक्खं जेण अज्ज एव्व अत्ताणं वावादअन्ती मए कहं वि णिवारिदा । एदं उत्तन्तं भट्टिणो णिवेदेहित्ति वसन्तअं भणिअ आअदह्मि ।)

(ततः प्रविशति काञ्चनमाला ।)

काञ्चनमाला—कथमन्विष्यन्त्यापि मया भगवती साङ्कृत्यायनी न दृष्टा । (विलोक्य ।) तदेतामपि तावन्मनोरमां प्रक्ष्यामि । (उपसृत्य ।) मनोरमे अपि जानासि कुत्र भगवती साङ्कृत्यायनीति । (कहं अण्णेसन्तीए वि मए भअवई सङ्किच्चाअणी ण दिट्ठा । ता एदं वि दाव मणोरमं पुच्छिस्सं । मणोरमे अवि जाणासि कहिं भअवई सङ्किच्चाअणित्ति ।)

मनोरमा—(विलोक्याश्रूणि प्रमृज्य ।) हला काञ्चनमाले दृष्टा । किं पुनस्तया प्रयोजनम् । (हला कञ्चणमाले दिट्ठा[2] । किं उण ताए पओअणं ।)

काञ्चनमाला—मनोरमे अद्य देव्याङ्गारवत्या लेखः प्रेषितः । तस्मिन्वाचिते बाष्पपूर्णनयना दृढं संतप्तुमारब्धा देवी । तद्विनोदननिमित्तं तस्या भगवतीमन्विष्यामि । (मणोरमे अज्ज देवीए अङ्गारवदीए लेहो पेसिदो[3] । तस्सि वाचिदे बप्फपुण्णणअणा दिढं संतप्पिदुं आरद्धा देवी । ता विणोदणणिमित्तं ताए भअवदिं अण्णेसामि ।)

अथ चतुर्थाङ्के अवशिष्टौ अवमर्शनिर्वहणसन्धी निर्वाह्येते । तत्र निष्क्रान्ता मनोरमा ततः प्रविशति मनोरमया धृता सविप्रवेगमात्मानं नाटयन्ती आरण्यिका एत्येतावपर्यन्तं वासवदत्ताप्रसत्या निरपायप्रियदर्शिकाप्राप्त्यवसायात्माऽवमर्शसन्धिः । अथ वासवदत्ताप्रसादमिच्छतो वत्सराजस्य प्रवेशं सूचयितुं प्रवेशकमारभते ततः प्रविशति मनोरमेति । तपस्विन्यनुकम्पार्हा । अङ्गारवती प्रद्योतस्य पत्नी वासवदत्ताया माता । तद्विनोदननिमित्तं तस्या दुःखस्यापमार्जनार्थमित्यर्थः ।

---

1 कहं एत्तिअं. 2 दिट्ठाए ताए किं पओ०. 3 अणुप्पेसिदो.

मनोरमा—हला किं पुनस्तस्मिंल्लेख आलिखितम्। (हला किं उण तस्सिं लेहे आलिहिदं।)

काञ्चनमाला—या मम भगिनी सा तव जनन्येव। तस्या भर्ता दृढवर्मा तातस्ते। तत्तव किमेतदाख्यातव्यम्। तस्य समधिकं संवत्सरं कलिङ्गहतकेन बद्धस्य। तन्न युक्तमेतं वृत्तान्तमनिष्टं श्रुत्वा समीपस्थितस्य समर्थस्य भर्तुस्त एवमुदासीनत्वमवलम्बितुमिति। (जा मह भइणी सा तव जणणी एव्व। ताए भत्ता दिढवम्मा तादो दे। ता तव किं एदं आअक्खिदव्वं। तस्स समहिअं संवच्छरं कलिङ्गहदएण बद्धस्स। ता ण जुत्तं एदं उत्तन्तं अणिट्ठं सुणिअ समीवट्ठिदस्स समत्थस्स भत्तुणो दे एव्वं उदासीणत्तणं ओलम्बिदुंत्ति।)

मनोरमा—हला काञ्चनमाले। यदा तावदयं वृत्तान्तो भट्टिन्यै न केनापि विज्ञापितव्य इति भर्त्राज्ञप्तं तत्केन पुनरिदानीं स लेखः श्रावितः। (हला कञ्चणमाले जदा दाव अअं उत्तन्तो भट्टिणीए ण केण वि विण्णविदव्वोत्ति भट्टिणा आणत्तं ता केण उण दाणिं सो लेहो सुणाविदो।)

काञ्चनमाला—अनुवाच्य तूष्णींभूताया मम हस्ताद्गृहीत्वा स्वयमेव भट्टिन्या वाचितः। (अणुवाइअ तुह्णींभूदाए मह हत्थादो गेण्हिअ सअं एव्व भट्टिणीए वाइदो।)

मनोरमा—तेन गच्छ त्वम्। एषा खलु देवी तयैव सह दन्तवलभ्यां तिष्ठति। (तेण गच्छ तुमं। एसा क्खु देवी ताए एव्व सह दन्तवलहीए चिट्ठइ।)

काञ्चनमाला—तेन हि भट्टिनीसकाशं गमिष्यामि। ((इति निष्क्रान्ता।) (तेण हि भट्टिणीसआसं गमिस्सं।)

मनोरमा—चिरं खलु म आरण्यिकासकाशादागतायाः। दृढं च निर्विण्णा सा तपस्विन्यात्मनो जीवितेन। कदाचिदत्याहितं भवेत्। तत्तत्रैव गच्छामि। (इति निष्क्रान्ता।) (चिरं खु मे आरण्णिआसआसादो आअदाए। दिढं च णिव्विण्णा सा तवस्सिणी अत्तणो जीविदेण। कदाइ अच्चाहिदं भवे। ता तहिं एव्व गच्छह्मि।)

(**इति प्रवेशकः।**)

समर्थस्य प्रभाववतः। दन्तवलभी हस्तिदन्तविरचिता चन्द्रशाला तस्याम्। अत्याहितं महाभीतिरनिष्टमित्यर्थः। प्रवेशकःतद्वदेवानुदात्तोक्त्या नीचपात्रप्रयोजितः।

---

१ भइणिआ. २ वुत्तन्तं अनाचक्खिअ समीव० (वृत्तान्तमनाख्याय समी०). ३ जदो (यतः). ४ वाइदव्वो (वाचयितव्यः). ५ ता (ततः).

(ततः प्रविशति सोद्वेगासनस्था वासवदत्ता साङ्कृत्यायनी विभवतश्च परिवारः।)

साङ्कृत्यायनी—राजपुत्रि अलमुद्वेगेन । नेदृशो वत्सराजः । कथमित्थंगतमपि भवत्या मातृष्वसृपतिं विज्ञाय वत्सराजो निश्चिन्तं स्थास्यति ।

वासवदत्ता—(सास्रम्।) भगवति अतिऋजुकेदानीं त्वम् । यस्य मया न कार्यं तस्य मदीयेन किं कार्यम् । मातुर्युक्तं ममैतदालिखितुम् । सा पुनर्न जानात्यद्यापि तादृशी न वासवदत्तेति । तव पुनरेष आरण्यिकावृत्तान्तः प्रत्यक्षः । तत्कथमेतद्भणासि । (भअवदि अदिउज्जुआ दाणिं तुमं । जस्स मए ण कज्जं तस्स ममकेरएण किं कज्जं । अज्जुआए जुत्तं मम एदं आलिहिदुं । सा उण ण आणादि अज्जवि तारिसी ण वासवदत्तेति । तुह उण एदं आरण्णिआए उत्तन्तं पच्चक्खं । ता कहं एदं भणासि ।)

साङ्कृत्यायनी—यत एव मे प्रत्यक्षं तत एव ब्रवीमि । तेन ननु कौमुदीमहोत्सवे त्वां हासयितुं तथा क्रीडितम् ।

वासवदत्ता—भगवति एतदत्र सत्यम् । तथा हासितास्मि येन भगवत्याः पुरतो लज्जया कथमपि तिष्ठामि । तत्किं तदीयया कथया । नन्वेतेनैव पक्षपातेनैतावतीं भूमिं नीतास्मि । (इति रोदिति ।) (भअवदि एदं एत्थ सच्चं । तह हासिदह्मि जेण भअवदीए पुरदो लज्जाए कहं वि चिट्ठामि । ता किं तक्केरकाए कहाए । णं एदेण एव्व पक्खवादेण एत्तिअं भूमिं णीदह्मि ।)

साङ्कृत्यायनी—अलं राजपुत्रि रुदितेन । नेदृशो वत्सराजः । (विलोक्य ।) अथवा प्राप्त एवायं यस्ते मन्युप्रमार्जनं करोति ।

वासवदत्ता—मनोरथा इदानीमेते भगवत्याः । (मणोरहा दाणिं एदे भअवदीए ।

(ततः प्रविशति राजा विदूषकश्च ।)

राजा—वयस्य क इदानीमभ्युपायः प्रियां मोचयितुम् ।

विदूषकः—भो वयस्य मुञ्च विषादम् । अहं त उपायं कथयिष्यामि । (भो अवस्स मुञ्च विसादं । अहं दे उवाअं कहइस्सं ।)

प्रवेशोद्द्वयस्यान्ते नीचपात्रप्रयोजितः ॥ इति । अतिऋजुका अतिशयेन सरलस्वभावा । कपटमजानानेत्यर्थः । मया न कार्यं मामेवावधीरयति आरण्यिकासंक्रान्तप्रेमत्वादिति यावत् । आर्याया मन्मातुः। तादृशी तथानुरक्तभर्तृका। हासितास्मि हास्यास्पदं कृतास्मि । पक्षपातेन राज्ञः पक्षग्रहणेन ।

---

१ अर्जुकायाः २ पुनर्जानानि...तादृशी एव (एव्व) वास०. ३ अयं वत्स०.

राजा—(सहर्षम् ।) वयस्य त्वरिततरमभिधीयताम् ।

विदूषकः—भो त्वं तावदनेकसमरसंघट्टप्रभाववाहुशाली । पुनरप्यनेकगजतुरगपदातिदुर्विषहबलसमुदितः । तत्सर्वबलसंदोहेनान्तःपुरं सुपीडितं कृत्वेदानीमेवारण्यिकां मोचय । (भो तुमं दाव अणेअसमरसंघट्टप्पहावबाहुसाली । पुणो वि अणेअगअतुरअपआइदुव्विसहबलसमुदिदो । ता सव्वबलसंदोहेण अन्तेउरं सुपीडिअं करिअ दाणिं एव्व आरण्णिअं मुञ्चावेहि ।)

राजा—वयस्य अशक्यमुपादिष्टम् ।

विदूषकः—किमत्राशक्यम् । यतस्तावत्कुब्जवामनवृद्धकञ्चुकिवर्जितो मनुष्योऽपरो नास्ति तत्र । (किं एत्थ असक्कं । जदो दाव कुज्जवामणबुड्ढकञ्चुइवज्जिदो मणुस्सो अवरो णत्थि तहिं ।)

राजा—(सावज्ञम्) मूर्ख किमसंबद्धं प्रलपसि । देव्याः प्रसादं मुक्त्वा नान्यस्तस्या मोक्षणाभ्युपायः । तत्कथय कथं देवीं प्रसादयामि ।

विदूषकः—भोः मासोपवासं कृत्वा जीवितं धारय । एवं देवी चण्डी प्रसत्स्यति । (भो आसोववासं करिअ जीविदं धारेहि । एव्वं देवी चण्डी पसीदिस्सदि ।)

राजाः—(विहस्य ।) अलं परिहासेन । कथय कथं देवीं प्रसादयामि ।

धृष्टः किं पुरतोऽवरुध्य विहसन्गृह्णामि कण्ठे प्रियां
किं वा चाटुशतप्रपञ्चरचनाप्रीतां करिष्यामि ताम् ।
किं तिष्ठामि कृताञ्जलिर्निपतितो देव्याः पुरः पादयोः
सत्यं सत्यमहो न वेद्म्यनुनयो देव्याः कथं स्यादिति ॥१॥

अनेके ये समरेषु संघट्टाः शत्रुभिः संघर्षास्तत्र प्रभावः ययोस्तादृग्भ्यां बाहुभ्यां शालतेऽसौ । पाठान्तरे अनेकसमरसंघट्टेषु ये प्रहारास्तैः अङ्कितः बाहुः सालः सर्जतरुरिव यस्य सः । अनेके च ते गजाश्च तुरगाश्च पदातयः पत्तयश्च तै दुर्विषहं शत्रुभिः सोढुमशक्यं यद्बलं सेना तेन समुदितः युक्तः उन्नतो वा । बलसन्दोहेन बलसमुदायेन । कुब्जाः वक्रपृष्ठा वामनाः खर्वा वृद्धाः कञ्चुकिनश्च । सर्वेपि दुर्बला इत्यर्थः । प्रसत्स्यति प्रसादमेष्यति । **धृष्ट इति** । धृष्टः धैर्यं दर्शयन् पुरतः स्थित्वेति शेषः । तस्या गतिमवरुध्य निरुध्य विहसन् प्रियां कण्ठे गृह्णामि आश्लिष्यामि । किंवा तां चाटूनां मधुरभाषणानां शतस्य प्रपञ्चेन विस्तारेण प्रीतां करिष्यामि ।

---

१ प्पहाराङ्किदबाहुसालः (प्रहाराङ्कितबाहुसालः). २ मुद्धघेर (मुग्धगृह०). ३ मोक्षाभ्यु०. ४ जाव एव्वं. ५ प्रसादयिष्यामि. ६ पुनः.

तदेहि । देवीसकाशमेव गच्छावः ।

विदूषकः—भोः गच्छ त्वम् । अहं पुनरिदानीमेव बन्धनात्कथमपि परिभ्रश्यागतोऽस्मि । तन्न गमिष्यामि । (भो गच्छ तुमं । अहं दाणिं एव्व बन्धणादो कहं वि परिब्भंसिअ आअदोह्मि । तो ण गमिस्सं ।)

राजा—(विहस्य कण्ठे गृहीत्वा बलान्निवर्तयति ।) मूर्ख आगम्यतामागम्यताम् । (परिक्रम्यावलोक्य च ।) इयं देवी दन्तवलभीमध्यमध्यास्ते । यावदुपसर्पामि । (सलज्जमुपसर्पति ।)

(वासवदत्ता सखेदमासनादुत्तिष्ठति ।)

राजा—

किं मुक्तमासनमलं मयि संभ्रमेण
नोत्थातुमित्थमुचितं मम तान्तमध्ये ।
दृष्टिप्रसादविधिमात्रहृतो जनोऽय-
मत्यादरेण किमिति क्रियते विलक्षः ॥ २ ॥

वासवदत्ता—(मुखं निरूप्य ।) आर्यपुत्र विलक्ष इदानीं त्वं भवसि । (अज्जउत्त विलक्खो दाणिं तुमं होसि ।

राजा—प्रिये सत्यमहं विलक्षः । यत्प्रत्यक्षदृष्टापराधोऽपि भवतीं प्रसादयितुं व्यवसितोऽस्मि ।

साङ्कृत्यायनी—(आसनं निर्दिश्य ।) महाराज क्रियतामासनपरिग्रहः ।

राजा—(आसनं निर्दिश्य ।) इत इतो देव्युपविशतु ।

(वासवदत्ता भूमावुपविशति ।)

राजा—आः कथं भूमावुपविष्टा देवी । अहमप्यत्रैवोपविशामि । (इति भूमावुपविश्य कृताञ्जलिः ।) प्रिये प्रसीद प्रसीद । किमेवं प्रणतेऽपि मयि गम्भीरतरं कोपमुद्वहसि ।

किंवा देव्याः पुरः पादयोः निपतितः तिष्ठामि । देव्याः प्रसादने प्रतिपत्तिमूढः अहं सत्यं सत्यं देव्या अनुनयः कथं स्यादिति न वेद्मि । शार्दूलवि० वृत्तम् ॥ १ ॥ **किं मुक्तमिति** । किं किंकारणमासनं मुक्तम् । मयि सम्भ्रमेण उपचारत्वरया अलम् । सम्भ्रमो मास्तु । हे तान्तमध्ये तान्तः क्लेशकृशः मध्यो यस्यास्तादृशि । इत्थमुत्थातुं नोचितम् । दृष्टिः मयि दृष्टिपात एव प्रसादस्तस्य विधिना करणेनैव केवलेन हृतः आत्मसात्कृतोयं जनः । अहमित्यर्थः । अत्यादरेणातिसम्मानप्रदर्शनेनेत्यर्थः । किमिति विलक्षः सलज्जः क्रियते । वसन्ततिलकं वृत्तम् ॥ २ ॥ निरूप्य निपुणं दृष्ट्वा । गम्भीरतरमत्यारूढं सहसापनेतुमशक्यमित्यर्थः ।

---

१ ता गमि०. २ भीमध्यास्ते. ३ एतन्नास्ति पुस्तकान्तरे. ४ गभीर.

भ्रूभङ्गं न करोषि रोदिषि मुहुर्मुग्धेक्षणे केवलं
नातिप्रस्फुरिताधरानवरतं निःश्वासमेवोज्झसि ।
वाचं नापि ददासि तिष्ठसि परं प्रध्याननम्रानना
कोपस्ते स्तिमितो निपीडयति मां गूढप्रहारोपमः ॥ ३॥

प्रिये प्रसीद प्रसीद । (इति पादयोः पतति ।)

वासवदत्ता—अतिसुखितो नन्वसि । किमिदानीं दुःखितं जनं विकारयसि । उत्तिष्ठ कोऽत्र कुपितः । (अदिसुहिदो णं सि । किं दाणिं दुक्खिदं जणं विआरेसि । उट्ठेहि को एत्थ कुविदो ।)

साङ्कृत्यायनी—उत्तिष्ठ महाराज । किमनेन । अन्यदेव तावदुद्वेगकारणमस्याः ।

राजा—(ससंभ्रमम् ।) भगवति किमन्यत् ।

(साङ्कृत्यायनी कर्णे कथयति ।)

राजा—(विहस्य ।) यद्येवमलमुद्वेगेन । मयापि ज्ञातम् । सिद्ध एवास्मिन्प्रयोजने देवीं तु दिष्ट्या वर्धयिष्यामीति नोक्तम् । अन्यथा कथमहं दृढवर्मवृत्तान्ते विस्रब्धस्तिष्ठामि । तत्कतिपयान्यहानि तद्वार्ताया आगतायाः । इदं च तत्र वर्तते ।

अस्मद्बलैर्विजयसेनपुरःसरैस्तै-
राक्रान्तबाह्यविषयो विहतप्रतापः ।
दुर्गं कलिङ्गहतकः सहसा प्रविश्य
प्राकारमात्रशरणोऽशरणः कृतोऽसौ ॥ ४ ॥

भ्रूभङ्गमिति । हे मुग्धेक्षणे चारुनयने । तदर्हेऽपि मयि भ्रूभङ्गं न करोषि । सरोषं भ्रुकुटिं न बध्नासि । केवलं मुहुः रोदिषि । नातिप्रस्फुरितोऽधरो यस्यास्तादृशी अनवरतमजस्रं निश्वासमेव उज्झसि मुञ्चसि । वाचमपि न ददासि परं प्रत्युत प्रध्यानेन प्रकृष्टचिन्तया नम्रमवनतमाननं यस्याः तथासि । एवंस्तिमितो बहिरदत्तावकाशस्तव कोपः गूढः प्रहारस्तेनोपमा यस्य तत्सदृशो वा मां निपीडयति क्लिश्नातितराम् । शार्दूलवि० वृत्तम् ॥ ३ ॥ अतिसुखित इति सोपालम्भम् । सिद्ध एवेति अस्मिन्कार्ये लब्धसिद्धिरेवास्मि । देवीं तु तस्मिन्सिद्ध इति शेषः । दृढवर्मवृत्तान्ते दृढवर्मण्यापद्ग्रस्ते इत्यर्थः । **अस्मद्बलैरिति** । तैः प्रसिद्धैः विजयसेनः पुरःसरो येषां तैः अस्मद्बलैः आक्रान्तो व्याप्तो बाह्यो विषयो यस्य सः । विहतः प्रतापो यस्य स च तथोक्तः । असौ कलिङ्गश्चासौ हतकश्च कलिङ्गहतकः अशरणः अगतिकः सन् सहसा दुर्गं प्रविश्य । स्थित इति शेषोऽन्यथा ल्यबनुपपत्तेः । प्राकारमात्रं शरणं रक्षितृ यस्य तथा कृतः । वसन्ततिलकं

---

१ नोतिपी०. २ उत्तिष्ट उत्तिष्ठ. ३ देवीं तुष्टया. ४ णः किल वर्ततेसौ.

तदवस्थं च तं

निर्दिष्टाक्रान्तमन्दं प्रतिदिनविरमद्वीरदासेरवृत्तं
शश्वत्संशीर्यमाणद्विपतुरगनरक्षीणनिःशेषसैन्यम् ।
अद्य श्वो वा विभग्ने झटिति मम बलैः सर्वतस्तत्र दुर्गे
बद्धं युद्धे हतं वा भगवति न चिराच्छ्रोष्यसि त्वं कलिङ्गम् ॥ ५ ॥

साङ्कृत्यायनी—राजपुत्रि प्रथमतरमेव भवत्याः कथितं मया कथमप्रतिविधाय वत्सराजः स्थास्यतीति ।

वासवदत्ता—यद्येवं प्रियं मे । (जइ एव्वं पिअं मे ।)

(प्रविश्य ।)

प्रतीहारी—जयतु जयतु भर्ता । एष खलु विजयसेनो दृढवर्मकञ्चुकिसहितो हर्षसमुत्फुल्ललोचनः प्रियं निवेदयितुकामो द्वारे तिष्ठति । (जेदु जेदु भट्टा । एसो क्खु विअअसेणो दिढवम्मकञ्चुईसहिदो हरिससमुप्फुल्लोअणो पिअं णिवेदिदुकामो दुवारे चिठ्ठइ ।)

वासवदत्ता—(सस्मितम् ।) भगवति यथा तर्कयामि परितोषितास्म्यार्यपुत्रेणेति । (भअवदि जह तक्केमि परिदोसिदाह्मि अज्जउत्तेणेत्ति ।)

साङ्कृत्यायनी—वत्सराजपक्षपातिनी खल्वहं न किंचिदपि ब्रवीमि ।

राजा—शीघ्रं प्रवेशय तौ ।

प्रतीहारी—तथा । (इति निष्क्रान्ता ।) तह ।

(ततः प्रविशति विजयसेनः कञ्चुकी च ।)

विजयसेनः—भोः कञ्चुकिन् । अद्य स्वामिपादा द्रष्टव्या इति यत्सत्यमनुपमं कमपि सुखातिशयमनुभवामि ।

वृत्तम् ॥ ४ ॥ **निर्दिष्टेत्यादि** । हे भगवति साङ्कृत्यायनीमुद्दिश्यैतत् । अद्य श्वो वा मम बलैः तत्र तस्मिन् दुर्गे झटिति शीघ्रं सर्वतः विभग्ने विध्वस्ते त्वं कलिङ्गं कलिङ्गराजमचिरादेव युद्धे बद्धं हतं वा श्रोष्यति । कथंभूतमित्याह । निर्दिष्टेनोपरिकथितेन आक्रान्तेन अभिद्रवेण मन्दं निरुत्साहं । निर्दिष्टाक्रन्दमन्देति पाठे निर्दिष्टो य आक्रन्दो दारुणो रणः । आक्रन्दो दारुणे रणे इत्यमरः । प्रतिदिनं दिने दिने विरमत् क्षीयमाणं वीराणां दासेराणां किंकराणां च । भृत्ये दासेरदासौ च इत्यमर । वृत्तं युद्धादिव्यापारो यस्य तम् । शश्वदजस्रं शीर्यमाणा ध्वस्यमाना द्विपा गजाः तुरगा नरा योधाश्च यस्मिन् । अतः क्षीणं निःशेषं बलं सैन्यं यस्य तम् । स्रग्धरा वृत्तम् ॥ ५ ॥ वत्सराजपक्षपातिनी एतेनैव पक्षपातेनेत्यादि वासवदत्तावचनं मनसि कुर्वत्याः सोल्लुण्ठनोक्तिरियम् ।

---

१ टाक्रन्द. २ सध्वंसं. ३ वापि.

कञ्चुकी—विजयसेनै अवितथमेतत् । पश्य ।

सुखनिर्भरोऽन्यथापि स्वामिनमवलोक्य भवति भृत्यजनः ।
किं पुनररिबलविघटननिर्व्यूढप्रभुनियोगभरः ॥ ६ ॥

उभौ—(उपसृत्य ।) जयतु जयतु स्वामी ।

(राजा उभावपि परिष्वजते ।)

कञ्चुकी—देव दिष्ट्या वर्धसे ।

हत्वा कलिङ्गहतकं ह्यस्मत्स्वामी निवेशितो राज्ये ।
देवस्य समादेशो निर्व्यूढो विजयसेनेन ॥ ७ ॥

वासवदत्ता—अयि भगवति अभिजानास्येतं कञ्चुकिनम् । (अइ भअवइ अहिजाणासि एदं कञ्चुइं ।)

साङ्कृत्यायनी—कथं नाभिजानामि । ननु स एष यस्य हस्ते मातृष्वसा ते पत्रिकामनुप्रेषितवती ।

राजा—साधु विजयसेनेन महान्व्यापारोऽनुष्ठितः ।

(विजयसेनः पादयोः पतति ।)

राजा—देवि दिष्ट्या वर्धसे । प्रतिष्ठितो राज्ये दृढवर्मा ।

वासवदत्ता—(सहर्षम् ।) अनुगृहीतास्मि । (अणुग्गहिदह्मि ।)

विदूषकः—ईदृशेऽभ्युदयेऽस्मिन्राजकुल एतत्करणीयम् । (राजानं निर्दिश्य वीणावादनं नाटयन् ।) गुरुपूजा । (आत्मनो यज्ञोपवीतं दर्शयन् ।) ब्राह्मणस्य सत्कारः । (आरब्धिकां सूचयन् ।) सर्वबन्धनमोक्ष इति । (ईरिसे अब्भुदए अस्सिं राअउले एदं करणिज्जं । गुरुपूआ । बह्मणस्स सक्कारो । सव्वबन्धणमोक्खोत्ति ।)

राजा—(वासवदत्तामपवार्य छोटिकां ददत् ।) साधु वयस्य साधु ।

अवितथं सत्यम् । **सुखेति** । अन्यथापि महत्प्रभुकार्यकरणाभावेपि स्वामिनमवलोक्य भृत्यजनः सुखेन निर्भरः नितरां पूर्णो भवति । किं पुनः अरिबलस्य विघटनेन ध्वंसेनेति यावत् निर्व्यूढः साकल्येनोढः प्रभोर्नियोगस्य निर्दिष्टकार्यस्य भरः येन सः । सुखनिर्भरोभवेदिति वक्तव्यमित्यर्थः ॥ ६ ॥ **हत्वेति** । विजयसेनेन कलिङ्गहतकं हत्वा अस्मत्स्वामी राज्ये निवेशितः प्रतिष्ठापितो हि । देवस्य समादेशः निर्व्यूढः स्वनुष्ठितः च ॥ ७ ॥ अभ्युदये इष्टसम्पादनोत्सववेलायाम् । गुरुपूजा इष्टार्थनिवेदनेन सत्कारः । छोटिका अङ्गुष्ठमध्यमयोश्चटिति संघर्षजन्यो ध्वनिविशेषः ।

---

१ एतन्नास्ति पुस्तकान्तरे. २ सोस्मत्, अस्मत्स्वामिनि निवेशिते. ३ देशोऽवस्थापितः, देशाद्रिपुजायिना. ४ काद्वयं–युगम्. ५ महान्. ६ अस्मात्परं जयतु आर्यपुत्रः (जेदु अय्यवुत्तो) इत्यधिकं पुस्तकान्तरे.

विदूषकः—भवति कथं त्वं न किमप्यत्र समादिशसि । (होदि कहं तुमं ण किं वि एत्थ समादिससि ।)

वासवदत्ता—(साङ्कृत्यायनीमवलोक्य सस्मितम् ।) मोचिता खलु हताशेनारण्यिका । (मोइदा क्खु हदासेण आरण्णिआ ।)

साङ्कृत्यायनी—किं वा तपस्विन्यानया बद्धया ।

वासवदत्ता—यथा भगवत्यै रोचते । (जह भअवदीए रोअदि ।)

साङ्कृत्यायनी—यद्येवमहमेवैं गत्वा तां मोचयिष्यामि । (इति निष्क्रान्ता ।)

कञ्चुकी—इदमपरं संदिष्टं महाराजेन दृढवर्मणा । त्वत्प्रसादात्सर्वमेव यथाभिलषितं संपन्नम् । तदेते प्राणास्त्वदीयाः । यथेष्टमिमान्विनियोक्तुं त्वमेव प्रमाणमिति ।

(राजा सलज्जमधोमुखास्तिष्ठति ।)

विजयसेनः—देव न शक्यैमेव देवं प्रति प्रीतिविशेषं दृढवर्मणः कथयितुम् ।

कञ्चुकी—यद्यपि तुभ्यं प्रतिपादितायाः प्रियदर्शिकाया अस्मद्दुहितुः परिभ्रंशान्न मे संबन्धो जात इति दुःखमासीत्तथापि वासवदत्तायाः परिणेत्रापि त्वया तदपनीतमेव ।

वासवदत्ता—(सास्रम् ।) आर्य कञ्चुकिन् कथं मे भगिनी परिभ्रष्टा । (अज्ज कञ्चुइ कहं मे भइणी परिब्भट्ठा ।)

कञ्चुकी—राजपुत्रि तस्मिन्कलिङ्गहतकावस्कन्दे विद्रुतेष्वितस्ततोऽन्तःपुरजनेषु दिष्ट्या दृष्टामिदानीं न युक्तमत्र स्थातुमिति तामहं गृहीत्वा वत्सराजान्तिकं प्रस्थितः । ततः संचिन्त्य तां विन्ध्यकेतोर्हस्ते निक्षिप्य निर्गतोऽस्मि । यावत्प्रतीपमागच्छामि तावत्कैरपि तत्स्थानं सह विन्ध्यकेतुना स्मर्तव्यतां नीतम् ।

प्रतिपादितायाः संकल्पदत्तायाः । परिभ्रंशात्स्वहस्तस्खलनाद्विनाशाद्वा । कलिङ्गहतकस्यावस्कन्दः अभिद्रवः तस्मिन् । दिष्ट्या सुदैवात् । संचिन्त्य कार्ययुक्ततां विचार्य । प्रतीपमागच्छामि परापतामि ।

---

१ मेष तावन्मोचयामि. २ शक्यते...प्रीतिविशेषः.

राजा—(सस्मितम् ।) विजयसेन किं कथयसि ।

कञ्चुकी—तत्र चान्विष्यता मया न प्राप्ता । तदाप्रभृति नाद्यापि विज्ञायते क्व वर्तत इति ।

(प्रविश्य मनोरमा ।)

मनोरमा—भट्टिनि प्राणसंशये वर्तते सा तपस्विनी । (भट्टिणी पाणसंसए वट्टइ सा तवस्सिणी ।)

वासवदत्ता—(सास्रम् ।) किं पुनस्त्वं प्रियदर्शनावृत्तान्तं जानासि । (किं उण तुमं पिअदंसणाउत्तन्तं आणासि ।)

मनोरमा—न खल्वहं प्रियदर्शनावृत्तान्तं जानामि । एषा खल्वारण्यिका कल्यव्यपदेशेनानीतं विषं पीत्वा प्राणसंशये वर्तत इत्येवं मया निवेदितम् । तत्परित्रायतां भट्टिनी । (रुदती पादयोः पतति ।) (ण हु अहं पिअदंसणाउत्तन्तं जाणामि । एसा क्खु आरण्णिआ कल्लववदेसेण आणीदं विसं पाइअ पाणसंसए वट्टदित्ति एव्वं मए णिवेदिदं । ता परित्ताअदु भट्टिणी ।)

वासवदत्ता—(स्वगतम् ।) हा धिक् हा धिक् । प्रियदर्शनादुःखमपि मेऽन्तरितमारण्यिकावृत्तान्तेन । अतिदुर्जनः खलु लोकः । कदाचिन्मामन्यथा संभावयिष्यति । तदेतदत्र युक्तम् । (प्रकाशं ससंभ्रमम् ।) मनोरमे लघ्विहैवानय ताम् । नागलोकाद्गृहीतविषविद्य आर्यपुत्रोऽत्र कुशलः । (हद्धि हद्धि । पिअदंसणादुक्खं वि मे अन्तरिदं आरण्णिआउत्तन्तेण । अदिदुज्जणो क्खु लोओ । कदाइ मं अण्णहा संभावइस्सदि । ता एदं एत्थ जुत्तं । मणोरमे लहु इह एव्व आणेहि तं । णाअलोआदो गहिदविसविज्जो अज्जउत्तो एत्थ कुसलो ।)

(निष्क्रान्ता मनोरमा । ततः प्रविशति मनोरमया धृता सविषवेगमात्मानं नाटयन्त्यारण्यिका ।)

आरण्यिका—हला मनोरमे कस्मादिदानीं मामन्धकारं प्रवेशयसि । (हला मणोरमे कीस दाणिं मं अन्धआरं पवेसेसि ।)

मनोरमा—(सविषादम् ।) हा धिक् हा धिक् । दृष्टिरप्यस्याः संक्रान्ता विषेणैव । (वासवदत्तां दृष्ट्वा ।) भट्टिनि लघु परित्रायस्व लघु

प्रियदर्शना प्रियदर्शिका । मनोरमावाक्ये सा तपस्विनी इत्यत्र सेत्यनेन कञ्चुकिप्रोक्ता राजकन्यैव परामृष्टा इति मन्यमानाया उक्तिरियम् । कल्यव्यपदेशेन कल्यं प्रातराशः तस्य व्यपदेशेन मिषेण यद्वा कल्या इति संस्कृतं तत्र कल्या मद्यम् । कल्यं प्रभाते क्लीबं स्यात्... । उपायवचनेपि स्यात्रिषु मद्येतु योषिति । इति मेदिनी । अन्यथा संभावयिष्यति अतयैव तस्यै विषं दत्तमिति तर्कयेत् ।

---

१ ततः. २ ततः प्रविशति म०. ३ एसा. ४ एतन्नास्ति क्वचित्. ५ दृष्टिदेशे आक्रान्तं (दिट्ठिदेसे अक्कन्तं.)

परित्रायस्व । गुरूभूतमस्या विषम् । (हद्धि हद्धि । दिट्ठि वि से संकन्ता विसेणेव्व । भट्टिणि लहु परित्ताएहि लहु परित्ताएहि । गुरुईभूदं से विसं ।)

वासवदत्ता—(ससंभ्रमं राजानं हस्ते गृहीत्वा ।) आर्यपुत्र उत्तिष्ठोत्तिष्ठ । लघु विपद्यते खल्वेषा तपस्विनी । (सर्वे पश्यन्ति ।) (अज्जउत्त उट्ठेहि उट्ठेहि । लहु विवज्जइ क्खु एसा तवस्सिणी ।)

कञ्चुकी—(विलोक्य ।) सुसदृशी खल्वियं मम राजपुत्र्याः प्रियदर्शनायाः । (वासवदत्तां निर्दिश्य ।) राजपुत्रि कुत इयं कन्यका ।

वासवदत्ता—आर्य विन्ध्यकेतोर्दुहिता । तं व्यापाद्य विजयसेनेनानीता । (अज्ज विञ्झकेउणो दुहिदा । तं वावादिअ विजयसेणेण आणीदा ।)

कञ्चुकी—कुतस्तस्य दुहिता । सैवेयं मम राजपुत्री । हा हतोऽस्मि मन्दभाग्यः । (इति निपत्य भूमावुत्थाय ।) राजपुत्रि इयं सा प्रियदर्शिका भगिनी ते ।

वासवदत्ता—आर्यपुत्र परित्रायस्व परित्रायस्व । मम भगिनी विपद्यते । (अज्जउत्त परित्ताएहि परित्ताएहि । मम भइणी विवज्जइ ।)

राजा—समाश्वसिहि समाश्वसिहि । पश्यामस्तावत् । कष्टं भोः कष्टम् ।

संजातसान्द्रमकरन्दरसां क्रमेण
पातुं गतश्च कलिकां कमलस्य भृङ्गः ।
दग्धा निपत्य सहसैव हिमेन चासौ
वामे विधौ न हि फलन्त्यभिवाञ्छितानि ॥ ८ ॥

मनोरमे पृच्छ्यतां तावत्किं ते बोध इति ।

मनोरमा—सखि किं ते बोधः । (सास्रं पुनश्चालयन्ती ।) सखि ननु भणामि किं ते बोध इति । (सहि किं दे बोधो । सहि णं भणामि किं दे बोधोत्ति ।)

प्रियदर्शिका—(अविस्पष्टम् ।) यदेतदवस्थायापि मया न महाराजो दृष्टः । (इत्यर्धोक्ते भूमौ पतति ।) (जं एदं अवत्थानं गदाए वि मए ण महाराओ दिट्ठो—

गुरूभूतमत्यारूढम् । संजातेति । क्रमेण भ्रमणपरिपाट्या अवसरक्रमेण च । भृङ्गः संजातः सान्द्रः निबिडः मकरन्दरसो यस्यास्तां कमलस्य कलिकां पातुं गतश्च हिमेन तुषारेण सहसैव निपत्य असौ कलिका दग्धा च । द्वौ चकारौ कार्यस्य यौगपद्यं दर्शयतः । विधौ-वामे प्रतिकूले सति अभिवाञ्छितानि न फलन्ति सिद्ध्यन्ति हि निश्चयेन । अर्थान्तरन्यासः ।

---

१ चासौ २ एदाए वि (एतयापि.) ण मए ।

राजा—(सास्रम् ।)

एषा मीलयतीदमीक्षणयुगं जाता ममान्धा दिशः
कण्ठोऽस्याः प्रतिरुध्यते मम गिरो निर्यान्ति कृच्छ्रादिमाः ।
एतस्याः श्वसितं हृतं मम तनुर्निश्चेष्टतामागता
मन्येऽस्या विषवेग एव हि परं सर्वं तु दुःखं मम ॥ ९ ॥

वासवदत्ता—(सास्रम्) प्रियदर्शने उत्तिष्ठोत्तिष्ठ । पश्यैष महाराजस्तिष्ठति । कथं वेदनाप्यस्या नष्टा । किमिदानीं मयापराद्धमजानत्या येन कुपिता नालपसि । तत्प्रसीद प्रसीद । उत्तिष्ठोत्तिष्ठ । न खलु पुनरपरात्स्यामि । (ऊर्ध्वमवलोक्य ।) हा दैवहतक । किमिदानीं मयापकृतं येनैतदवस्थां गता मे भगिन्यो दर्शिता । (प्रियदर्शिकाया उपरि पतति ।) पिअदंसणे उट्ठेहि उट्ठेहि । पेक्ख एसो महाराओ चिट्ठइ । कहं वेअणा वि से णट्ठा । किं दाणिं मए अवरज्झं अआणन्तीए जेण कुविदा णालवसि । ता पसीद पसीद । उट्ठेहि उट्ठेहि । ण हु पुणो अवरज्झिस्सं । हा देव्वहदअ किं दाणिं मए अवकिदं जेण एदावत्थं गदा मे भइणी आदंसिदा ।)

विदूषकः—भो वयस्य कथं त्वं मूढ इव तिष्ठसि । नैष विषादस्य कालः । विषमा खलु गतिर्विषस्य । तद्दर्शयात्मनो विद्याप्रभावम् । (भो वअस्स कहं तुमं मूढोविअ चिट्ठसि । ण एसो विसादस्स कालो । विसमा क्खु गई विसस्स । ता दंसेहि अप्पणो विज्जापहावं ।)

राजा—सत्यमेवैतत् । (प्रियदर्शिकामालोक्य ।) मूढ एवाहमेतावतीं वेलाम् । तदहमेनां जीवयामि । सलिलं सलिलम् ।

विदूषकः—(निष्क्रम्य पुनः प्रविश्य ।) भोः एतत्सलिलम् । (भो । एदं सलिलम् ।

(राजोपसृत्य प्रियदर्शनाया उपरि हस्तं निधाय मन्त्रस्मरणं नाटयति । प्रियदर्शिका शनैरुत्तिष्ठति ।)

वासवदत्ता—आर्यपुत्र दिष्ट्या प्रत्युज्जीविता मे भगिनी । (अज्जउत्त दिट्ठिआ पच्चुज्जीविदा मे भइणी ।)

वसन्ततिलकं वृत्तम् ॥ ८ ॥ **एषेति** । एषा प्रियदर्शिका विषाक्रान्त्या ईक्षणयुगं मीलयति । दिशो मम अन्धा जाताः । अस्याः कण्ठः प्रतिरुध्यते स्वरो निरुध्यते इमा मम गिरः शब्दाः कृच्छ्राभिर्यान्ति । एतस्या श्वसितं हृतं मम तनुर्निश्चेष्टतां निर्व्यापारतामागता । अतः अस्या विषवेग एव मन्ये परं सर्वं तु दुःखं विषवेगजा पीडा मम । असङ्गतिरलंकारः । शार्दूल० वृत्तम् ॥ ९ ॥

---

१ हृतं. २ मयि. ३ मां (मं) नाल. ४ रप्यप०. ५ भगिनी प्रियदर्शना.

विजयसेनः—अहो देवस्य विद्याप्रभावः ।

कञ्चुकी—अहो सर्वत्राप्रतिहता नरेन्द्रता देवस्य ।

प्रियदर्शिका—(शनैरुत्थायोपविश्य च जृम्भिकां नाटयन्ती सविषादमवि-लोक्य ।) मनोरमे चिरं खलु सुप्तास्मि । (मणोरमे चिरं खु सुत्तह्मि ।)

विदूषकः—भो वयस्य निर्व्यूढं ते वैद्यत्वम् । (भो वअस्स णिव्वूढं दे वेदित्तणं ।)

(प्रियदर्शिका साभिलाषं राजानं निरूप्य सलज्जं किंचिदधोमुखी तिष्ठति ।)

वासवदत्ता—(सहर्षम्) आर्यपुत्र किमिदानीमप्येषान्यथैव करोति । (अज्जउत्त । किं दाणिं वि ऐसा अण्णहेव्व करेदि ।)

राजा—(सस्मितम् ।)

स्वभावस्था दृष्टिर्न भवति गिरो नातिविशदा-[3]
स्तनुः सीदत्येषा प्रकटपुलकस्वेदकणिका ।
यथा चायं कम्पः स्तनभरपरिक्लेशजनन-
स्तथा नाद्याप्यस्या नियतमखिलं शाम्यति विषम् ॥१०॥

कञ्चुकी—(प्रियदर्शिकां निर्दिश्य ।) राजपुत्रि एष ते पितुराज्ञाकरः । (इति पादयोः पतति ।)

प्रियदर्शिका—(विलोक्य ।) कथं कञ्चुक्यार्यविनयवसुः । (सास्रम् ।) हा तात । हा मातः । (कहं कञ्चुई अज्जविणअवसू । हा ताद । हा अज्जूए ।)

कञ्चुकी—राजपुत्रि अलं रुदितेन । कुशलिनौ ते पितरौ । वत्स-राजप्रभावात्पुनस्तदवस्थमेव राज्यम् ।

वासवदत्ता—(सास्रम् ।) एह्यलीकशीले । इदानीमपि तावद्भगि-नीस्नेहं दर्शय । (कण्ठे गृहीत्वा ।) इदानीं समाश्वसितास्मि । (एहि अलि-असीले । दाणिं वि दाव भइणिआसिणेहं दंसेहि । दाणिं समस्ससम्मि ।)

वेदना चेतना । मूढः कर्तव्यतानभिज्ञः । नरेन्द्रत्वं प्रभुत्वं विषवैद्यता च । नरेन्द्रो वार्तिके राज्ञि विषवैद्ये च कथ्यते । इति विश्वः । **स्वभावस्थेति**—अस्या दृष्टिः स्वभावे प्रकृतौ तिष्ठतीति स्वभावस्था न भवति । गिरो वाचो नाति विशदाः परिस्फुटाः । प्रकटाः स्फुटं दृश्यमानाः पुलका रोमाञ्चाः स्वेदकणिकाश्च यस्यास्तथोक्ता एषा तनुः सीदति ग्लायति । यथा च अस्या स्तनभरस्य परिक्लेशः पीडा तस्य जननः कारकः कम्पस्तथा । अद्यापि अस्याः अखिलं विषं नियतं न शाम्यति । अस्या विष-बाधाद्यापि साकल्येन नापनीतेत्यर्थः । शिखरिणी वृत्तम् ॥ १० ॥ समाश्वसितास्मि मनः-

---

१ णिरूढं दे मन्तवादित्तणं (निरूढं ते मन्त्रवादित्वं). २ बिसं अपत्थं करेदि (विषम-पथ्यां करोति). ३ गिरा नातिविशदा. ४ करः प्रणमति. ५ अज्जुके.

विदूषकः—भवति त्वं भगिनीं गृहीत्वा कण्ठ एवं परितुष्टासि। वैद्यस्य पारितोषिकं विस्मृतम्। (होदि तुमं भइणिं गेह्णिअ कण्ठे एव्वं परितुट्ठासि। वोदिअस्स पारिदोसिअं विसुमरिदं।)

वासवदत्ता—वसन्तक न विस्मृतम्। (वसन्तअ ण विसुमरिदं।)

विदूषकः—(राजानं निर्दिश्य सस्मितम्।) वैद्य प्रसारय हस्तम्। भगिन्या अग्रहस्तं ते पारितोषिकं दापयिष्यामि। (वोदिअ पसारेहि हत्थं। भइणीए अग्गहत्थं दे पारिदोसिअं दाविस्सं।)

(राजा हस्तं प्रसारयति।)

(वासवदत्ता प्रियदर्शिकाहस्तमर्पयति।)

राजा—(हस्तमुपसंहृत्य।) किमनया। संप्रत्येव कथमपि प्रसादितासि।

वासवदत्ता—कस्त्वमग्रहीतुम्। प्रथममेव तातेनेयं दत्ता। (को तुमं अगण्हिदुं। पुढमं एव्व तादेण इअं दिण्णा।)

विदूषकः—भो माननीया खलु देवी। मास्याः प्रतिकूलं कुरु। (भो माणणीआ क्खु देवी। मा से पडिऊलं करेहि।)

(वासवदत्ता राज्ञो हस्तं बलादाकृष्य प्रियदर्शिकामर्पयति।)

राजा—(सस्मितम्।) देवी प्रभवति। कुतोऽस्माकमन्यथा कर्तुं विभवः।

वासवदत्ता—आर्यपुत्र अतोऽपि परं किं ते प्रियं क्रियताम्। (अज्जउत्त अदो वि परं किं दे पिअं करीअदु।)

राजा—किमतःपरं प्रियम्। पश्य।

निःशेषं दृढवर्मणा पुनरपि स्वं राज्यमध्यासितं
त्वं कोपेन सुदूरमप्यपहृता सद्यः प्रसन्ना मम।
जीवन्ती प्रियदर्शना च भगिनी भूयस्त्वया सत्कृता
किं तत्स्यादपरं प्रियं प्रियतमे यत्सांप्रतं प्रार्थ्यते॥ ११॥

स्वास्थ्यं लम्भितास्मि। विभवः सामर्थ्यम्। निःशेषमिति। दृढवर्मणा पुनरपि निःशेषं स्वराज्यमध्यासितमधिष्ठितम्। कोपेन सुदूरमपहृता त्वमपि सद्यो मम प्रसन्ना। प्रियदर्शना भगिनी जीवन्ती सती त्वया भूयः पुनरपि सत्कृता। अतः हे प्रियतमे किं

---

१ वैज्जम्म. २ परिहृत्य. ३ नु स्यात्.

तथापीदमस्तु ।

(भरतवाक्यम् ।)

उर्वीमुद्दामसस्यां जनयतु विसृजन्वासवो वृष्टिमिष्टा-
मिष्टैस्त्रैविष्टपानां विदधतु विधिवत्प्रीणनं विप्रमुख्याः ।
आकल्पान्तं च भूयात्स्थिरसमुपचिता संगतिः सज्जनानां
निःशेषं यान्तु शान्तिं पिशुनजनगिरो दुःसहा वज्रलेपाः ॥ १२ ॥

(इति निष्क्रान्ताः सर्वे ।)

इति[3] चतुर्थोऽङ्कः

समाप्तेयं प्रियदर्शिका नाम नाटिका ।

तदपरं स्याद्यत्साम्प्रतं प्रार्थ्यते । न किंचिदप्यवशिष्टमित्यर्थः ॥ ११ ॥ भरतवाक्यं नटवाक्यम् । नाटकाभिनयसमाप्तौ सामाजिकेभ्यो नटेनाशीर्दीयते इत्यर्थः । प्रस्तावनानन्तरं नटवाक्याभावादत्र भरतवाक्यमित्युक्तिः । इति शाकुन्तलटीकायां राघवभट्टः । **उर्वीमिति** । वासव इन्द्रः इष्टामभिलषितां वृष्टिं वर्षं विसृजन् मुञ्चन् उर्वीं पृथ्वीमुद्दामानि उत्कटानि सस्यानि धान्यानि यस्यां तथा जनयतु करोतु । विप्रेषु मुख्या विप्रमुख्या द्विजश्रेष्ठा विधिवद्यथाविधि इष्टैः कृतैः यज्ञैः । नपुंसके भावे क्तः । त्रिविष्टपं स्वर्गस्तत्र भवाः त्रैविष्टपा देवास्तेषाम् । तत्र भव इत्यण् । प्रीणनं विदधतु प्रीतिं जनयन्तु । सज्जनानां सङ्गतिश्च आकल्पान्तं प्रलयपर्यन्तं स्थिरा चासौ समुपचिता सम्यग्वृद्धा च भूयात् । दुःसहा दुर्जया इति पाठे जेतुं कठिणाः । वज्रलेपा वज्रं सुधालेपनविशेषः । तस्य इव लेपः प्रसक्तिर्यासां तास्तथोक्ताः पिशुनजनगिरः खलवाचः निःशेषं यथा तथा शान्तिं यान्तु । अत्राशीर्नाम नाट्याङ्गमुक्तम् । स्रग्धरा वृत्तम् ॥ इति प्रियदर्शिकाटीकायां चतुर्थोऽङ्कः ॥

---

१ स्थिरतरमुपचिता. २ दुर्जयाः. ३ इति श्रीमहाकविश्रीहर्षदेवविरचितायां प्रियदर्शिकानाटिकायां च०.

तृतीयाङ्कगतस्य व्यक्तिर्व्यञ्जनेति पद्यस्य नागानन्दान्तर्गतस्य शिवरामकृतटीका यथा—

व्यञ्जनधातुनेति । धातुर्वाद्यवादनविधिः । यदुक्तं-विस्तारः करणश्चैव आविद्धो व्यञ्जनस्तथा । चत्वारो धातवो ज्ञेया वादित्रकरणाश्रयाः ॥ इति । तत्र व्यञ्जनधातुर्वीणा०—... बिन्दुरधरश्च ॥ (पृ. ३८ टीका द्रष्टव्या) । अङ्गुष्ठाभ्यां तु यत्तन्त्रीस्पर्शनं स्यात्कलं तु तत् । वामाङ्गुष्ठकमूलेन पीडनं तु तलं स्मृतम् ॥ सर्वाङ्गुष्ठप्रहारश्च निष्कोटितमिहोच्यते । सव्यप्रदेशिन्याघात उत्कृष्टं परिकीर्तितम् ॥ सर्वाङ्गुलिसमाघातो रेफ इत्युच्यते बुधैः । तन्त्रीषु त्रिप्रकारं वा व्यवमृष्टमिति श्रुतम् ॥ कनिष्ठाङ्गुष्ठसंयुक्तं पुष्पं तु परिकीर्तितम् । तलस्थानेधरन्यासस्तथानुस्वनितं भवेत् ॥ गुर्वक्षरमयी तन्त्री बिन्दुरित्यभिधीयते । कनिष्ठाङ्गुष्ठकाभ्यां तु तन्त्रीभ्यामधरो गतम् ॥ व्याससमासादेषामनुबन्धः सार्वधातुको ज्ञेयः ॥ आसारप्रसारविधिना सकलशाखासु सामग्रीमनुभवन् विस्तारः । शाखाभेदमात्रविधायी करणः । तदन्योन्यानुरूपमेलनकृदाविद्धः । सर्वस्याप्यस्य मूलभूतो व्यञ्जयति विशेषानिति व्यञ्जनधातुः । दशविधेनापीति । बहुभिरपि धात्ववयवैरहमहमिकयात्र वादिते तत्तत्काले स्वप्राकाश्यं प्रथीक्रियते । अमुना त्रिधा विस्पष्टेयं लय इति व्यक्तिमुपगच्छता व्यञ्जनधातुनैव सह लयभेदाप्यभिव्यक्तः । + + + नामतोपि लयभेदानुदीर्य पुनस्त्रिधेत्युक्तिस्तत्रैव राद्धादिभेदानुयातिव्यञ्जिका । पाणीनां त्रिविधः संयोगो राद्धं विद्धं शय्यागतमिति । एषु व्यवस्थितपाणिप्रयोगाणां लयानां यतीनां च संश्लेषनियमः । तद्यथा-समा यतिर्लयश्चैव द्रुतो यत्र भवेदिह । तथैवोपरिपाणिश्च राद्धं वाद्यं तु तद्भवेत् ॥ अवपाणिस्तु यत्र स्यात्प्रयोगो लम्बितो लयः । गोपुच्छा च यतिर्वाद्यं तद्वै शय्यागतं भवेत् ॥ स्रोतोगता यतिर्यत्र लयो मध्यस्तथैव च । समपाणिप्रयोगश्च विद्धवाद्यं तु तद्भवेत् ॥ एषु पुनस्तत्त्वौघानुगता इति त्रयो भेदाः । एते सर्वे लयादयः प्रयोगे परस्परपरिस्यूताः । अपि शब्देन व्यञ्जनधातोः परिपूर्णत्वमुक्तम् । द्रुतमध्येति । लम्बित इति विलम्बित उच्यते । यदुक्तं तालान्तरालवर्ती यः सकालो लय उच्यते । त्रिविधः स च विज्ञेयो द्रुतो मध्यो विलम्बितः ॥ यतिर्विच्छेदः । तदुक्तं—तालच्छन्दोवगतिविधये वाद्यते यो विरामो वाद्यैर्हीनः श्रवणसुभगो नामतः सा यतिः स्यात् । इति । लयगानाद्यतिः सम्यक् कथिता दत्तिलादिभिः । समा स्रोतोवहा चैव गोपुच्छा चेति सा त्रिधा ॥ इति च । तत्त्वौघानुगता इति । अत्रोक्तं—त्रिविधं गीते कार्यं इत्यादिः वाद्यमथौघो द्विधातव्यम् ॥ इत्यन्तोंऽशः टीकायामन्तर्भावितः ३८ पृष्ठे द्रष्टव्यः । अत्र संख्यानिर्देशेन लब्धा विस्पष्टं संवादिता दर्शिता इति विशेषकथनेन च पूर्णत्वं प्रयोगे जितश्रमत्वं च प्रतिपाद्यते । अत एव अहो इति विस्मयहेतुत्वं समर्थितम् ॥

An Alphabetical Index of Verses occurring in the play.

TRANSLATION.

ACT I.

I May Gaurî be propitious unto you ; she, who at her १
marriage rite had her sight troubled by the smoke (of the
nuptial fire), but again whose eyes were gladdened
by the rays of the moon (on Śiva's head); who looking
with longing at the bride-groom, had again her face
hung down through Brahma's shame; who was full of
jealousy at (when she beheld) Hara, reflected into
the mirror of the moon-like nails of her feet, bearing
Gangâ ; and whose hair stood on end at his touch
(as he seized her hand) !

Moreover, may Śiva, who—though angry as the mount Kailasa, being upheaved, quaked, when the *ganas* had their amazment rising, when Kumâra (Ka'rtikeya) was lurking under the lap of his mother, when the serpent (on the body of Śiva) was looking about with rage, and when the ten-headed one (Ra'vana) with his body groaning under the firm planting of his foot (to press down the mountain) was sinking to the depth of Pâtála—was yet delighted at being closely embraced through fear by Umá, protect us !!

(*At the end of the Benediction*) २

Stage-manager—(*After walking round*) To-day, at the spring-festival, I being very respectfully called, have been thus addressed by the multitude of kings, dependent on the lotus feet of the illustrious king Sriharsha, and here arrived from the regions in different directions—"We have heard it, coming from ear to ear, that our master, Śri Harshadeva, has composed a Nâtîkà, Priyadars'ikâ by name, graced with a novel arrangement of plot. But we have not seen it staged. Out of great deference, therefore, to that very king, the delighter of the hearts of all people, and with a disposition on your part to favour us, you should represent the same with proper performance'. I will, therefore, in the first place arrange the costumes (or the tiring room) and then do as desired. (*Looking around*) I am quite convinced that the minds of the spectators have been won over (or favourably disposed). For,

Śri Harsha is a skilled poet; and this assembly too is appreciative of merits; the story of king Vatsarája is attractive (popular) in the world; and we, on our part, are expert in acting : each one of these circumstances is, by itself, the source of the attainment of the desired object; how much more so must then be this combination of all excellences that has come about through the greatness (*lit.* increase) of my good luck !

(*Looking towards the tiring room*).

Ah, how now ! When I was just about to begin the prologue, my brother, having known my intention, has assumed the part of the chamberlain of Dṛdhavarman, king of Angas, and is coming hitherwards. I will also then put on the costume of the character to enter next. [*Exit*].

End of the INDUCTION.

ACT I.

(*Enter the* Chamberlain)

CHAMB :—(*Jesticulating fatigue accompanied by sorrow, and sighing*)

Alas ! Oh, pity !

The king's misfortune; grief caused by separation from my kinsfolk; exile from the country; and the fatigue of a difficult journey—thus is tasted by me this fruit of my longevity of life, that has been bitter and fruitless. (4).

(*With sorrow and amazement*). That such a disaster should have been brought over even such a one as king Dṛdhavarman, whose three regal powers were unobstructed, and who was a peer of Raghu, Dilīpa and

Nala, with a sudden attack, by the cursed king of the Kalingas, who had cherished a feeling of resentment at the thought that he had betrothed (promised) his daughter to Vatsarâja, although solicited for himself by him, and who found an opportunity (*lit.* a weak point) in that king Vatsa did not return till then from captivilty —this, to tell the truth—I do not believe though it has come to pass. How is it that fate has been exceedingly cruel and thus disposed (adverse) towards us! For, that princess I bore away from the tumult of the assault of that sort and terrible like the destruction time of the world and placed in the house of the forest-king, Vindhyaketu, connected with a friendly bond with king Dṛdhavarman, thinking that I might some how take her to king Vatsa and thereby free my master from his obligation (*lit.* debt of promise). But when I had gone to Agastya's holy pool to bathe, as it was not far off, some people fell upon Vindhyaketu in an instant, slew him, and depopulating the place like demons, burnt it; and it is not known in what plight the princess too now is. The whole place was carefully searched by me; but I did not find out whether she was carried off by those marauders or burnt by them. So what am I, luckless one, to do! (*Reflecting*) Ah! I have heard that Vatsarája has escaped from imprisonment and returned to Kauśambî, carrying off with him Pradoyata's daughter. What! shall I go just there then? (*Sighing and observing his own condition.*) But what sort of thing shall I say, going there without the princess? Ah! Vindhyaketu had said to me to-day —"Don't you fear. His honour, the great king Dṛdhavarmâ, is alive; and is in captivity greatly disabled by severe wounds. I will, therefore, go to my master and make the remaining part of my life blissful (*lit.* fruitful) by serving his feet. (*Going about and looking up*). Oh the extreme rigour of the autumnal sun! since it is found to be extremely severe even by me heated as I am by many afflictions.

This sun that is freed from the screen (*lit.* bond) of clouds and has reached Libra after occupying Virgo, is indeed, blazing fiercely, having regained his effulgence, as Vatsarája, freed from close imprisonment is shining pre-eminently, having attained eminence after securing the princess and regained his own abode (*i. e.* capital or power). (5) (*Exit*)

End of the Vishkambhaka.

(*Enter the* King and Vidûshaka.)

King—The constancy (*lit.* the being unaffected) of my servants was known; the talent of ministers was witnessed; even friends were observed (as regards their sincerity); the affection (loyalty) of the townsmen was realised all the more; the passion for adventures in battle was quite satisfied; and the jewel of women was obtained: what, indeed, have I not obtained from captivity, as from piety practised without hypocrisy (sincerely)? (6)

Vidu ;—(*With displeasure*) O friend, how do you praise that whore's son, cursed Captivity.' And that is forgotten now, *viz*—How you, like a newly captured lordly elephant, with feet (steps) stumbling on account of the shackles of clanking iron chains, with the burning of the heart indicated by the pale lotus-like face (the dry tip of the trunk), with eyes up-raised and steady owing to the force of rage, and with the path along the ground cleared with the huge hands (torn up with the huge trunk), did not get the comfort of sleep even during the nights.

King—Vasantaka, you are, indeed, a wicked man. Mark—

You saw the prison gloomy with darkness but not the splendour of her moon-like face; you felt pain at the clank of the chains, but heard not her sweet accents; the cruel prison-guards are present to your mind to-day and not her loving side-glances: you behold the faults of confinement but not the merits of Pradyota's daughter. (7)

Vidû.—(*With an air of pride*). If at all confinement brings in its train happiness, why do you then fasten your wrath upon the Kalinga-King for having taken Dṛdhavarman a captive ?

KING—(*Smiling;*) Fie upon you, fool! Every one is not Vatsarája who can escape in this way from prison taking a Vásavadattá with him. So let this matter (*lit*-topic) be dropped. It is many days since Vijayasena was sent against Vindhyaketu. And no one has come (brought tidings,) from him till now. Let therefore, the minister Rumaṇwan be called at once. I wish to say something to him.

(Having entered—)

The Portress—Victory, victory, to Your Majesty! Here are arrived at the door-region Vijayasena and the minister, Rumaṇvat.

KING —Quickly usher them in.

POR.—As Your Majesty commands!

[*Enter* RUMANVAT and VIJAYASENA.]

Ruma.—(*Musing.*)

Although gone out the very moment, servants generally enter a royal palace, full of apprehension, as if they were guilty, even though without guilt. (8)

(*Approaching*) Prosperity to Sire ?

KING—(*Pointing to a seat*) Rumaṇvat, be seated here.

RUMAN.—(*Sitting down, with a smile*). Here is Vijayasena, the conqueror of Vindhyaketu, bowing (to you).

VIJA.—(*does accordingly.*)

KING.—(*Embracing him graciously.*) Is Your Honour well ?

VIJA.—(I am) to-day by Sire's favour.

KING—Vijayasena, please be seated (VIJAYA. *sits down*).

KING—Vijayasena, tell Vindhyaketu's acount.

VIJA—Sire, what more can I tell? It is as it should be when Sire is angry.

KING—Still I wish to hear it in detail.

VIJA.—May Your Majesty hear–Starting from here according to Your Majesty's order, with an army of elephants, cavalry and infantry, as directed, we traversed the road though long in three days, and unexpectedly fell upon Vindyaketu at the time of day-break.

KING.—Then, then ?

VIJA.—Then roused by hearing the tumultuous din of our forces, he, Vindhyaketu, too, rushed out like a lion from a cave of the Vindhya mountain and without waiting for (the mustering of) his army and conveyances and having a few followers that happened to be at hand, proceeded at once to engage us, proclaiming his name.

KING—(*Looking at* RUMAṆVAT *with a smile*). That was creditably done by Vindhyaketu. What then ?

VIJA.—Then when his companions were killed to a man in a fierce onslaught by us, whose envy and energy were doubled at the thought—'Here is he, ' he, with the fury of his anger and strength enhanced by the crushing blow, fought in a still fiercer manner.

KING—Bravo, Vindhyaketu ! Excellent, excellent !

VIJAYA—What description can be given, Sire ! I will tell in brief—

Having first of all, himself fighting on foot, crushed the foot-soldiers by merely striking them hard with his chest, and dispersed the terrified cavalry like a herd of deer in the quarters with volleys of arrows from afar, he discharged on all sides the whole stock of his weapons and then quickly unsheathing his sword, proceeded to enjoy the sport of cutting off the plantain-grove of the mass of elephants' trunks. (9).

१ Making havoc, single-handed, in this way in our three-fold army, with his towering shoulders covered with the rays of his sword, Vindhyaketu, with his broad chest shattered by hundreds of weapons, and exhausted after a long time, was slain in the battle. (10)

KING—Rumaṇvan, to tell the truth, we are quite put to shame by the death of Vindhyaketu, following the path proper for worthy (*i. e.* brave) persons.

Ruman.—Sire, even the merits of an enemy produce joy in persons of your type who side with virtues alone.

King—Vijayasena, has Vindhyaketu a child, whereon I may bestow (*lit.* show) the fruit of gratification ?

Vijaya.—Sire, about this too I will tell you. When Vindhyaketu had been thus slain with his kinsmen and followers, and his wives followed him in death, when the country people had taken shelter on the peaks of the Vindhya mountains and the place had been desolate, there was a maiden in Vindhyaketu's house whose beauty was in keeping with her high birth and who was uttering the piteous lament—oh father, oh mother ! She is brought here by us being taken to be his daughter, and she is waiting at the door. Your Majesty is to decide with regard to her (*i. e.* as to how she is to be dealt with). १०

King.—Yaśodharâ, go yourself and deliver her over to Vâsavadattâ and say to the Queen—She should be always looked upon by you in the light of a sister and should be taught everything proper for a maiden of high birth, singing, dancing, playing upon instruments and other accomplishments. And when she becomes fit for being given away in marriage, you should remind me.

Portbess—As Your Majesty commands.

(*Behind the curtain*—A Bard).

By the breasts, gleaming with their beauty disclosed owing to the garments slipping down through exertion of the multitude of courtezans in the harem, getting ready the auspicious articles and cosmetics necessary for your pleasure-bath, your bathing room is adorned (as if) with other kinds of raised golden pots (11).

King—(*Looking upwards*) Ah ! how now ! The divine sun is occupying mid-heaven.' For now ;

The water of the ponds (in the gardens) appears to be boiling as it were with the heat of the rays of the sun on account of the leapings of the Śafaras ; the peacock spreads out his tail looking like an umbrella, though drooping from his sportive dance; the fawn covetous of the water in the basins seeks the circle of shades of the trees; and the bee, having at once left the cheek of the elephant, lurks (*lit.* enters) under the lobe of his ear. (12)

Rumanvan, get up; do get up. Having just entered the inner apartment and performed the usual rites, we will honour Vijayasena and dispatch him for annihilating the king of Kalinga.

[*Exeunt Omnes.*]

END of **ACT I**

ACT II

(*Enter* VIDU'SHAKA).

Indîvarikâ has, indeed, said to me–Noble Sir, Queen Vásavatta, who has been observing the vow of a fast, might call yau to receive the *Svastivâchana*. I will, therefore, bathe in the pond attached to the shower-house and having gone into the presence of the Queen will utter something in the manner of a cock (*i. e.* in a gradually raised voice). Otherwise, how are Brâhmaṇas like us to accept a donation in the royal palace? (*Looking towards the tiring room*) Ah ! Here my dear friend has started to go to the very showerhouse-garden to dispel the longing caused by the queen's separation. So I will go with my friend himself and do as (I said.).

१२ (*Enter the love-sick* KING).

My mind yearns, to-day, to see that beloved of mine who is emaciated, who wears only the auspicious ornaments, who speaks slowly and with effort, who subdues the beauty of the morning moon by her face having a palish hue, and who is full of longing owing to the observance of the rules of her fast, as if she were in the condition produced by first love. (1).

VIDU.—(*Approaching*) Hail to your Honour! May you prosper!

KING.—(*Looking at him*) Vasantaka, for what do you appear to be delighted!

VIDU.—Because the Queen is going to honour a Brâhmaṇa.

KING.—If so, how does it benefit you?

VIDU.—(*With pride*) Oh, such a Bráhmana, indeed, that I get the Svastivâchana-present first from the Queen in the palace crowded with thousands of Brâhmaṇas, versed in four, five or even six Vedas.

KING.—(*Laughing*) Your Bráhmanaship (Vedic scholarship) is shown by the number of the Vedas (mentioned by you). Come then, great Brâhmana. To the shower-house garden itself we go now.

VIDU.—As your Majesty commands.

KING.—Lead the way.

VIDU.—Come, oh! Let us go. (*Walking round and* १३
looking on) O friend, see, the loveliness of the shower-house-garden, the surface of the stone-slab in which is soft on account of the various kinds of flowers ceaselessly falling upon it, wherein the bunches of the Bakula and the Jasmine flowers are broken by the weight of the bees buried in the fragrance, where the cups of the Bandhûka flowers are opened by the breezes richly charged with the perfume of lotuses, and where the light of the sun is obscured by the dense *tamâla* trees.

KING.—Friend, you have well described it. For, here,

By the stems of the Śephalikâ flowers (scattered about) the ground appears as if covered with small bits of corals; the scent of the Saptachhada flowers at once gives rise to the false idea of its being the odour of the rut of elephants; and these bees here, having the colour of their bodies tawny with (or having the tawny unguents of) the thick mass of pollen dropped from the expanded lotuses, and intoxicated with the drafts of liquor (honey), are humming something in indistinct accents. (2).

Vidu.—O friend ! look, look at this too–this Saptaparṇa tree here, the mass of the flowers of which is unceasingly falling and which, therefore, still looks as if it has the drops of water falling through the interstices of its leaves at the close of the rainy season (or at the end of a shower).

१४ King.—Friend, happily observed. There is much that is like the rainy season (yet). For

Bearing softness (of surface) by the meadows which rob (possess or surpass) the beauty of the Śirîsha flowers, and therefore having at once a pavement made with the washed pieces (or powder) of emerald, the ground here, on account of the heaps of Bandhûka flowers dropped from their stems, now appears as if covered with hundreds of cochineal insects. (3)

(*Enter a* Maid).

Maid.—I am ordered by Queen Vàsavadattà—Girl Indivarikâ, to-day I have to present an Argha (offering of worship) to the great sage Agastya. Do you go then and come back quickly taking with you a garland of S'ephâlikâ flowers. Let this Araṇyikà, too quickly gather the full-blown lotuses from the pond in the shower-house-garden before they are closed up by the sun when going to set and come back. The poor girl does not know that pond. So I will take her with me and go. (*Looking towards the scenes*). This way, A'ranyikâ, come this way.

(*Enter* Aranyika).

१५= Aranyika'.—(*With tears and dejection, to herself*). That I, who was born in that sort of (so high a) race in that way and who lived commanding others, should now do the bidding of others ! So it must be said that there is nothing difficult for fate to bring about. Or rather it is my fault, since knowing this I did not destroy myself. So what shall I do now ! Or* it is now difficult for

---

* The passage may also be interpreted as—Or why ? A hard thing I have thought of now (*viz.* committing suicide)..........I will do as I said (*i. e.* kill myself). But this does not appear to be intended. See notes.

me to do what I had thought of. Better even this (state of things) than that I should lower myself by disclosing my illustrious race. What help is there ! I will do as I am asked to do.

MAID.—Come here, Araṇyikâ.

Arà—Here I come. (*Showing fatigue*) Maid, is the pond still far off ?

MAID.—It is here, hidden by the clumps of S'ephâlikás. Come then ; let us descend into it. (*They jesticulate descent*).

KING.— Friend, why do you seem to be thinking of some other thing ? Do I not say—' There is much that is like the rainy season. (*He repeats—Bearing softness* &c.)

VIDU.—(*Angrily*) You divert yourself, being full of longing, by looking at this and some other thing. But the time of me, a Bráhmaṇa, to receive the *Svastivachana* is passing—so I will quickly bathe and go into the Queen's presence.

KING.—Ah, fool ; we have already gone beyond the pond. Although thus experiencing the excess of gratification caused to all the senses, how do you not mark it ? See—

The cackle of the swans here sounding like the tinkle of the loved one's anklets delights the ears ; the side of the white mansion seen through the intervals of the trees on the bank brings joy to the eyes ; by the perfume of the lotuses, clever in diffusing their fragrance, the nose feels gratified ; and these breezes, cool by their contact with water, cause delight to the limbs. (4)

Come then. Let us approach the margin of the pond. (*Walking about and looking*). Friend, look, look.

This silvery pond, captivating by the lustre of its full-blown lotuses, delights me by its mere sight, as though it were the eye of the goddess of the garden. (5)

VIDU....(*With curiosity*). O friend, behold—Who is this female that is seen, with a cluster of bees round her braid fragrant with the perfume of flowers, with tender hands red like a coral-creeper, and with her creeper-like arms radiant, thin and delicate,—like the very garden-nymph moving in a visible form, with the row of bees for her braid, fragrant &c., having the sprouts for her hands rosy like &c., and the bright, slender and delicate creepers for her arms?

King.—(*Observing with curiosity*). Friend, she is one who gives rise to many surmises by the grace of her unsurpassed beauty. In short, I too do not know definitely. See—

१७ Is she a Nâga damsel that has risen from the nether world intent on beholding the earth! That is, indeed, a vain supposition; I have seen it (Pátala); whence can there be such a one in it; can she be moonlight in a bodily form come here? The sight of that is not possible during the day. Who is she then that appears like S'rî with a lotus held in the hand? (6)

Vidu.—(*Observing carefully*) Here is, indeed, the Queen's maid-servant, Indîvariká. So hiding ourselves behind a clump let us see.

(Both *do so*).

Maid.—(*Acting the plucking of a lotus-leaf.*) A'raṇyikā, you gather the lotuses; I too will gather the S'ephàlikà flowers in this lotus-leaf and repair to the Queen.

King.—Friend, a conversation seems to go on. Let us therefore listen attentively. Perhaps it (who she is) will be clear from it.

(The Maid *acts going*).

Ara'nyika'.—Friend Indîvarikà, I am not able to stay here even for a *muhurta* without you.

Maid.—(*Smiling*) According to the sort of speech of the Queen I heard to-day, you will have long to stay without me.

१८ A'ranyika'.—(*With dejection*). What was said by the Queen?

Maid.—This—I was then told by the king thus—When this daughter of Vindhyaketu becomes fit for marriage, I should be reminded of that", so I will put the king in in mind of that, so that he will be engaged in thoughts about a husband for her.

KING.—(*With joy*) This then is that daughter of Vindhyaketu. (*With regret*) Long have we been foiled (or, robbed of her sight). Friend, this is indeed, a maiden, to look at whom is not sinful. We shall see her now without hesitation (or freely).

A'RAN.—(*Angrily stopping her ears*) Go you then. I have nothing to do with you who talk nonsense.

(*The* maid-servant *goes and gesticulates the collecting of flowers.*

KING.—Oh, her nobility of birth has been greatly manifested by her firmness (of mind). Friend, blessed, indeed, will be he who will be the object of the happiness of the touch of her body.

(ARANYIKA' *acts the collecting of lotuses*).

VIDU.—O friend, mark, mark; wonderful, wonderful! As she plucks the lotuses, she puts into the background the beauty of the lotus-beds by the spreading lustre of her hand moving in the water.

KING—Friend, this is quite true. See— १९

Having become the object of the touch of the hand of her, who gives delight by her glances similar to that of (given by) a continuous shower of the drops of nectar, and who has assumed a peculiar loveliness owing to the slipping of her breast garment, as of the rays of the body of the moon that gives delight with a fitting shower of nectareous drops and that becomes peculiarly charming owing to the veil of clouds being removed, it is wonderful, indeed, that these lotuses do not become closed up at once. (7)

A'RANY.—(*Gesticulating torment from bees*) Oh fie! oh fie! These other wicked bees, greatly annoying me as they alight on the beds of blue lotuses, after leaving the lotus plant, torment me here. (*Covering her face with her upper garment, in alarm*) Friend Indīvarikā, save me, save me. These horrid bees will, indeed, assail me.

VIDU.—Oh friend, your wishes are fulfilled. Before that daughter of a born slave comes, you too, being silent, approach her. She, on her part, knowing Indīvarikā to be coming from the movement of feet indicated by the sound of water, will just cling to you.

KING.—Bravo, friend, bravo! Your advice is opportune. (*He approaches* ARANYIKA').

२० A'RANY.—(*Gesticulating the hearing of the sound of footsteps*) Indīvarikā, come to me quickly, come to me quickly. I am harassed by these wicked bees. (*Clings to the* KING).

(*The* KING *clasps her at the neck.* A'RANYĪKA', *removing her upper garment from her face and without seeing the* KING *acts looking at the beees.*)

KING.—(*Keeping off the bees with his upper garment*).

O you, give up this dispiritedness (depression of spirits); O timid one, these bees, drawn by their liking for perfume light on the lotus of your face; if again with your long eyes agitated through fear you will still diffuse the beauty of a bed of blue lotuses, how will they leave you?

ARANY.—(*Exhibiting flurry on seeing the* KING). How now! this is not Indīvarikā! (*Leaving the* KING *and moving aside in alarm*). Indīvarikā, come quickly, come quickly; protect me.

VIDU.—Lady, when you are protected by Vatsarāja, able to protect the whole world, you call out for the maid-servant, Indīvarikā?

(*The* KING *repeats—O you, give up &c.*).

A'RANY.—(*Looking at the* KING *with longing and bashfulness, to herself*). This is the great king to whom I was given (betrothed) by my father. In the right place was my father's preference, indeed!

MAID—A'ranyiká is, indeed, harassed by the wicked २१
bees. So I will at once approach her and comfort her. A'ranyiká, fear not; here I come.

VIDU.—Move away, O, move away. Here Indîvariká is just coming. Seeing (if she sees) this affair, she will inform the Queen of it. (*Pointing with the finger*). So having entered this plantain-bower we shall wait for a while.

(*Both do accordingly*).

MAID.—(*Approaching and touching her cheeks*). Friend A'ranyaká, this is the fault of your face resembling a lotus that the bees thus come to be guilty (or, the offenders—*i.e.*, torment you). (*Taking her by the hand*) Come then; let us go. The day has drawn to its close. (*They gesticulate departure*).

A'RANY.—(*Looking towards the plaintain-bower*) Friend Indīvariká, owing to the extreme coldness of the water my thighs seem to be benumbed. So slowly, slowly, we shall go.

MAID.—As you say. (*Exeunt both*).

VIDU.—O, come; let us issue forth. Having taken her with her, that slave's daughter, Indivariká, has gone away.

KING.—(*Sighing*) What, gone! Friend Vasantaka, not indeed is the desired object gained without impediment by those who are not lucky. (*Looking*) Friend, mark, mark! २२

The bed of lotuses, although its lotuses are closed up, yet being thorny (horripilated) tells, as it were, of the pleasure derived from the touch of her tender sprout-like hand. (४).

(*Sighing*) Friend, what is the means now to see her again?

VIDU.—Sir, having yourself broken the doll you are crying now; you do not act according to the words of me, a Bráhmana.

KING.—What did I not do!

VIDU.—That you have forgotten now. For I said—Be silent and approach her. Since you, having entered into a very critical position, reproved her, in your affected wisdom due to vain knowledge, saying—Ah you, give up this dispiritedness, &c., and such other words, why do cry now? And again ask me the means to see her.

KING.—Oh, how does the fool call what was comfort-giving a reproof!

VIDU.—It is just known who is a fool in this case. Then why go on with this? The divine one having a thousand rays (sun) is about to set. Come then; let us enter just the inside (of the palace).

KING.—(*Looking*). Ah, the day has almost drawn to its close. Alas! For now—

The splendour of the day, like my beloved, has gone, taking away the beauty of the groups of lotuses; there is observed a greater glow of Râga (redness—passion) in the orb of the sun as in this heart of mine; the wheel-named bird (ruddy goose) like me, is standing on the margin of the lotus-pond, thinking of his mate; and the directions have been suddenly darkened (void of interest) to the world also, as to me. (10).

(*Exeunt Omnes*)

End of Act II.

ACT III.

२३ (*Enter* MANORAMA')

MANORAMA'—I have been commanded by Queen Vàsavadattá saying—Manoramá, my girl, to-day on the occasion of the Kaumudî festival you have to perform the remaining part of the episode about my husband and myself which has been dramatised by Sāmkrityáyanî. Yesterday, indeed, her part was wrongly played by my dear friend, A'raṇyikā, being absent-minded. But if again the same be done by her to-day when appearing in the role of Vāsavadatta', the Queen will necessarily get angry. Where shall I find her then and reprove her?

(*Looking on*). Here is A'ranyikà entering the plantain-bower on the bank of the pond, saying something to herself. So hiding myself behind a bush I will listen to her unrestrained (free) utterings.

(*Enter* AR'NYIKA', *seated and acting love-sickness*.) २४

AR'ANY.—(*Sighing*) My heart, seeking an unobtainable person, why dost thou afflict me ?

MANO—This is then the cause of her absent-mindedness. But what again does she long for? Being attentive I will hear her.

AR'ANY.—(*With tears*) How does the great king, being of a pleasing appearance in that way, thus torment me (now) ! Wonderful, wonderful ! (*Sighing*) Or rather, this is my misfortune, and not the great king's fault.

MANO.—(*Fearfully*) How now ! the great king himself is the object of her longing ! Noble, dear friend, noble ! Your desire is in accordance with your high birth.

AR'ANY.—To whom, indeed, shall I relate this matter and make the pain of my misery somewhat bearable ? (*Reflecting*) Or why ! I have my dear friend, Manoramá, who is not different from my heart. But to her even I am not able to tell this through bashfulness. All considered, whence can there be solace to my heart other than death ! २५

MANO.—(*With tears*) Alas ! alas ! the poor girl's passion has reached its climax. So what shall I do in the matter ?

ARANY.—(*With longing*) This is the spot where, tormented by the bees, I was supported by the great king and comforted in the words—"O timid one, be not afraid ".

MANO.—(*Joyfully*) What ! She also is seen by the king ! Then by all means there is a way for her to live. I will then at once approach her and cheer her up. (*Suddenly advancing*) Proper, indeed, it is to be bashful even towards one's heart.

AR'ANY.—(*Bashfully to herself*) Oh fie, fie ! Every thing has been heard by her. So it will be quite proper to disclose all to her. (*Aloud; seizing her by the hand*). Dear friend, do not be angry, pray do not. It is bashfulness that is at fault.

MANO.—(*Joyfully*) Friend, away with hesitation. Tell me this. Have you been really seen by the king or not?

AR'ANY.—(*Bashfully with face hung down*) My dear friend has already heard everything.

MANO.—If you have been seen by the king, then don't you be worrying yourself. He himself will be eagerly engaged in devising some means to see you.

६ AR'ANY.—This my friend speaks with partiality. O you, lover of (blinded by love for) a friend, how can this be (expected) from a person who is, indeed, bound by the chains of the Queen's virtues.

MANO.—(*Laughing*) O you, silly girl (*Lit.* wanting in clever perception), although the bee has its love for the lotus plant, how can it, when it has seen the Màlati (jasmine) and is eager to taste its new flavour, rest quiet without obtaining it!

AR'AN.—What is the use of talking about this which is impossible? Come away then. My limbs, which are all the more tormented by the autumnal heat, do not give up their heat even now.

MANO.—O you bashful one, it is not proper for you, even when reduced to such a plight, to conceal the real state of your heart.

(AR'ANYIKA' *hangs down her face.*)

MANO.—O you naturally unconfiding one, what can you conceal now! Does not your passion, manifesting itself (*lit.* coming out) day and night, in the guise of sighs, as though it were the *hum* sound caused by the incessantly falling shower of the shafts of the flower-arrowed God (Cupid) tell it. (*To herself*) Or rather, this is not, indeed, the time for chiding her. So in the first place I will put some lotus-leaves on her bosom. (*Rises, and having taken some totus-leaves from the pond places them on* AR'ANYAKA'*s heart.*) Let my friend take comfort, let my friend take comfort.

(*Enter* VIDU'SHAKA)

VIDU'.—Very great, indeed, is my dear friend's passion for Ar'anyika'. For having set side the affairs of state he has been diverting himself by thinking about a remedy to obtain her sight only. (*Reflecting*) Where shall I find her then? Or why; I will search for her just there, on the margin of the pond. (*Walks on*).

MANO.—(*Hearing*) A sound like that of foot-steps is heard. So becoming concealed in the clump of plantains we shall see who is this (that is coming). (*Both do accordingly and see*).

AR'AN.—Ah, he is the very Bràhmana, who is always at the side of the king.

MANO.—How, Vasantaka himself! (*Joyfully to herself*) May it be that way (*i.e.* as I wish it)?

VIDU'.—(*Looking in all directions*) What! Has A'ranyikà really become Ar'anyikà (acting like a forest-bred girl; or, gone to a forest, as she is not found here) now.

MANO.—(*With a smile*) Friend, the king's companion, the Brahmana, is talking with respect to you. So let us listen attentively.

(AR'ANYIKA' *listens eagerly and bashfully*.)

VIDU'.—(*Dejectedly*) When in the first place, at the bidding of my dear friend whose body has become languid owing to the very great torment of love, I looked for her at the residence of the queens Vâsavadattâ, and Padmâvatî and of other queens, and did not find her there, I came here, thinking I should search the place also where she was seen at the pond. But then she is not here also. What shall I do now?

MANO.—Did my dear friend hear this?

VIDU'.—(*Reflecting*) Or why! It was already said to me by my friend—If you do not find her, after searching for her, then come, taking from that very pond at least the lotus-leaves that have had their pleasure-giving coolness doubled by the touch of her hand. Then how am I to know these?

MANO.—This is my opportunity. (*Approaching and taking* VIDU'. *by the hand*). Vasantaka, come on. I will show (also; expose) you.

VIDU'.—(*In alarm*) Expose me ! to whom ? To the Queen ? I have not, at all, said any thing.

MANO.—Vasantaka, dismiss this fear. As you have described to have been the condition of your dear friend on account of Aranyikà, double of that has been the state of my dear friend on account of our lord. So see it, see it.

२९ VIDU'.—(*Seeing, with joy*) My labour has borne fruit. Hail to your ladyship !

(ARANYIKA' *bashfully casts off the lotus-leaves and rises*).

MANO.—Noble Vasantaka, at your mere sight my dear friend's affliction has vanished, so that she is herself removing the lotus-leaves. So your noble self should favour them (by taking them).

AR'ANYIKA'—(*With agitation*), O you given to joking, why do you put me to shame ? (*She stands with her face slightly turned back*).

VIDU.—(*With dejection*) Let the lotuses remain. Your dear friend is extremely bashful. So how is their union to take place ?

MANO.—(*Musing for a moment, joyfully*) Vasantaka, in this way, it seems. (*She whispers into his ear*).

VIDU.—Excellent, dear friend ; cleverly suggested !

(*Aside*) By the time you two put on your costumes, I will come taking my friend with me. (*Exit*).

MANO.—O passionate one, get up, get up, We have to act the remaining part of that very play. Come then; let us go to the play-house. (*Walking round and seeing*) Here is the play-house. Come then ; let us enter in. (*Gesticulating entrance and looking about*), Well done, well done ! Every thing is got ready ; the Queen must be coming.

(*Enter the* QUEEN, ŚAMKRITYAYANĪ *and the retinue according to rank.*)

VA'SAVADATTA'—Revered lady, how wonderful is your poetic genius! For this story of my husband, with its secret incidents, although a mattter of experience, being dramatised (by you) raises our interest in it all the more, when being seen, as though it had not been seen before. ३०

SA'MK—O you of long life, the merit of this subject is such that a poem though without excellence (insipid) necessarily causes delight to the ears of its hearers. See,

Generally even an insignificant thing attains eminence by its connection with what is great; for even ashes come to be a decoration when applied to the broad temples of a rutting elephant. (1)

VA'SAVA.—(*With a smile*) Revered lady, it is a patent fact (*lit.*, is but known) that the son-in-law is loved by every one. So what is the use of thus continuing the conversation? It is better to see the very same representation.

SA'MKR.—Just so. Indîvarikâ, lead the way to the play-house.

MAID—Come, come, my Queen. (*They all walk on.*)

ŚA'MK.—(*Looking on*) Oh the loveliness of the play-house!

Charming with the huge strings of pearls hanging from the golden posts decked with hundreds of jewels, and occupied by the youthful damsels that have conquered (surpass in beauty) the nymphs of heaven, this play-house appears like the (aerial vehicle, or) residence of the gods. (2).

MANO. and ARAN.—(*Approaching*) Prosperity, prosperity, to the Queen!

VASAVA.—Manorama, the twilight has indeed, passed. Go you then, and quickly put on your costumes.

BOTH—As the Queen commands. (*They start to go*).

VA'SA.—Aranyikâ, go to the dressing room and decorate yourself with these very ornaments that are put on my person. (*She removes the ornaments from her person and hands them over to* A'ran.). Manoramá, you too take from Indîvariká the ornaments that were given to my husband by my father when pleased by his capture of Nalagiri and decorate yourself, so that you will look quite like the King.

(MANORAMA' *takes the decorations from* INDIVARIKA' *and exit with* ARANYIKA').

INDĪVARIKA'—Here is a seat; may your Majesty sit down.

VA'SAVA.—(*Pointing to a seat*) May your reverence sit down.

(BOTH *sit down*).

(*Enter the* CHAMBERLAIN *having put on his dress*).

Looking after the management of the inner apartments, guarding against stumblings at every step, and now led by a staff, being broken down by old age, I imitate all the actions of a king, who, following the science of government, maintains order within cities and avoids errors of policy at every step. (3).

३२ I am commanded by Mahâsena, who bears a significant name and who has put to chagrin (overpowered) all the armies of his enemies, to inform the ladies of the harem thus—Tomorrow we are to celebrate the Udayana festival. Therefore you are to repair to the garden of Love with your retinue splendid with dresses befitting the festival.

SA'MK.—(*Pointing to the* CHAM.) Princess, the play has commenced. Please see it.

CHAM.—So this is what I have to tell them—that they should go accompanied by their attendants and not attendants with their decorations put on. For,

Among these (inmates of the harem) even the servants of the maids-in-attendance of the queens are conspicuous with their feet adorned with anklets, with their broad hips having gingling girdle-bands, with their large breasts decked with (*lit.* having beauty imparted to them by) pearl necklaces, with their arms having *Keyuras* (armlets) on them, and with their ears furnished with *Kundalas*, their hands with bracelets and their hair with *Swastikas*. (4)

There is nothing, indeed, unusual that is to be done here. Thinking that it is my master's order, I will simply communicate the remaining part of the king's order to the Princess. २३

(*Walking about and seeing.*) Here has that (princess) Vâsavadattâ entered the music-hall followed by Kânchanamâlâ, lute in hand.. I will just tell her. (*Walks forth.*)

(*Enter* A'RANYIKA, *in* VASAVADATTA''s *costume, seated, and* KANCHANAMA'LA, *with a lute in her hand*).

A'RAN —Friend, Kânchanamâlâ, why again is the music-master tarrying even to-day ?

KA'NCH :—Princess, he has seen a crazy fellow ; and overpowered by wonder at hearing his words he has stayed there enjoying the fun (*lit.* laughing at him).

A'RAN.—Maid, well does he ask him. Both are mad men, as it is said--'The like take pleasure in the like.'

SA'MKR—I see that her form is like that of a princess; so with such a form she is sure to act your part well.

CHAM —(*Advancing*) Princess, His Majesty sends word to you—To-morrow we are sure to hear you playing the lute. So you should be ready with Ghoshavatî fitted with new strings.

AR'ANY—Sir, if so, quickly send the music-master.

CHAMB.—Here I send Vatsarâja to you. (*Exit*).

A'RANY.—Kánchanamalá, bring me the lute (Ghoshavatî). I will just examine its strings.

(KA'NCHANAMA'LA' *hands over the lute.*)

A'RANYIKA' *puts it on her lap and strikes* (*or, adjusts*) *the strings*).

(*Then enter* MANORAMA' *having put on* VATSARA'JA'S *decorations*). २४

MANORAMA'—(*To herself*) Surely the King tarries. Is it that Vasantaka did not tell him, or is he afraid of the Queen? If he comes now it will be a nice thing

[*Enter the* King, *and* Vidûshaka *with his body veiled*].

King—The cool-rayed one (moon) does not cause affliction to me just to-day as at first; now only hot sighs do not parch my lip as they did constantly before; just now my mind is not vacant nor are the limbs languid as formerly; and my torment becomes reduced even as the desires of my heart are thought of (as near fulfilment). (5).

Friend, did Manoramá really say—"Since my dear friend is kept even out of the path of the King's sight by the Queen, this is the way to bring about their union. To-day at night we are to enact before the Queen the play called Udayanacharita. In it A'raṇyiká will be Vásavadattá and I too Vatsarája. Everything is to be learnt (acted) according to his own doings. So having come and acting his part himself, let him enjoy the pleasure of her company."

Vidû.—If you do not believe me, here is Manoramá waiting, wearing your costume. So approach her and ask her yourself.

King—(*Approaching* Manoramá) Manoramá, is what Vasantaka says true?

Manoramá—Sire, quite true. Decorate yourself with these ornaments. (*With these words she takes off the ornaments from her person and hands them over to the* King).

(*The* King *puts them on*).

Vidû.—Here, indeed, are kings thus made to dance (act) even by a maid-servant. Oh the importance of business (the object to be achieved)!

King—(*Laughing*) Fool, this is not the time for joking. Silently enter the picture gallery and wait there with Manoramá, beholding our acting.

(Both *act accordingly*).

A'rany.—Kánchanamálá, let alone the lute. Just I wish to ask you something.

KING—Let me hear (to know) which part of the story is being acted. (*He listens attentively*).

KA'NCH—May the Princess ask.

A'RANY.—Does my father really say so, *viz.*—"If playing on the lute Vatsarâja captivates me I will necessarily free him from captivity."?

KING—(*Entering with a toss of the curtain, joyfully ties a knot in the hem of his garment*). Thus it will be. What doubt is there ?

Having filled Pradyota with his attendants with wonder by my performance on the lute, I see that ere long I shall take away Vásavadattâ. (6)

For all things have been well arranged by Yaugandharâyaṇa.

VA'SAVA.—(*Rising at once*) Prosperity ! prosperity to my husband !

KING—(*To himself*) How is it that I am recognized by the Queen ?

SA'MKR.—(*With a smile*) Princess, away, away with this hurry (or, confusion). This is a play.

KING—(*To himself joyfully*) Now I am made to ३६
breathe freely.

VA'SAVA.—(*Sitting down with a smile of embarrassment*) What ! this is Manorama' ! I thought it was my husband. Bravo, Manoramâ, bravo. Excellently acted.

SA'MKR.—Princess, rightly, indeed, was confusion caused in you by Manoramá. Consider—

Hers is that same form (of Vatsarája), the cause of delight to the eyes ; the same is the splendid costume ; self-same is this her gait here, that characterises an intoxicated elephant; the same is the exceedingly lofty dignity ; her grace the same, and the very same is her voice that resembles the rumble of water-charged clouds : here is presented before us, in his very person, the lord of the Vatsas himself by her, clever (in acting). (7).

VA'SAVA.—O Indîvarikâ, I was taught to play on the lute by my lord in fetters; so fetter him with this garland of blue lotuses. (*Taking off from her head the garland of blue lotuses she gives it to her*).

(INDIVARIKA' *does as directed and sits down in the same place.*

A'RANY.—Kânchanamâlâ, tell me, pray tell me. I ask—Does my father really say this, *viz.*—" If Vatsarâja captivates me by his playing on the lute, then I will necessarily set him free from captivity. "

KA'NCHA.—Princess, he does, really. Act in such a way that, as a matter of fact, you will be highly esteemed by Vatsarâja.

३७ KING—Kânchanamâlâ has actually brought to pass what was then desired by me.

A'RANY.—If so I will play with care.

(*Plays upon the lute, singing*).

Observing the sky densely crowded with chains of clouds the royal swan longs to go to the Mânasa lake, his residence, taking with him his mate. The swan among kings—Vatsarâja,—seeing the prison vault closed up with thick chains, desires to repair to his own abode, taking his beloved with him in order to reach (please her heart). (8).

(VIDÛ,—*gesticulates sleeping*).

MANO.—(*Shaking him with her hand.*) Vasantaka, see, see ; my friend is playing her part.

VIDU.—(*Angrily*) Slave's daughter, you too do not allow me to sleep ! From the time my dear friend saw A'ranyikâ, I have not seen, along with him, what sleep is. So I will go to some other place and sleep. (*Goes out and sleeps*).

(A'RANYIKA' *sings again*).

Hurled into (powerfully affected with) a new passion, by the perverse Kâma, the female bee pines, eagerly longing to see her mate, of a charming sight. (9).

KING—(*Hearing the song the very moment and suddenly going forth*) Commendable, princess, commendable! How charming the singing, how charming the playing (on the lute)! For,

Distinctness has now been attained here (in this performance) by the *Vyañjana* mode of playing (on the lute) in all its ten parts; this *laya* (tempo) here, distinguished by its three varieties of quick (allegro) intermediate (moderato) and slow (adagio) has been clearly marked in three ways; all the three *pauses*, Gopuchcha' and the rest, have been accomplished in due order: and the three modes of playing on instruments have been properly exhibited. (10)

A'RANY.—(*Clasping the lute rises from her seat and longingly looking at the* King) Preceptor, I bow to you.

KING—(*With a smile*) May you have that which I wish for you!

KA'NCH.—(*Pointing* to A'RANYIKA''s *seat*) The preceptor should please sit just here.

KING—(*Having sat down*) Where should the Princess sit now?

KA'NCH.—(*With a smile*) The Princess has just now been complimented by you with commendation of her skill. So she deserves to share the seat of the preceptor.

KING—Let her sit here; she deserves (to occupy) half of the seat. Princess, sit down.

(A'RANYIKA' *looks at* KA'NCHANAMA'LA').

KA'NCH.—(*Smilingly*) Princess, sit there. What is wrong in this?

(A'RANYIKA' *sits down bashfully*).

VA'SAVA.—(*Blushingly*). The subject-matter has been added to by your reverence. I did not, at all, sit on the same seat with my husband at that time.

KING—Princess, I wish to hear again. Play on the lute.

AR'ANY.—(*With a smile*) Kánchanamálá, having played for a long time I feel exhausted. So I shall not be able to play.

KANCH.—Preceptor, the Princess is greatly fatigued. See, how drops of perspiration are formed on her cheeks and her fingers (or fore—hands) tremble. So let her be refreshed (by resting) for a short while.

KING—Kánchanamála, you have said what is proper. (*Wishes to seize her by the hand.* A'rany. *withdraws her hand*).

४० VASAVA.—(*Sarcastically*) Lady, this also has been overdone by you. I am not certainly Kánchanamalá that can be misled by (such) composition. [Or, I should not be deceived (misrepresented) by Kānchanamàlâ's dramatic speech].

SA'MKR.—(*Smiling*) O you of long life, dramatic composition must be of this nature.

A'RANY.—(*With seeming anger*) Go away, Kanchan., go away. I do not like you.

KA'NCH.—(*With a smile*) If you do not like me standing here, here I walk off. (*Starts to go.*)

AR'ANY.—(*In confusion*) Kânchana., stay, stay; here is the fore-hand offered to him.

KING—(*Taking the hand of* A'RANYIKA').

Can it be a lotus-bud at once cooled by the contact of dew-drops? Not such methinks is its power to delight (now); it has it at dawn only when it is left by (free from) the sun; are there five moons in the form of fingers shedding a shower of coolness (or dew). Even that (the shower) burns (causes affliction). I know it—this is clearly ambrosia flowing under the guise of perspiration. (11)

By you, moreover, is implanted in my heart this Rāga (passion—redness), with your hand clever in robbing the tender coral sprout of its beauty. (12).

४१ A'RANYIKA'—(*Exhibiting the peculiar sensation of touch*) Oh fie, oh fie! my limbs commit a havoc in me (experience a thrill of overpowering emotion) as I touch this Manoramá.

VA'SAVADA.—(*Rising suddenly*) Revered lady, *you* see the representation. I, for myself, cannot bear to see what is false.

SA'MKR.—Princess, this *Gandharva form of* marriage is sanctioned by the religious codes of law. What is the matter for shame in this? This is a dramatic representation. So it is not proper to go away causing a break in the interest when there is no occasion for it.

VA'SAVA.—(*Walks away*).

INDÍVARIKA'—(*Looking on*) Your Highness, Vasantaka, is lying in deep sleep at the door of the Picture-gallery.

VA'SAVA—(*Observing carefully*). This is Vasantaka, indeed. (*Reflecting.*) The King also must be here. So having roused him I will just ask him. (*Wakes him up.*)

VIDÛ.—(*Rising dull with sleep and looking up suddenly*) Manoramā, has my dear friend come back after having played his part; or is he acting still?

VA'SAVA.—(*With dejection*) What! My husband is acting? Where is Manorámá now?

VIDÛ.—Here, waiting in the Picture-hall.

MANORAMA'—(*With alarm, to herself*) How was it that the Queen asked him taking quite a different view of the matter; and this foolish fellow too understanding her in quite a different way spoiled the whole matter?

VA'SAVA.—(*Laughing angrily*) Bravo! Manoramá, ४२
bravo! nicely have you acted!

MANORAMA'—(*Falling at her feet, trembling with fear.*) Your Highness! It is not, indeed, my fault in this case. By this rascally fellow standing at the door I was detained here, after taking the decorations from me. And again, my voice, as I cried, was not heard by anyone, as it was drowned in the sound of the tator.

VA'SVA.—Get up, girl, I know it all. Vasantaka is the chief manager in the play—The story of Âranyikā.

VIDU.—Just think yourself–where is A'ranyikà and where Vasantaka !

VA'SAVA.—Manoramá, having well-secured him just come after me. The acting he has arranged I will see now.

MANORAMA'—(*To herself*) Now life is put in me. (*Binds Vidu. by the hand and then aloud*) Miscreant, now reap the fruit of your evil policy.

VA'SAVA.—(*Approaching in a hurry*) My lord, may this evil be averted ! (*Removing with these words the garland of blue lotuses from his feet, ironically–*) My Lord should forgive me that I, thinking that it was Manoramá, caused you to be bound with a garland of blue lotuses.

(ARANYIKA' *stands, having moved away in fear*).

४३ KING.—(*Rising suddenly and seeing* MANORAMA', and VIDUSHAKA, *to himself.*) How am I discovered by the Queen ?

(*Acts being abashed*).

SA'MKṚTYA'YANI'—(*Seeing all, with a smile*) How has the representation turned out to be quite a different thing ? This is not the proper place for persons of my sort. (*Exit*).

KING—(*To himself*) Unusual is this way of showing anger. I see that reconciliation is difficult to be brought about in this case. (*Musing*) I will do this. (*Aloud*). My Queen, let anger be set aside.

VA'SAVADATTA'—Husband, who is angry here ?

KING—How, are you not angry ?

Although your glance is affectionate, still the lustre of your eyes is red; this your choked voice, though there is sweetness in it, falters at every word; your hard breathings, though suppressed, are well observed from the heaving of your full bosom : so this your anger, though restrained with evident effort, is clearly seen. (13).

(*Falling at her feet*) Be pleased, my dear, be pleased.

VA'SAVA.--A'ranyikā, thinking that you are angry, my husband is saying to you-" Be pleased, my dear, be pleased. " So approach him.

(*With these words she pulls her*).

A'RANYIKA'—(*In fright*) Your Highness, I know nothing of this.

VA'SAVA —A ranyiká, how don't you know anything? Here I will teach you. Indivarikà, seize her.

VIDŪ.—Madam ! To-day it being the Kaumudî festival, my friend performed the acting to divert your heart.

VA'SAVA—When I see this misbehaviour of your both, I am moved to laughter.

KING—My Queen, away with misconception. See—

Why for nothing is this spot produced on the moon of your forehead by the knittings of the eyebrows ? Why is this throbbing lip made to resemble the *bandhujīva* flower shaken by the breeze ? And again this your waist is oppressed by the weight of your breasts throbbing all the more : give up your anger towards me : for the amusement of your mind alone this acting was performed by me. (14).

Queen, be pleased, be pleased. (*He falls at her feet.*)

VA'SAVA.—Girl, the playing is over. Come then ; let us enter the inner apartment. (*Exit*).

End of the mimic Play.

KING—(*Looking*) How is it that the Queen has gone without showing favour ?

When I look at the face of the Queen and also at that of my beloved here pictured before me: the one streaked with the particles of perspiration and with eye-brows very fiercely contracted through anger, and the other with its lotus-like eyes greatly agitated through fear like those of a gazelle bounding with great speed, I, alarmed and yet having my mind full of longing, am thrown into a great difficulty. (15).

So I will just now go to my couch and think about the means of propitiating the Queen.

(*Exeunt Omnes.*)

END OF ACT III.

---

४५ ACT IV

(*Enter* MANORAMA')

MANORAMA'—Oh the long continuity of the Queen's anger! She does not take pity on my dear friend A'ranyikà, though confined for so long a time. The poor girl is not distressed so much by the hardships of her own imprisonment as by her despair to see the King. And such is her affliction that to-day I prevented her with great difficulty from killing herself. I have come having asked Vasantaka to communicate the matter to the King.

(*Then enter* KA'NCHANAMA'LA).

KA'NCHA.—Strange that I did not find the revered Sàmkṛitàyanî though searching for her. (*Looking on*) I will then ask this Manoramà. (*Going forth*) Manoramà, do you know where the revered Śámkrityàyanî is?

MANORAMA'—(*Looking at her and wiping off her tears.*) Friend, Kánchanamálà, I have seen her; but what have you to do with her?

KA'NCHANA.—To-day a letter was sent by her Highness Angâravatî. That being read, the Queen, with eyes filled with tears, began to feel greatly pained. So for her diversion I am searching for the venerable lady.

:४६ MANORAMA'—Friend, but what was written in that letter?

KA'NCHANA.—She who is my sister is just like your mother; and her husband is (as) your father. So need this be told to you? It is more than a year since he has been taken a captive by the accursed king of the Kalingas. It is not proper, therefore, for your husband, who is his neighbour and powerful, thus to observe indifference on hearing of this undesirable occurrence.

MANORAMA'.—Friend Kànchanamálà, but who read the letter to the Queen when, indeed, it was ordered by our lord that the matter should not be communicated by any one to Her Highness.

KA'NCHANA.—As I remained silent after reading it to myself, the Queen took it from my hand and read it herself.

MANORAMA'—Then go you; here is the Queen sitting with the very lady in the upper ivory chamber.

KA'NCHANA.—I will go there to the Queen. (*Exit*).

MA'NORAMA'.—It is a long time since I came leaving Ar'anyiká. The poor girl is quite tired of her life. Something disastrous might perchance happen. So I will go just there. (*Exit.*)

(*Enter seated* VA'SAVADATTA' *in distress*, SA'MKRITYA'YANÍ *and the* retinue *in order of rank.*)

SA'MKRIT.—Princess, away with agitation. Vatsarája is not such. How can Vatsarája rest unconcerned on knowing very well that the husband of your mother's sister is in such a plight?

VA'SAVADATTA'.—Holy lady, now you are extremely simple-minded. What can he, who has nothing to do with me, have to do with one connected with me? It was meet for my mother to write to me about this. But she does not know that Vásavadattá is not such now (as she was before). This A'ranyiká affair again has been witnessed by you with your own eyes. How do you say this then?

SA'MKRIT.—Since it was witnessed by me, for that reason I say so. He surely acted that way at the Kaumudi festival to make you laugh (enjoy the fun).

VA'SAVA.—Holy dame, this much is true here. I was so made to be laughed at that it is with difficulty that I stand before your reverence through shame. So why continue that topic? Surely it is by this partiality that I have been raised to such a high level (reduced to this state). (*Weeps*).

SA'MKRIT.—Do not weep, Princess. Vatsarája is not such (as would remain indifferent). (*Looking about*) Or why; here comes he who will himself remove your sorrow.

VA'SAVA.—These are now your ladyship's fancies!

(*Enter* KING *and* VIDUSHAKA).

KING.—Friend, what is the way now to get my beloved released?

VIDU.—Friend, give up your dejection. I will tell you the way.

४८ KING.—(*With joy*) Friend, mention it very quickly.

VIDU—Friend, in the first place you are distinguished by your two arms that have proved their valour in conflicts with your enemies in many a battle; and again rendered more powerful by (or, and again possess) an irreistible army consisting of numerous elephants, horsemen and foot-soldiers. So having now hardpressed the harem with the whole bulk of your forces, set Aranyiká free.

KING.—Friend, you have advised what is impracticable.

VIDU.—What is impracticable in this (since there is surely not a single man there save the hunch-backs, dwarfs, and the old chamberlain.

KING.—(*Despisingly*) Fool, what nonsense you talk! Excepting the Queen's favour there is no other means to procure her release. So tell me how I shall gain the Queen's favour.

VIDU.—Sir, support your life observing a month's fast. Thus will the fierce Deví (wrathful Queen) be pleased.

KING.—(*Smiling*) Do not joke. Tell me how I should propitiate the Queen?

Shall I, being bold, obstruct her (course) standing before her and smiling, clasp the dear one at the neck? Or shall I cause her to be delighted by framing a speech couched in hundreds of flattering expressions? Or shall I remain with folded hands having fallen before the Queen at her feet? Truly, truly, I know not how the Queen's conciliation is to be effected. (1).

Come then; let us go into the Queen's presence. ४९

VIDU'.—Go you, yourself. As for me I have come just now having escaped from confinement with difficulty. So I will not go.

KING.—(*Smiling and clasping him by the neck, makes him turn back by force.*) Fool, come on. (*Walking round and looking on.*) Here is the Queen sitting in the centre of the ivory-chamber. I will approach her. (*Approaches abashed*).

(Vāsavadatta' *rises from her seat languidly*).

Why have you left your seat? away with this hurry to show respect to me. It is not proper thus to stand for me, O you with your waist wearied (thereby). Why is this person, who is won over by the favour of the mere casting of a glance, made to feel abashed by excessive courtesy! (2).

VA'SAVA.—(*Closely observing his countenance.*) Husband, you are now abashed (indeed)!

KING.—My dear, I am really abashed. For, although my guilt was visibly seen, I am endeavouring to appease you.

SA'MKRIT.—(*Pointing to a seat.*) Sire, please sit down.

KING.—(*Pointing to a seat.*) Let the Queen sit here.

VA'SAVA.—sits on the ground.

KING.—Oh, the Queen has sat on the ground. I too will sit just here. (*So sitting on the ground, with folded hands.*) Beloved, be pleased, be pleased. Why do you cherish this deep-seated anger, when I have thus bowed to you?

O you with bewitching eyes, you do not knit your ५०
brows, but simply weep again and again; with your

lower lip not much quivering you heave sighs without cessation; you do not give a reply, but remain with your face hung down in deep meditation: your suppressed anger greatly pains me like a hidden stroke (*i. e.* wound caused by it). (3)

My beloved, be pleased.

VA'SA.—You are surely very happy. Why do you now torment an afflicted person? Rise, who is angry here?

SA'MKR.—Get up, sire; what is the use of this? Quite different is the cause of her affliction.

KING.—(*In haste.*) Revered lady, what is that other cause?

(SA'MKṚITYA'YANI *whispers it in the ear.*)

KING.—(*Laughing.*) If so, away with sorrow. I too knew it. But I did not say (anything about it) thinking that I should greet the Queen after the purpose had been accomplished. Otherwise how could I remain unconcerned in this Dhṛdhavarma matter? So several days have elapsed since tidings about it reached (here). This is the state of things there.

With his outward territory overrun by our forces led by Vijayasena, and his power destroyed, the accursed Kalinga, rendered helpless, has been forced to seek protection from the rampart after having at once entered his fortress. (4)

५१ And him, Kalinga, thus situated—, rendered powerless by our attack as described above, with the activities of his warriors and servants decreasing day by day, and having his entire army routed as his elephants, horses and men are falling so as to be destroyed—, you will hear before long, O revered lady, as being either captured or slain in the battle, when in a day or two his fortress is levelled down from all sides by our forces. (5)

SA'MKRIT.—Princess, I told your ladyship, at the earliest, that Vatsarája would not remain without making a counter move.

VA'SAVA.—If so, that is gratifying to me.

(*Enter Portress*).

PORTRESS.—Prosperity, prosperity to your Majesty! Here is Vijayasena, accompanied by Dṛdhavarman's Chamberlain. waiting at the door, with his eyes expanded through joy and wishing to communicate something agreeable.

VA'SAVA.—(*With a smile*) Revered lady, as I guess I am entirely compensated (lit., satisfied) by my lord.

SA'MKR.—I am, indeed partial to Vatsarája! So I say nothing.

KING.—Quickly ask them to come in.

PORTRESS.—I will. (*Exit*).

(*Enter* VIJAYASENA *and the* CHAMBERLAIN.)

VIJAYA.—Dear chamberlain, at the thought that I am to see my master's feet to-day, I am truly experiencing an ecstacy of joy, indescribable and beyond comparison.

CHAMBER.—This is true. See— ५२

Even ordinarily (lit., otherwise) a servant is filled with joy on beholding his master: how much more then must be he who has fully carried out the responsible task entrusted to him by his lord, by routing the enemy's forces? (6)

BOTH.—(*Approaching.*) Victory, victory, to our master!

(*The* KING *embraces them both*).

CHAMBER.—Sire, my congratulations to you.

Having slain the cursed Kalinga at your Majesty's command, Vijayasena, the conqueror of the foes, has set our master on the throne. (7)

VA'SAVA.—My revered lady, do you recognize this chamberlain?

SA'MKR.—How shall I not recognize him? Surely this is he by whom your aunt sent the letter to you.

KING.—A momentous business has been accomplished by Vijayasena.

(VIJAYASENA *falls at his feet*).

KING.—Queen, I congratulate you. Dṛdhavarman has been reinstated on his throne.

QUEEN.—(*With joy.*) It is a favour to me.

VIDU.—At the time of such good fortune, this must be done in this royal palace—(*Pointing to the* KING *and acting playing on the lute.*) worship of the Preceptor; (*showing his sacred thread*) honour to a Bráhmaṇa; (*indicating* AR'ANYIKA'.) and the release of all in custody.

KING.—(*Aside, with a fillip*) Well done, friend, well done!

५२ VIDU.—Madam, how is it that you do not pass any orders in this case.

VA'SAVA.—(*Looking at* SA'MKRITYANÍ, *with a smile.*) The knave has, indeed, got A'ranyaká out of prison.

SA'MKR.—What is the use of keeping the girl in custody?

VA'SAVA.—Just as your reverence likes.

SA'MKR.—If so, I myself will go and set her free. (*Exit.*)

CHAMBERLAIN.—Here is another message sent by Dṛdhavarman—By your favour everything has been accomplished as desired. So this my life is yours (at your disposal); you have the right to use it as you please.

(*The* KING *remains with his face hung down through modesty.*)

VIJAYASENA.—Sire, it is not possible at all to describe the great affection Dṛdhavarman feels for Your Majesty.

CHAMBERLAIN.—(*Continuing.*) And although pain was caused to me that there was no alliance formed with you on account of the loss of my daughter, Priyadarsiká, who was affianced to you, still the same has been removed by you as the husband of Vásavadattá.

VA'SAVA.—(*Tearfully.*) Noble chamberlain, how was my cousin lost?

CHAMBERLAIN.—Princess, when in the course of the attack by the accursed Kalinga the inmates of the harem had fled here and there, I took her who was fortunately seen by me, and thinking—'It is no longer advisable to stay here now', started to come to

Vatsarája. Then after due consideration I committed her to Vindhyaketu's care and went away. Just as I returned I found the place made, along with Vindhyaketu, a matter of memory by some people.

KING.—(*With a smile.*) Vijayasena, what do you say (to this)?

CHAMBERLAIN.—There although I searched for her I did not find her. And from that time to this day it is not known where she is—

(*Enter* MANORAMA').

MANORAMA'.—Your Highness, the poor girl is in danger of life.

VA'SAVA.—(*Weeping.*) What! Do you know what has happened to Priyadars'ana'?

MANORAMA.—Certainly I do not know what has happened to Priyadars'ana'. This A'raṇyiká here drank the poison brought to her under the guise of wine and is in peril of life. This is what I humbly said So your Highness should save her. (*Falls at her feet weeping*).

VA'SAVA.—(*To herself.*) Oh fie, fie! my grief for Priyadars'aná has been hidden (eclipsed) by this account of A'raṇyiká. People are, to be sure, extremely wicked. They might, perchance, mis-judge me. So this is proper to be done in this case. (*Loudly and with concern.*) Manoramá, bring her quickly just here. My husband who has learnt the art of poison-curing in the world of the Nàgas is an expert in this matter.

(*Exit* Manoramá; *then enter* Aranyiká, *supported by* Manorama, *and exhibiting herself as suffering from the effects of the poison.*)

A'RANYIKA'.—Dear Manoramá, why are you leading me into darkness?

MANORAMA'.—(*With dismay.*) Alas, alas! Her sight also is affected by the poison. (*To* Vàsavadattá) Mistress, quickly save her, quickly save her. The poison has affected her seriously.

VA'SAVADATTA'.—(*Taking the* KING *by the hand, in*

agitation.) Rise, rise, my lord. The poor girl is fast dying.

Chamberlain.—(*Observing her.*) She surely resembles very much our princess, Priyadars'iká. (*Referring to* Va'savadatta'.) Princess, whence is this maiden ?

Vasava.—Sir, she is Vindyaketu's daughter, brought here by Vijayasena after slaying him.

Chamber.—Whence could he have a daughter. This is the same, my princess. Alas ! I am undone, a luckless man ! (*Falling on the ground and rising up.*) Princess, this is that Priyadars'iká, your cousin.

Vasava'.—Husband, save her, save her. My cousin is dying.

King.—Be calm, be calm. Let me see first. (*Aside*) Pity, oh pity !

The bee in its course went to drink the lotus bud having abundant floral juice formed in it ; and at the same time it was scorched up by the frost having suddenly fallen on it. When fate is adverse desires bear no fruit. (8)

(*Aloud*) Manoramá, ask her if she has consciousness.

Manorama'.—Friend, are you conscious ! (*Shaking her again, with tears.*) Friend, I say, I ask you if you are conscious.

Priyadar.—(*Indistinctly.*) I say, even such as I am, I did not see His Majesty. (*With this half-uttered she falls on the ground.*)

५६ King.—(*With tears, aside.*)

She is closing this pair of her eyes (but) the quarters have been dark to me ; her throat is choked ; these words of mine escape me with difficulty ; her breathing has stopped (*lit.* is taken away); my body has become paralysed (*lit.* come to be in a state of motionlessness); I think the effect of poison only is hers ; but mine is all the affliction caused by it. (9)

Va'sava.—(*Weeping*) Priyadars'aná, rise, oh rise. See ; here is the King sitting. How is it that her consciousness is also lost ? What wrong have I done you unknowingly, angry at which you do not ;talk to me? Be pleased, then, be pleased. Arise, arise. I will not give offence again, Ah, cursed fate ! What evil deed was done by me now that my cousin is presented to me reduced to this plight ?

VIDU.—My friend, why do you stand like one bewildered ? This is not the time for dejection ! Very serious, indeed, is the working of the poison. So show the power of your art.

KING.—This is quite true, (*Looking at* PRIYADARS'IKA'.) I remained stupefied all this while. So I will restore her to life. Water, water.

VIDU.—(*Going out* and *coming back again.*) O here is water.

(*The* King *advancing and placing his hand on* Priyadars'ikâ, *acts the silent repeating of the incantation* ; Priyad'arsika' *slowly rises up.*)

VA'SAVA.—My lord, thank God, my cousin has revived.

VIJAYASENA.—Oh the power of his Majesty's know- ५७
ledge !

CHAMBERLAIN.—Oh, unobstructed everywhere is the power of His Majesty as *Narendra* (sovereign—Poison–physician) !

PRIYADARS'IKA'.—(*Slowly rising up and sitting, indicates yawning, then with dejection indistinctly.*) Manoramâ, I have, indeed, slept long.

VIDU.—O friend, your skill as a physician has been fully proved.

(PRIYADARS'IKA', *gazing longingly at the* KING *stands up bashfully, her face hung down a little.*)

VA'SAVA.—Husband, why does she still act differently (like one not fully restored to sense) ?

KING.—(*With a smile*).

Since her eye-sight is not restored to its natural state, her words are not very distinct ; this her body reels, with horripilation and the drops of perspiration clearly visible on it; and there is this tremor causing torment to her full bosom; it is certain the poison has not yet wholly ceased to operate on her. (10).

CHAMBERLAIN.—(*Referring to* PRIYADARS'IKA'.) Princess, here is your father's servant. (*With these words he bows at her feet.*)

PRIYADAR.—(*Looking at him.*) What! our chamberlain, the worthy Vinayavasu! (*Weeping*) Alas, father; Oh mother!

CHAMBERLAIN.—Princess, do not weep. Your parents are well. By the favour of Vatsarája, the kingdom is restored to its original position.

VA'SAVA.—(*With tears*) O cunning (lit. false-natured) one, come; now at least show your sisterly affection. (*Clasping her at the neck.*) Now I am pleased.

VIDU'.—Madam, you are gratified having clasped your cousin round the neck. But the reward to be given to the physician is forgotten.

VA'SAVA.—Vasantaka, not forgotten.

VIDU'.—(*Addressing the* KING *with a smile.*) Physician, hold forth you hand. I will cause the hand of her cousin to be given as a reward to you.

(*The* KING *stretches forth his hand*; VA'SAVADATTA *offers* Priyadar'siká's *hand.*)

KING.—(*Withdrawing his hand.*) What have I to do with her? You have been just now somehow conciliated.

VA'SAVA.—Who are you not to take it (the hand)? She was already given by her father.

VIDU'.—Sir, the Queen, indeed, ought to be honoured. Do not act against her wish. (Vásavadattá *forcibly draws forth the* King's *hand and offers up* PRIYADARS'IKA'.)

KING.—(*Smilingly.*) The Queen is all powerful. Whence can we have power to do otherwise.

VA'SAVADATTA'.—My lord, what other thing desired by you, beyond this, should be done?

KING.—What is there more than this that is to be coveted ? Observe—

His own kingdom has been occupied again in its entirety by Dṛdhavarman ; you, although possessed by anger to a great degree, have been at once reconciled with me. And your cousin, Priyadars'anā, living, has been united with you. So what other covetable thing is there further than this that can be sought ?

Still, let there be this—

(*The Bharata-Va'kya.*)

May Vásava, sending down the wished-for rain make the earth have a luxuriant growth of grain ; may the eminent Bráhmaṇas give satisfaction to the celestials by sacrifices duly performed ; may there be union among the good, firm and ever growing, to the end of the world ; and may the words of villainous people, unbearable and sticking indelibly (to the heart) fully disappear (lit. be laid at rest) ! !

(*Exeunt Omnes*).

END OF ACT IV.

Here ends the NA'TIKA' styled PRIYADARS'IKA'.

IMPORTANT ABBREVIATIONS.

Ak., *Amara.*—Amarakośa.

Bg.—Bhagavadgîtâ.

Bhar.—Bhartṛihari's Śatakas (N. and V.).*

Bhaṭṭi.–Bhaṭṭikâvya (I.–V.).*

Bṛih.-S.—Bṛihatsaṃhitá.

Col. U. Ed.—Columbia University Edition of the Play.

Cf.—Compare.

Ch.—Chapter.

Br. K. M.–Bṛhatkathámanjarî.

Com.—Commentary; commentator.

D. K.—Daśakumáracharita.*

D.-R.—Daśa-Rûpaka.

Gît.—Gîtagovinda.

Hitop.—Hitopadeśa.*

Kád.—Kádambarî.*

Kathá.—Kathásaritságara.

Káv., *K.-D.*—Kávyâdarśa.

K.-P.—Kávyaprakáśa.

Kum.—Kumárasaṃbhava. (I.–VII.).*

Málav.—Málavikágnimitra.*

Malli.—Mallinâtha.

Mál.-Mádh.—Málatî-Mádhava.*

M.-S.—Manusmṛiti.

Megh.—Meghadûta*.

Mṛich.—Mṛichchhakaṭika.*

Mudrá.—Mudrárákshasa*.

Nág.—Nágánanda.*

Pañchar.—Pañcharátra of Bhása.*

Priy.—Priyadarśiká.

Pt.—Pañchatantra.*

Ragh.—Raghuvaṃśa. (I.-X.)*

Râm.—Rámáyaṇa.

Ratn.—Ratnâvalî.*

Ṛitus.—Ṛitusaṃhára.*

S.—Sûtra.

S'ák.–Śákuntala of Kálidása.*

S.-D.—Sáhityadarpaṇa.

Sid.-Kau.—Siddhánta-Kaumudî.

Śree—Śreenivasacharear.

S'iś'.—Śiśupálavadha.

Subhá.—Subháshita.

Svap.-Vâs.—Svapnavâsavadatta of Bhása.

Uttar.—Uttararámacharita.*

Várt.—Várttika.

Veṇî.—Veṇîsaṃhára.*

Vikr.—Vikramorvaśîya.*

Vikr.-Ch.—Vikramâṅkadevacharita of Bilhaṇa.

*Annotated by the Editor.

NOTES.

ACT I.

P. 1. **प्रियदर्शिका**—Properly the name of the heroine; it then metaphorically (by the metaphorical transference of an epithet अभेदोपचार) signifies the play of which Priya. is the Heroine. The poet's other play, Ratnâvalî, is similarly named.

Following the custom of previous writers the poet begins his work with the usual *Mangala*, which consists of a salutation to the favourite deity or a benediction, and which is believed to have the power to remove obstacles in the way of, and to lead to a safe completion, the work undertaken. This is technically called *Nândî* in the case of dramas. The efficacy of a *Mangala* is thus stated by Patanjali in his Mahâbhâshya—मङ्गलादीनि मङ्गलमध्यानि मङ्गलान्तानि च शास्त्राणि प्रथन्ते वीरपुरुषकाण्यायुष्मत्पुरुषकाणि च भवन्त्यध्येतारश्च प्रवक्तारो भवन्ति । Śriharsha has glorified Pârvatî and Śiva in this play, as he has done in the Ratnâ. also. He pays his veneration to Pârvati first, owing to her being the more respectable of the two, as being the mother of the world (मातुरभ्यर्हितत्वात् as remarked by Malli. in his com. on Ragh. I. 1.).

Śl. 1. The śl. describes the emotion of Gauri (Pârvatî) at the time of her marriage with Śiva, wherein Brahmâ, as was meet, was the officiating priest joining their hands. *Cf.* Śiva Pu.—ब्रह्मा सर्वं च तत्रत्यं कारयामास वै तदा । आवाहनं तथा पाद्यं सर्वं च विधिपूर्वकम् ॥.........संस्थाप्याग्निं पुनस्तत्र वैवाहमकरोद्विधिम् ॥ &c. Construe—करग्रहविधौ धूमव्याकुलदृष्टिः पुनः इन्दुकिरणैः आह्लादिताक्षी उत्सुका वरं पश्यन्ती भूयः ब्रह्मणः ह्रिया आनतमुखी पादनखेन्दुदर्पणगते गङ्गां दधाने हरे सेर्ष्या स्पर्शाद् उत्पुलका गौरी वः शिवाय अस्तु ।

धूमव्या०—The smoke was due to the offerings made into the fire that witnessed the match; for the offerings *cf.* हविःशमीपल्लवलाजगन्धी पुण्यः कृशानोरुदियाय धूमः । Ragh. VII. 26. **व्याकुल** pained or disturbed. This was because the bride is required to inhale the smoke. लाजाहोमं कृत्वा धूममाजिघ्रेत् इति गृह्यविदः । *Cf.* Ragh. VII. 27. आचारधूमग्रहणाद्बभूव (वृद्धाचाराद्धूमग्रहणमित्येके); see Kum. VII. 81. and *cf.* for the smoke Par. p. I. 1. **इन्दुकिरणैः**—When she looked up the pain was removed by the soothing rays of the moon on Śiva's head. **उत्सुका**—This description is rather conventional. The bride is anxious to see her husband and gets the first opportunity to see him after the removal of the cloth held between the two when the Mangalâshtakas are over. But in

Gaurî's case she had already seen S'iva before the marriage ह्रिया—She felt shame for fear of being observed by Brahmâ who was there serving as the uniting priest. आनत०—may also be separated as नत०. भूयोह्रिया may also be taken as a comp. word (through excessive shame); but this is not very satisfactory. सेर्ष्या—Full of jealousy; for she saw *Gangá* on the head of Śiva's image as mirrored in her bright nails. At first she had not seen her as she dared not look long at Śiva in the presence of Brahmâ. Pârvatî is often represented as jealous of Gangá regarded as her co-wife. *Cf.* Mud. I. 1; तद्युक्तं बहुमार्गगां मम पुरो निर्लज्जबोद्धुस्तव; Ratná. I. ślॱ between 2 and 3. पादनखेन्दु०—For comp. see com.; the double comparison is rather unpoetic. Strangely enough Sans. poets represent the nails of fine ladies (and also of men) as lustrous enough to take in images. *Cf.* सिञ्जन्मणिनूपुरपुटेन ....अङ्कुष्ठेनाहूत इव चरणनखेषु निपपात । Kâd. p. 292.

स्पर्शानुत्पुलका—The standing of the hair on end caused by touch is one of the eight Sâtvika Bhâvas (or involuntary manifestations of strong feeling). It is considered as the first outward indication of love and is often referred to by poets; *cf.* Vik. I. 11; Kum. VII. 77 (रोमोद्गमः प्रादुरभूदुमायाः), Ragh. VII. 22. &c. *Cf.* with this śl. आदौ प्रेमकषायिता हरमुखव्यापारलोला शनैर्व्रीडाभारविघूर्णिता मुकुलिता धूमोद्गमव्याजतः । पत्युः संमिलिता कृशा सरभसव्यावर्तनव्याकुला पार्वत्याः परिणीतिमङ्गलविधौ दृष्टिः शिवायास्तु वः ॥ Pâr. p. I. 1. कैलासाद्रौ &c.—The reference here is to Rávana's lifting up the mountain Kailaśa when it was shaken to its foundation, causing alarm to Pârvatî and others who lived on it. To quiet Pârvatî's fear S'iva pressed down the mountain with his foot and Râvaṇa escaped being crushed under it only by pacifying the deity. This is also constantly referred to by poets; *cf.* कैलासश्रियमिव दशमुखोन्मूलनक्षोभनिपतितां; Kâd. p. 211; समुत्क्षिपन्यः पृथिवीभृतां वरं वरप्रदानस्य चकार शूलिनः । त्रसत्तुषाराद्रिसुतासंभ्रमस्वयंग्रहाश्लेषसुखेन निष्क्रयम् ॥ Sis. I. 50; गत्वा चोर्ध्वं दशमुखभुजोच्छ्वासितप्रस्थसन्धेः कैलासस्य &c. Meg. I. 61; see also Râmâ. Uttar. K. canto XVI. Construe उद्धस्ते कैलासाद्रौ परिचलति सति गणेषु उल्लसत्कौतुकेषु सत्सु, कुमारे मातुः क्रोडं विशति सति विषमुचि सरोषं पश्यति सति पादा०द्भुपुषि दशमुखे पातालमूलं याति सति क्रुद्धोपि उमया भयघनम् आश्लिष्टमूर्तिः अतः तुष्टः शिवः वः पातु.

उद्धस्ते—Trown or torn up. गणेषु—The *gaṇas* are the attendants of Śiva, being a race of demigods called Pramathas and are under the superintendance of Ganeśa, one of the demigods. They are thus described in the Kâlikâ P.—विचित्ररूपाभरणा जटाचन्द्रार्धमण्डिताः । आकाशमार्गे गच्छन्तमनुगच्छन्ति नित्यशः ॥ ध्यानस्थं परिचर्यन्ति सलिलाद्रिमिरीश्वरम् । नानाशस्त्रधराः शम्भोर्गणास्तु प्रमथाः स्मृताः ॥ &c. उल्लस०—Their curiosity was roused by the sudden shaking of the mountain. कुमारे—Kárttikeya, when an infant. विशति—*i. e.* through fear. विषशुचि—The serpent on the body of Śiva. Śiva is described as having huge serpents on his person, coiled round his neck, or arms, &c ; *cf* हित्वा तस्मिन् भुजगवलयं शंभुना दत्तहस्ता Meg. I. 63; करेण शम्भोर्वलयीकृताहिना Kum. V. 66. श्मशानचारी सततं व्यालाभरणभूषणः। S'iva P.

P. 2. पादावष्टम्भ०—पादेन अवष्टम्भः—supporting *i. e.* steadying it by the (pressure of the) foot., तेन; or पादस्य अवष्टम्भः the firm planting of. S'iva planted his foot firmly on the mountain to make it steady, which pressed down Rávana and hence सीदद्वपुषि whose body was pained or afflicted. पाताल०—He was sinking down to the surface of Pâtâla under the pressure exerted on the mountain by S'iva's foot. क्रुद्धः—He was angry that his mountain should have been torn up and his peace disturbed. आश्लिष्टमूर्तिः अनत्सुष्टः—For idea *cf.* the śl. from Sis. quoted above.

नान्द्यन्ते—नान्दी is the stanza or stanzas of benediction. For its difinition see com.; it is derived as नन्दन्ति देवता अस्यामिति नान्दी; fr. नन्द् and aff. घञ् (अ) with the fem. ई added. Another way is—आशीर्योगाद्विना नन्दतीति नन्दः; नन्द एव नान्दः by adding अ (अण्) स्वार्थे (प्रज्ञादित्वादण्); ततः स्त्रियां ङीप्. As the drama developed the cumbrous preliminaries of the prelude (पूर्वरङ्ग) were dispensed with, नान्दी the most important of them being retained. It then formed an essential part of the prologue. This Nândî is of four kinds, *viz.* नमस्कृतिर्माङ्गलिकी आशीः पत्रावली तथा। नान्दी चतुर्धा निर्दिष्टा नाटकादिषु धीमता ॥ The subject matter of the plot ought to be slightly indicated in the Nândî; and it is done in the present Nândî also. Thus धूमव्याकु० suggests Priya.'s long sorrow caused by her own state and her father's overthrow by the Kaling,a-king. इन्दुकिरणैः &c.—refers to the delight caused to her eyes by the sight of the king and later of her father's chamberlain. पश्यन्ती वरं refers to her looking longingly at the king Vatsa. and her desire for a union with him. आनतमुखी shows that she had to observe reserve for concealing her love from the Queen and her servants. The second śl. refers to Dṛdhavarman's overthrow and his being restored to power again by the interference of king Vatsa; as also to the queen's anger and her final reconciliation with him. See com.

नान्द्यन्ते सूत्र०—supply आह, ब्रूते or some such word to complete the sense. Now the question arises—Who recited the Nândî ? If the Sûtra., according to the precept.—सूत्रधारः पठेत्तत्र मध्यमं स्वरमाश्रितः । नान्दीं पदैर्द्वादशभिः &c. (Nát. Sû. V. 98), his name should have preceded the ślokas of the Nândî.

Two explanations are offered. The name of the Sûtra. is not put first because nothing but auspicious words can begin a work. *Cf.* in this connection the Sûtra of Pân. वृद्धिरादैच् which begins his अष्टाध्यायी (and not आदैज्वृद्धिः like अदेङ् गुणः). The other is—The Sûtra. or manager of the पूर्वरङ्ग recited the Nândî. And he having retired, the manager of the play (नाटकस्य सू०) entered and began the play. But as the discussion is immaterial to the ordinary reader we do not further enter into it here.

सूत्रधारः—The chief manager of the play, who held as it were the threads of the business of the play. He assigned to the various actors the parts they were to play, instructed them and took a leading part in the prologue.

वसन्तोत्सवे—The vernal festival seems to have been one of the occasions on which plays were publicly staged. The spring festival was formerly celebrated from about the middle of the bright half of Chaitra to the full-moon day to mark the return of spring, when Kâmadeva or the god of love was worshipped with great pomp. According to some, the festival began from the 5th of Mâgha and lasted for about two months. It is now identified with the Holi-festival in which people of all grades of society mix with one another and make merry. The Bhavishyottara Purâna gives a full description of this, for which see Wilson's H. T. p. 264. The passage from अद्याहं to सर्वो गुणानां गणः is almost the same in all the three plays of the poet, with इन्द्रोत्सवे instead of वसन्तोत्सवे (which is an optional reading there also) in the Nâgânanda.

श्रीहर्षः—For Harsha see Introd.; देवस्य-देव fr. दिव् to shine originally meant one shining or brilliant; then it came to mean 'a god (Lat. *deus*), and lastly came to be added to the names of kings as a term of respect and greatness; *cf.* Vikramadeva, Vikramânkadeva, &c. पादपद्मो०—living or subsisting by (the support of) the lotus-like-feet &c.—a respectful way of saying —the humble servants or vassals of. राजसमूहेन—This refers especially to the eighteen kings that owed allegiance to Harsha and his two allies, the king of Valabhi and Bhâskaravarman, king of Prâgjyotisha (Assam). अपूर्व—goes with रचना; such as has not been shown before; novel, extraordinary. We cannot take अपूर्व as qualifying वस्तु as the theme of the play was not invented by the poet. रचना is the skilful arrangement of the various parts and incidents leading to a charming end. The poet means that he has borrowed the theme but presented it in a new charming way. प्रियदर्शिका—named after प्रिय०, the princess of Anga, and the heroine of the play.

P. 3. नाटिका—see Introd. Sec I. परम्परा—is a word by itself (अव्युत्पन्नं प्रातिपदिकं) meaning a series or succession of. श्रोत्र०—coming from ear to ear, hearsay. श्रुतं—श्रुता *v. l.* is bad as it cannot be syntactically connected with नाटिका owing to the presence of इति; or इति ought to be dropped. प्रयोगतः—प्रयोग is the representation or exhibition on the stage. अनुग्रहबुद्ध्या—With the thought or object of, *i. e.* with the wish to favour us. *Cf.* प्रणयिषु वा दाक्षिण्यादथवा सद्वस्तुपुरुषबहुमानात्। &c. Vik. I. 2. यथावत्—separately-in due form, in a proper way; or as compounded (यथावत्प्र०),. representation in toto, or as it is; leaving out nothing. नेपथ्यरचनां—The word नेपथ्य is derived as निनः (नि *neu.* the eye) or नेः (ने a leader) पथ्यं good, pleasing or beneficial to, and means—(1) dress, or (2) decoration; it also means, (3) the tiring room (where the decorations are made, or the actors put on their dress); and (4) the drop curtain (जवनिका). –रचना (here) the arrangement of the tiring room (such as the assignment of parts to the actors, giving them instructions as to costume, acting and so on). आवर्जितानि—p. p. p. of वृज् cau. with आ to incline, &c.; drawn to us, attracted. सामाजिकाः—Those who gather in an assembly, the audience; ठक् (इक) is added to a word denoting combination in the sense of 'those who assemble there'; or समाजं रक्षन्ति those who keep an assembly by their presence.

निपुणः—skilled in the art of poetry, *i. e.* having the skill attained by the observation of the ways of the world and by the study of the Śástra and good poems; *cf.* शक्तिर्निपुणतालोकशास्त्रकाव्याद्यवेक्षणात्। Kâv. Pra. I. 2. गुणग्राहिणी—otherwise our skill will be vainly exhibited. This is an encouraging fact. *Cf.*

> " And as you are known,
> the first and happiest hearers of the town, "
> Shakespeare's Henry VIII, Prologue.

हारि—हर्तुं शीलमस्य naturally attractive; the word is generally used as the last part of a comp., as मनोहारि, हावहारि; दुष्टे विष्टपहारिणीदृक्हरो Bh. N. 25, &c. वत्सराज०—वत्सानां राजा वत्सराजः the king of the Vatsa country (for which, see Introd., geography of the play). This was Udayana, the son of Sahasrânîka, a king of the lunar race. This geneology is thus given in the Kathâs.—पाण्डु–अर्जुन–अभिमन्यु–परीक्षित्–जनमेजय–शतानीक–सहस्रानीक–उदयन. According to the Vishnu P., he was the son of a second Sahasrânîka,

19th in succession from Janamejaya, which appears to be more probable. Mahâsena, also called Chanda-Mahâsena, the king of Ujjayinî, had a daughter of exquisite beauty, named Vâsavadattâ, whom he wished to give in marriage to Vâtsarâja. (According to another account to a king named Sanjaya; see the quotation, from. Mâl. Mâd. below). With this object he enticed* Udayana to his city and kept him a captive there. Being engaged to teach music to Vâsavadattâ he gained her heart and by the advice of his minister Yaugandharàyaṇa, managed to escape with her to his capital. They were afterwards married in great pomp. For the full account see Kathâ. Lambaka II. tar. 11, 12. **हारि चरितं**—This is proved by the various references to his name; *cf.* प्राप्यावन्तीनुदयनकथाकोविदग्रामवृद्धान् । Meg. I. 30; प्रद्योतस्य प्रियदुहितरं वत्सराजोऽत्र जह्रे । Ibid. I. 33; उत्तेजयामि सुहृदः परिमोक्षणाय यौगन्धरायण इवोदयनस्य राज्ञः । Mṛch. IV. 26. वासवदत्ता च राज्ञे संजयाय पित्रा दत्तमात्मानमुदयनाय प्रायच्छत् । Mâl. Mad. II. **नाट्ये**—नाट्य here means dramatic representation. **वयं**—by this he refers to himself and the other actors. **वस्तु**—a thing, an item; this is different from वस्तु in अपूर्ववस्तुरचना above. **एकैकं**—एक repeated is to be taken as a Bah. comp. (by एकं बहुव्रीहिवत् । Pân. VIII. 1. 9) and dissolved as एकमेकं, the case term. of the first word being dropped in being compounded. **०फल**—is here reputation and money. **पदं**—an abode, *i. e.* source of. **पुनः**—implies पक्षान्तर (what then when &c.). **मद्भाग्योप०**—Here he refers to himself, as he is the principal person concerned. **गुणानां**—Favourable circumstances, advantages. *Cf.* एकैकमप्यनर्थाय किमु यत्र चतुष्टयम् । Hit. I.

This *śl.* is quoted in the Sâh. D. and D.-R. as an instance of प्ररोचना (or that which attracts the attention of the audience to the representation by a commendation of the poet, the play, the

---

* Mahâsena, though an enemy of Udayana, wished to give his daughter Vâsavadattâ in marriage to him, but doubting if he would accept her, he thought of the following expedient for bringing about the union. Seeing that Udayana spent his days and nights in the forests he thought of making him a prisoner, and with this view he caused a woooden elephant to be made and concealed some armed men in it. It was then placed in the forest. When Udayana came across it, the armed men came out and seeing him alone, seized and made him a prisoner. He was then brought before Mahâsena who gave his daughter Vâsavadattâ in his charge and told him that he would be set at liberty when he gave his daughter instructions and training in music (गन्धर्वविद्या). Gadre.

proficiency of the actors, &c.) one of the *angas* of भारतीवृत्ति, which is thus defined—निवेदनं प्रयोज्यस्य निर्देशो देशकालयोः । काव्यार्थसूचकैः शब्दैः सभायाश्चित्तरञ्जनम् । कविकाव्यनटादीनां प्रशंसा च प्ररोचना ॥

नेपथ्याभि°—Towards the curtain or screen (that separated the tiring room behind the stage from the stage itself. अये—shows surprise. —नाम्युपते—engaged in, busy with; this reminds one of Bhâsa, who begins some of his plays with अये कथं or किन्नु खलु विज्ञापनव्यग्रे, मयि (see Svap., Pancha., Mad. Vyá., &c.). अङ्गाधि°—For Anga, see Introd. वृद्धवर्मणः—does not seem to be the name of a real historic personage. It is probably invented by the poet. भूमिका—part. अस्मद्भ्राता—In the Ratnâ. also the younger brother of the Sûtra. is introduced as assuming the character of Yaugandharâyaṇa. This form of introduction is called प्रयोगातिशय. प्रस्तावना—प्रस्तावयति (that which introduces the subject matter) इति; fr. प्रस्तु+अन (युच्) added कर्तरि, with the fem. आ. The प्रस्ता° is also called आमुख; for its definition, see com. The प्रस्ता° here is a simple affair, as in the plays of Bhâsa, no other character than the Sûtra. being introduced.

P. 4. कञ्चुकी—The Kanchukî forms almost a necessary character of Sans. plays. He is generally introduced as an old man lamenting over his misfortune, having to serve even when worn out by age. *Cf.* Vik. III. 1, Mud. III. 1, &c. He was probably so called from the long cloak (कञ्चुक) he wore. He was the superintendent of the female apartments of kings, was a Brâhmana by caste and had various good qualities-see com. नाटयन्—नाटयित्वा &c. are used to indicate that the Actor shows that he does something or represents by some conventional gesture or expression a particular state of feelings or mood.

राज्ञो विपत्—shows how sincerely the Chamberlain loved his king. दुर्गम°—देशच्युति there was, but to make matters worse, he had to pass through tractless regions, as he had to bear with him secretly the princess. अस्याः—this, *i. e.* marked by such happenings. कटु°—कटुः अत एव निष्फला. कटु cannot be taken separately, as the happenings mentioned above were not the result of his long continued old age. Śl. quoted in Dhanika's com. on D. R. IV. 9, as an example of dejection caused by misfortune (आपद्).

नाम—as was well known (प्राकाश्ये); or it may be कुत्सने (and yet, oh irony of fate). अप्रतिहत—Unobstructed, always successful. शक्तित्रय—The three regal powers, *viz.* प्रभावः or प्रभुश°—

the power arising from an efficient army and a good treasury (स प्रभावः प्रतापश्च यत्तेजः कोषदण्डजं Amara); मन्त्रश॰ or the power arising from good counsel (*i. e.* a wise ministry), and उत्साह or the personal energy of the king. रघु॰—रघु॰ was the celebrated son of Dilîpa; नल king of Nishada–names well known to the Indian student. प्रार्थ्यमाना—earnestly sought, solicited. बद्धानु॰—who entertained a deep feeling of resentment. लब्धरन्ध्रेण—who found a loop-hole, *i. e.* a weak point, as Vatsarâja was not expected to come to Dṛdh.'s assistance. कलिङ्ग॰—For कलिङ्ग see Introd.; कलिङ्गानां जनपदानां राजा कलिङ्गः स चासौ हतकश्च । यसत्यं—To speak, the truth, truly. उपपन्नं—Although come to pass or happened, a fact. यथाकथंचित्—Lit. as circumstances would permit, somehow. अनृणं—Free from debt. He believed that his master had contracted a debt as it were, when he promised to give his daughter in marriage to king Vatsa and that he (Kanch.) would free him from it by taking the princess to king Vatsa. अवस्कन्दसम्भ्रम—The flurry and confusion caused by the attack, the comparison to प्रलयकाल shows that the attack was sudden and caused terrible havoc. अपवाह्य—The object is तां (राजपुत्रीं). आटविकस्य—अटव्यां भवः आटविकः ruling over a forest tract, a forest king. विन्ध्यकेतोः—Vind. seems to have been a petty king, as he was so easily routed. अगस्त्यतीर्थ—appears from the context to be some holy place in the Vindhya regions, near the hermitage of Agastya described by Bâna in his Káda. An Agastyatîrtha, a place of pilgrimage, is located in the province of Tinnevelly in the extreme south of India. निपत्य—Having attacked. दस्युभिः—By marauders or robbers. दस्यु is one of the old Vedic words (a class of demons or enemies of gods and men, slain by Indra) that remain in classical Sans. प्रद्योत॰—Another name of Mahâsena or Chanda-mahâ., so say the commentators on Kâli.'s Meg. I. 34. wherein there is a reference to this king—प्रद्योतस्य प्रियदुहितरं वत्सराजोऽत्र जह्रे) and this appears to be correct from Bhâsa's Svap. Vâ. According to the Katha. Pradyota was the king of Magadha and a person different from Mahâsena. The name of his daughter also was Padmâvatî. See Kathâ. XV. 19. 20 and our note on प्रद्योत, at Meg. I. 34. कौशाम्बी—the capital of the Vatsa country, was once a flourishing city, though now remaining as an insignificant village. See Intro.

P. 5. जर्जरीकृतः—Hacked or terribly disabled by, mangled. सफलयिष्यामि—सफलय् a denom. from सफलं (सफलं करिष्यामि). शरदातपस्य—The autumnal heat is described as very fierce. तीक्ष्णः—Hot, burning.

S'l. 5. घनबन्धन &c.—This and the other words in this S'l. are paronomastic (श्लिष्ट); *cf.* for a similar use of ślesha, Rat. I. 8. Cons.—घनबन्धनमुक्तः कन्याग्रहणात्परं तुलां प्राप्य अधिगतस्वधामा अर्थे रविः घनबन्ध० स्वधामा वत्सराज इव प्रतपति। घनब०—(1) The covering or screen formed by clouds; (2) close imprisonment. कन्या०—(1) entering into the sign Virgo; (2) The seizing of the Princess. परां तुलां *v. l.*—the sign libra coming next after कन्या; (2) High eminence, supreme greatness. अधिगतस्व०—(1) who had regained his usual brilliancy; (2) who had come back to his abode or country. प्रतपति—(1) burns fiercely; (2) shows his power eminently. See com.

विष्कम्भकः—For def. see com.; it is an interlude at the beginning of an act, briefly indicating the events past and those to come. It is called S'uddha when introduced by one or more minor characters (मध्यपात्र) and संकीर्ण when introduced by minor and low (नीचमध्यम) characters. See also note on प्रवेशक *infra* Act IV, p. 46.

विदूषकः—The confidant and constant companion of the hero and one of the necessary characters of the Sans. plays. Although a Bráhmana he is represented as ugly in appearance, fond of food and easily falling asleep. He generally assists his chief in love-matters; but his principal duty is to stir laughter by his fantastic dress, &c.; see com.

Śl. 6. In this śl. the king states how his temporary imprisonment was beneficial to him in more ways than one. With the feeling of satisfaction expressed here *cf.* Rat. I. 9 and Nag. I. 7. अविकारिता—विकार एषामस्तीति विकारिणः न विका० अविकारिणः तेषां भावः अविकारिता the state of being unaffected by disloyalty, &c., hence sincere loyalty, steady love. परिगता—Fully known; for this sense *cf.* परिगतपरिगन्तव्य एव भवान्। Veni. III. p. 15. प्रथमपरिगतार्थस्तं रघुं संनिवृत्तं Ragh. VII. 71. मतिः—mental ability, insight in political matters. पौराणां—See Kathá. II. 4. 34, 35. निर्व्यूढा—Fully carried out, put into execution. रणसाहस—see com. व्यसनिता—Extreme fondness for, love of. निर्व्याजात्—Free from guile or hypocrisy; practised with sincere devotion to God; *cf.* धर्मः प्रोज्झितकैतवः &c. Bhag. P. I. 1. 1; किमिव न प्राप्तं—For धर्म (religious merit obtained by the proper performance of religious rites) leads to the accomplishment of every thing. *Cf.* नोपुष्टे कोपि धर्माय सर्वाभिप्रेतहेतवे।; and Mah. Bhár. त्रिवर्गोयं धर्ममूलो नरेन्द्र राज्यं चेदं धर्ममूलं वदन्ति। The rhetorical fig. in this śl. is Vibhávaná.

P. 6. दास्याः पुत्रं—may also be a comp. word. There is an optional अलुक् of the Gen. when censure is implied and the word

पुत्र forms the second member (षष्ठ्या आक्रोशे । पुत्रेऽन्यतरस्याम् । Pân. VI. 3. 21, 22); lit.—a whore's son, used humourously by the Vidû. as a term of contempt; that cursed (imprisonment). It is used with persons or with inanimate objects as here; *cf.* एते दास्याः पुत्रा अर्थकल्यवर्ताः &c. Mṛch. I. p. 13. खलखलायमान०—This and the other epithets apply to the king as well as to the गजपति. खलखलायमान is the pres. p. of the Atm. verb formed from खलखल an onomatopoetic word, by adding य (क्यष्). A final आ (डाच्) is added to the final half of a word indicating sound when the word consists of at least two syllables; and words ending in आ take the denom. aff. य (क्यष्) by लोहितादिडाज्भ्यः क्यष् । Pân. III. 1. 13. For comp. see com. प्रतिस्खलत्—stumbling at evey step. शून्य०—शून्य properly lonely, solitary (शूनायै प्राणिवधाय हितं रहस्यस्थानत्वात्); fr. शूना animal slaughter and aff. य (यत्); here (1) शून्य without animation, dejected; मुखपुष्कर lotus-like face or countenance; (2) शून्य dry, devoid of moisture मुखं cavity यस्य तादृशं पुष्करं the tip of the trunk; तेन पिशुनितः indicated, हृदयसंतापो यस्य. The passage here is somewhat obscure. Mr. Gadre following Jîv.'s ed. reads शून्यदुष्कर (दुःखर) पिशुनयद्धृदय०; but as remarked by him, it is difficult to assign a meaning to this. It is explained as शून्यं unaffected by any feeling दुष्करं experiencing pain, (दुःखरं *v. l.* दुःखं राति इति) पिशुनयत् indicating internal affliction (अन्तःसन्तापसूचकं) यद् हृदयं तस्य संतापो यस्य. But this is not satisfactory. शून्यदुष्करहृदयसन्तापः *v. l.* is also equally unintelligible. It may be explained as शून्यश्चासौ दुष्करहृदयसन्तापश्च. उत्तम्भित—raised and fixed upwards. शुण्डकर—(1) huge arms; (2) large trunk. अधिगतधरणिपृष्ठः—*v. l.* (1) lying on the bare ground; (2) throwing himself on the surface of the earth. अनिद्रासुखं—may also be taken as an adv. comp.; अविद्यमानं निद्रासुखं यस्मिन्कर्मणि तद्यथा तथा । It is also explained as निद्रासुखस्याभावः अनिद्रासुखं (अर्थाभावेऽव्ययीभावः). The reading of the Mad. ed. निद्रासुखं न प्राप्नोषि is easier. अनुवाचयसि—may mean-you repeatedly spoke of. वसन्तक—This name occurs in the Rat. also and is taken from the story of Udayana.

Śl. 7. चारकं—also *mas.*, a prison; see Das. ch. p. 59. निगल—same as निगड a chain, fetters; ल may be substituted for ड. The śl. shows how the impression made on the king's mind by the charms of Vâsa. quite overshadowed the hardships of imprisonment. And this was a fact; *cf* तस्य दृष्ट्वा तु तां कन्यां वत्सराजस्य मानसम् । तथा स्नेहाक्रममभवन्न यथा मन्युमेक्षत । Kathâ. II. 4. 29. सगर्वं—Because he thought that he could here hit the king on his own ground. Mark the pun on the word बध्नासि.

P. 7. विजयसेनस्य—In the Rat. it is Vijayavarman (the son of Ruma.'s sister) who figures as a general under Rumaṇvat. Why the expedition was sent against Vindhyaketu is not stated here. Káli., when he makes his hero Agnimitra send an expedition against an enemy furnishes a reason for it. अमात्यः रुम०-Ruma. spoken of here as a minister appears in the Rat. (see p. 92) and elsewhere as a general of king Vatsa. In Bhâsa's Sva. Vâs., however, he is called अमात्य; अस्ति रुमण्वानमात्यो वृद्धं प्रयत्नवान् &c. I. In the Kathâsar, he is mentioned as a general assisting Yaugandharáyaṇa in state matters-यौगन्धरायणश्चास्य महामन्त्री विनिर्गशम्। सेनापती रुमण्वांश्च राज्यभारमुदूहतुः॥ Lamb. III. 1. 4. तत्क्षणमपि &c.—It is usual with ministers (and other servants) to pour forth such a complaint when going into the presence of their masters. This shows that even in ancient times the ministerial office was as not a rosy bed. *Cf.* Rat. I. 7, IV. 20 last lines; Mud. V. 12; and for a similar thought Mâl. अहो दुरासदो राजमहिमा। न च परिचितो न चाप्यगम्यश्चकितमुपैमि तथापि पार्श्वमस्य। I. 11. ०मपि—The force of अपि is this—though the interval between their first visit and the next be extremely short and so there is very little chance of their having committed a fault, still.

P. 8. यादृशः &c.—This is meant as a compliment to the king. He means—as disastrous as can be expected when he is angry. यथादिष्टेन—A Karm. Comp. पदाति—पादाभ्यामतति गच्छति इति पदातिः a foot-soldier; from पाद् changed to पद् (by पादस्य पदाज्यातिगोपहतेषु Pân. VI. 3. 52) and अत् to go with affix अ (अण्). The mention of the threefold army here shows that the use of the chariots in battle, the fourth element of the ancient Hindu army, was abandoned at least in Harsha's time. तुमुल—Tumultuous.

बलवाहनः—बल army; वाहन vehicles, conveyances; *cf.* for this sense अपवर्जितं च कोशवाहनं; p. 63, तत्कोशवाहनमवशीर्णं p. 201, Das. ch. I, VIII; or बल infantry and वाहन horse, *i. e.* cavalry; for वाहन meaning a horse *cf.* विना वाहनहस्तिभ्यो मुच्यतां सर्वबन्धनम्। Mud. VII. 17; Ragh. I. 48, IX. 25. अनवेक्षित०—*v. l.* Without inspecting and equipping &c. यथासंनि०—For comp. see com. स्वनाम उद्घोषयन्—It was customary for warriors to declare their names before engaging in combat; for it was held derogatory to the dignity of a hero of family to fight with a nameless person. शोभितं—What is worthy or creditable. अयमसाविति—*i. e.* at the sight of one whom we had to annihilate. विमर्दः—Hard-pressing. महता विमर्देन—By a fierce attack, or charge. निःशेषित—To a man, totally. विमर्दिताधिक०—विमर्दितं is used as a noun here by the wholesale slaughter (of his followers); for comp. see com. संप्रहारः—a fight, battle; or striking, dealing out blows; *cf.* तद्वीरघात्यसुपसंहृतसंप्रहारः Uttar. VI. 7 (where संप्र० may have both the meanings); युधि संप्रहारं प्रचक्रतु रामनिशाविहारौ। Bhatti. II. 36.

Śl. 9. पादातं—The body of foot-soldiers; fr. पदाति and aff• अण् (अ) by Pân. IV. 2. 38. See com. दूरात्—standing afar; दूरं *v. l.* is not good as the idea is included in आशाः नीत्वा. अश्वीयं—cavalry; by Pân. IV. 2. 48 (see com.), the affixes छ (ईय) and अण् (अ) are added to अश्व; so आश्वं also.

P. 9. प्रहरणनिवहः—*Cf.* for these चापचक्रकृपाणशक्तितोमरगदाप्रभृतिषु। Kâd. I. p. 26 उत्खाय—Having drawn out or unsheathed. ०कानन-च्छेदलीलां—छेद एव लीला (the sport of) तां is equivalent to स लीलया छेदनं cutting of with the ease with which &c.; *cf.* Ragh. XII. 96 (तां कूटशाल्मलीं चिच्छेद कदलीसुखम्);

Śl. 10. बलत्रितयं—see com. खचित—inlaid or covered with. अंसकूटः—The shoulder blade; his towering shoulders. जर्जरित—Shattered. P. p. p. of जर्ज् (cau. which also occurs as झर्झ्) " the resolution into जर्जरित-ऊरु (thighs) वक्षाः ' having wounded thighs and chest would be equally possible according to the rules of Sans. grammer, though not of Hindu chivalry. *Cf.* MBh. IX. 60. 5 V Col. Ed. p. 105. सत्पुरुषोचितं—Worthy of a man leading a pious life. A warrior killed while fighting face to face with an enemy also attains heaven; see com. and *cf.* Ragh. VII. 51. व्रीडिताः—Because he fought valiantly like a true hero and fell only when overpowered by odds. See com.

अनुमृतास्—Followed him in death; *i. e.* immolated themselves along with the dead body of their husband. सहधर्मचारिणी—A wife; सहधर्मचरण is one of the principal objects of a Hindu marriage; husband and wife (a धर्मपत्नी) must perform the holy rites together; *cf.* तदियं प्रतिगृह्यतां सहधर्मचरणाय। Śak. V. p. 125. विन्ध्यशिखरा०—The constr. is जनपदेषु विन्ध्यशिखराश्रितेषु. The additional reading विनष्टेषु (had fled away) makes no good sense; for the whole will mean ' when the people of the country who had already fled to the peaks of the Vind. mountain had fled away. But we are not told that they were pursued by the victors. कृपणः—miserable, pitiable. आभिजात्या०—endowed with a beauty in keeping with or befitting her noble birth. अभिजातरूपा *v. l.*—possessed of excellent beauty. तां प्रति—As regards her *i. e.* how she is to be dealt with or what is to be done with her.

P. 10. यशोधरे—This is the name of the Portress. भगिनी-बुद्ध्या—in the light of, considering her as, your sister. It will be seen in the last Act that this she turns out to be. गीतनृत्त°—These are the first three of the 64 arts often referred to by Hindu writers and mentioned by Vátsyáyana in his Kámasûtras, For these see our notes on Bha. Nit. Śat. p. 42. नृत्त–is different from नृत्य and consists of the rhythmical movement of the body (without gesticulation) and is regulated by the marking of musical intervals and time (नृत्तं ताललयाश्रयम् Das. R. I. 9). By आदि may be meant painting (आलेख्य) and others. These were considered as a necessary part of the accomplishments of a maiden of high family.

वैतालिकः—A bard or minstrel, whose principal duty in ancient times it was to announce metrically the close of the divisions of the day; *vide* Vik. II. 1; Rat. I, 23, &c.; sometimes two bards are mentioned; see Śák. V. 7, 8; Mudr. III. 20–28; &c.

Śl. 11. The cons. is ते स्नानभूमिः लीला...संपादिनः सर्वा......लोकस्य °वृत्तैः स्तनैः उत्क्षिप्त° कलशैः इव अलंकृता. For comps. see com. उपकरण—Articles necessary at a bath. स्नानीयं—Unguents or perfumed powders to be rubbed against the body; or a bathing garment; or a garment for wiping off the body after a bath, as at Mál. V. 12 (स्नानीयवस्त्रक्रियया). वारविभ्रमवती—वार a multitude; विभ्रमवती a woman; *cf.* विलासवती; hence वारवि°—a woman of the multitude, a courtezan or harlot; वार with any word meaning स्त्री has this sense. The courtezans formed also a part of the attendants of the harem. *Cf.* Kautilya's Arth.s I. 20. आयास—Exertions in the discharge of their several duties. स्खलत्—dropping or slipping down. अव्यहित—not concealed, exposed to view. व्यवहित—*v. l.* spreading out. छाया—splendour, gleam. अवदात—white, fair. शातकुम्भ—gold; or golden; fr. शतकुम्भ gold (said to be found in the शतकुम्भ mountain); in this latter case the form should be शातकौम्भ according to some. Their uncovered breasts on account of their size and colour looked like other pots of gold. For the presence of courtezans at the king's bath *cf.* राज्ञः समन्तादुपतस्थुः—गृहीतजलकलशाः स्नानार्थमभिषेकदेवता इव वारयोषितः । Kad. p. 32. सहस्रदीधितिः—सहस्रं दीधितयो यस्य; दीधीते that which shines इति दीधितिः *fem.*, a ray of light.

अये कथं &c.—We have almost the same words in the Nâga. introducing a description of the midday-sun with which the first Act of that play as of this closes. Here the poet has used the device of introduing a bard, as done by his great predecessor

2

Kálidása in his Mál. II. 12. to announce the mid-day which enables the king to bring the Act to a close.

Śl. 12. क्कथत्—shows the intensity of the summer heat; *cf.* तप्तं वारि विहाय &c. Vik. II. 23. शफर—a small fish, very active and sparkling. उद्वर्तन—a darting or turning upwards; *cf.* चटुलशफरोद्वर्तनप्रेक्षितानि Meg. I. 43. दीर्घिका—A large pond oblong in shape containing lotus-plants and attached to large houses; *cf.* विकचतामरसा गृहदीर्घिकाः Ragh. IX. 37; also XVI. 13. छत्राभं—छत्रस्य इव आभा यस्य; or better छत्रेण सदृशः; a nityasamása; *cf.* Amara—स्युरुत्तरपदे त्वमी। निभसंकाशनीकाशप्रतीकाशोपमादयः। बर्हभारं—बर्ह a peacock's tail; hence बर्हिन्, बर्हिण a peocock;—भारं the mass of feathers, plumage.

P. 11. आलवालं—(आ + लव + ला to take with आ and affix क *i. e.* अ) a basin for water round the root of a tree; *cf.* Ragh. I. 51; also Vik. II. 23. कपोलं—to which it was attracted by the presence of ichor there. कर्णपाली—the lobe of the ear. प्रविश्याभ्यन्तरं—The midday was the time when the king could retire to the interior of the palace and enjoy his leisure according to his pleasure; *cf.* षष्ठे भागे त्वमपि दिवसस्यात्मनश्छन्दवर्ती। Vik. II. 1 कृतयथोचितक्रियाः—Bathing, offering worship to the deities, &c.; see Kád. p. 33. कलिङ्गोच्छित्तये—*cf.* कोसलोच्छित्तये Rat. I. p. 8. विजयसेनं प्रेषयामः—The reason for this expedition and the success achieved by Vija. are mentioned in Act IV. See pp. 46, 50, 52.

ACT II.

आर्य—A form of address for a Bráhmaṇa, a minister and an elder brother; विप्रामात्याग्रजाश्चार्याः &c. D. Ru. उपवास०—Queens are often mentioned as observing a fast and abiding by its attendant rules. A स्वस्तिवायन is given on such an occasion and the Vidû. being a Bráhmaṇa and a companion of the king naturally comes to be its recipient. See Vik. III. 12; Rat. I. pp. 17, 26.

स्वस्तिवाचन—(also —नक) fr. स्वस्ति (indec. meaning 'a blessing') and वच् cau. and aff. ल्युट् (अन); स्वस्ति वाच्यते अनेन that by which one is made to pronounce a blessing. Primarily it refers to a ceremony preliminary to the performance of a religious rite or some solemn observance in which the Bráhmaṇas say

'स्वस्ति' to the Yajamána, and secondarily to the gift accompanying such a ceremony. It also refers to a present (called वायन–in Maráthi वाण–for the Prákrit सोत्थिवाअन is also rendered as स्वस्तिवायन in Sans.) which consists of a small quantity of rice, a cocoanut, a piece of cloth for a bodice, a comb, &c.; or sometimes of sweetmeats only-and is given to a Bráhmaṇa by a married woman whose hushand is living (सुवासिनी). For other particulars, see Rat. I. p. 26 and our note on the word; Vik. III. pp. 158, 160 शब्दापयेत्—will call; fr. शब्द + आप the taking up or utterance of; शब्दापं करोति शब्दापयति by adding णिच् (अय) in the sense of तत्करोति; see com. If the Prákrit सद्दाएदि be rendedred as शब्दायेत then it is derived from शब्द and the affix क्यङ् (य) which forms Atm. verbs (शब्दायते) by शब्दवैरकलहाभ्रकरणे। Pân. III. 1. 17.

धारागृहं—A summer house or a large bath-room; lit. a house furnished with water jets or fountains of water. *Cf.* शिलाविशेषानधिशय्य निन्युर्धारागृहेष्वातपमृद्धिमन्तः। Ragh. XVI. 49—ह्योद्यानं—The garden containing the धारागृह. कुक्कुटवादं—Uttering anything imitating the cry of a cock in the morning (*i. e.* gradually raising the tone and protracting the voice) so as to give it the appearance of a Vedic passage. See Pán. I. 2. 27. Vidû. means that he would recite something assuming the Vedic tone when receiving the Vâyana. For Vidû.'s knowledge of the Vedas, comp. the king's remark below, वेदसंख्ययेव &c. p. 12.

प्रतिग्रह—has the technical sense of 'the acceptance of a gift by a Bráhmaṇa (which is his peculiar prerogative); see Manus. I. 88; Yáj.s. I. 118. उत्कण्ठा—An eager desire to see or a great longing for, a beloved person. चिन्ता तु स्मृतिराध्यानं स्मरणं, सस्पृहे पुनः। उत्कण्ठोत्कलिके। इति शब्दार्णवः।

P. 12. Śl. 1. मङ्गलमात्र०—For comp. see com.; there are certain ornaments and things, which are considered as auspicious (being the emblems of Saubhâgya) and which a Hindn wife cannot discard under any circumstances. These are-the *mangalasutra* (a wreath of small glass beads with gold ones, the Kumkuma mark on the forehead, glass bangles, &c. Hence the queen is described as wearing these even when under a vow, when other gaudy ornaments are to be dispensed with. *Cf.* Vik. III. 12 (सितांशुका मङ्गलमात्रभूषणा). मन्दोद्यमा०—मन्दोद्यतालापिनीं *V. l.* मन्दं यथा तथा उद्यत आलापो यस्याः speaking in words gently uttered (on account of the weakness caused by fasting,). ०द्यमालापिनीं gives rise to an awkward comp.; the comp. may also be taken as मन्द् उद्यमो यस्मिन् स मन्दोद्यमः; म० आलपो यस्याः; in either case it indicates extreme emaciation. प्रातस्तन—तन is affixed to adverbs of time in the sense of 'belonging to that time'; cf. प्राक्तन, सायंतन, अद्यतन, &c.—शेन्दुद्युति—cf. प्रविगलत्यमं प्रातश्चन्द्रद्युति वपुः Mâl. Mâd. IV. 4. निश्चमोष०—is to be taken with क्षामं and the other accusatives. प्रथमानुराग०—For the effects of first love not gratified and a maiden's being more attractive then, cf. क्षामक्षामकपोलमाननं, शोच्या च प्रियदर्शना च मदनक्लिष्टेयमालक्ष्यते। Śak. IV. 8.

अर्चति—The pres. in the sense of 'immediate future,'—is going to honour with gifts. चतुर्वेद &c.—is evidently meant to be jocular. For comp. see com. ब्राह्मण्यं—ब्रह्म the Veda अधीते (Pân. VI. 2. 59) ब्रह्म जानाति (Pân. VI. 2. 92) इति ब्राह्मणः; तस्य भावः; Vedic scholarslip. महाब्राह्मण—महत् when prefixed to such words as ब्राह्मण, वैद्य, is depreciatory (निन्दायां). So in the Rat. राजा—(सस्मितं) साधु भवन्तं महाब्राह्मणं मुक्त्वा कोन्य एवमृचामामभिज्ञः। II. p. 43.

P. 13. अविरतं—Ceaselessly, incessantly. सुकुमार—soft to touch; or secondarily, charming. उत्सङ्ग—the surface or upper part of; cf. इभवो वासितोत्सङ्गाः Ragh. IV. 74; or उत्सङ्ग, the vicinity of. निलीन—stuck fast. बकुल—also called केसर is a large and tall tree having darkish green leaves and small round flowers of a pale-brown or white colour and sweet-smelling. मालती—मां लक्ष्मीं लातीति takes up; or मालं a garland तनोति; fr. तन्+डः i. e. अ) also called सुमनाः (as it gratifies the mind by its smell) is a kind of jasmine (jasminum glandiforum) having flowers of an exceedingly pleasing smell. Its oil is much prized as a perfume. उद्दामा—दाम्नः उद्गतः (free from the fastening string, i. e. restraint); or उद्गतं दाम यस्य (may be उद्दामा or-मः); moving unchecked, freely; or proud, strong; the wind is poetically fancied as proudly moving being charged with the fragrance of. पर्यस्तकुसुम—completely (परि) opened. बन्धूक—(also called बन्धुजीवक—बन्धुरिव जीवं जलं यस्य) is an erect growing plant having flowers of a bright red colour which expand at noon and drop next morning. Cf. Ragh. XI. 25 (wherein drops of blood are compared to the बन्धुजीव flowers); Kir. IV. 7. बन्धन the cases or stems of. तमाल—A dark-barked tree but having white flowers. पिहित—also अपिहित the अ of अपि and अव being optionally dropped. सश्रीकता—Lit. its being possessed of beauty; grandeur, loveliness; so Rat. I. प्रेक्षस्व तावद् मदनमहोत्सवस्य सश्रीकताम्। p. 11.

Śl. 2. क्षुद्रप्रवाल—tiny pieces of coral. शेफालिका—शेरते शेफाः bees अस्यां; is a small tree with rough scabrous leaves but fragrant flowers; *cf.* शेफालिकाकुसुमगन्धमनोहराणि । Rs. III. 14. **सप्तच्छद**—(छद a leaf, hence also called सप्तपर्ण, सप्तपत्र &c. having seven leaves per twig) Alstonia scholaris, is a large tree often referred to by poets as having the strong odour of the ichor of elephants. *Cf.* प्रसवैः सप्तपर्णानां मदरागसुगन्धिभिः । Ragh. IV. 23. **गजमदामोद**—आमोद is not appropriate with मद; it simply means 'scent' here. **रजःपुञ्जपिञ्ज०**—अङ्गराग unguent or paint applied to the body. **वारुणी**—Liquor in the form of the honey of flowers. For a similar thought, *cf.* अमी गीतारम्भैर्मुखरितलतामंडपभुवः परागैः पुष्पाणां प्रकटपटवासव्यतिकराः ।........समन्तादापानोत्सवमनुभवन्तीव मधुपाः ॥ Nag. III. 8.

एतदपि—the Prákrit एदं should rather have been translated by एतं as it refers to सप्तपर्णपादप, which is mas. **अविरल**—In quick succession, or, in clusters. **वर्षाः**—fem. pl.

Śl. 3. **बिभ्राणा**—The Nom.s qualify क्षितिः. मृदुता बिभ्राणा may also be taken separately. **शिरीष**—is a tall tree, attaining the height of thirty feet. Its flowers are known for their extreme delicacy. *Cf.* Kum. I. 41. Its flowers are worn by young ladies as ornaments on their ears; *cf.* Śak. I. 4; Ragh XVI. 48; Meg. II. 2.

P. 14. **उत्प्रेक्षितं**—उत्प्रेक्षा कृता; expressed metaphorically. **श्रीहारिभिः**—which possess (or, surpass) the beauty of, the Śirisha flowers being also of a darkish green colour; *cf.* शुकावलिर्व्यक्तशिरीषकोमला । Kir. IV. 36. **क्षोदैः**—क्षोद which usually means 'powder' must be taken to mean pieces or fragments here, as the adj. क्षालितैः will be inappropriate otherwise. **उत्करैः**—heaps, collections. **इन्द्रगोपक०**—the Indragopa (cochineal) insects which appear in clusters in the rainy season are also of a bright red colour and hence the Utprekshâ.

हञ्जे—A vocative particle used by a lady when addressing a maid-servant. See com.; हला is used between females of equal rank or position. **अगस्त्यमहर्षये**—see the two quotations by Pandit Krishnamachariar given in the com. **अर्घः**—A respectful offering or oblation to a deity or a venerable person, &c. consisting of rice, water, rubbed sandal, &c. The usual ingredients are—आपः क्षीरं कुशाग्रं च दधि सर्पिः सतण्डुलम् । यवः सिद्धार्थकश्चैव अष्टांगोऽर्घः प्रकीर्तितः ॥ So these flowers must be added to these, as in Yaj. I. 289, as they are specially mentioned here. Some translate अर्घो by अर्घ्यं; this is got by adding य to अर्घ by पादार्घाभ्यां च । Pán. V. 4, 25. अर्घः पूजाविधिः तदर्थं द्रव्यमर्घ्यम् । Sid. Kau. According to the second śl. quoted in the com. an Arghya ought to be offered to Agastya at the close of Bhádrapada (August—September), when

Agastya (the bright star Canopus ' of the constellation Argo Naves in the Southern celestial hemisphere) rises, for the attainment of all desires. Varâh. in his Br. Sam. says that a king should offer an Arghya to Agastya for the attainment of great power; सांवत्सरावेदितदिग्विभागे भूपोऽर्घमुर्व्यां प्रयतः प्रयच्छेत् । ch. XII. 15; for other particulars see 16–18. अस्ताभि०—Lit. desiring *i. e.* about to set; occurs again at p. 22. मुकुलाय्यन्ते—Pres. pass. of मुकुलायते denom. from मुकुल; are closed; *lit.* are made to assume the condition of buds. तपस्विनी—Lit. a female ascetic; and as ascetics require protection from others तपस्विन् secondarily means. ' one helpless or deserving pity, poor '; *cf.* हतस्तपस्वी वैरोचकः Muds II. p. 112 Sak. p.132

P. 15. सबाष्पो०—बाष्पेण उद्वेगेन च सहितं यथा तथा; उद्वेग agitation, mental pain or distress. नाम—is प्राकाश्ये. आज्ञाप्य स्थितया—who used to command; स्था with the gerund shows continuity of the act. एष दोषः—*viz.* आज्ञप्तिकरणं; that I have to obey others. Sâgarikâ also similarly refers to her misfortune that she has to serve, but not with regret as she had obtained a sight of the king. (तत्परप्रेषणदूषितमपि मे जीवितमेतस्य दर्शनेनेदानीं बहुमतं संवृत्तम् । p. 27). दुष्करमिदानीं &c.—This at first appears to mean ' I have thought of doing a hard thing *i. e.* committing suicide. But this does not seem to be intended. A'rany. finds it necessary to yield to her misfortune and says अथवा (used पक्षान्तरे) or why मया चिन्तितमिदानीं दुष्करं it is difficult to carry out my resolve. Again अपि after एतद् in वरमेतदपि will have no force. She would rather prefer servitude than avoid it by revealing her high birth. Had the first meaning been intended she would have said एतदेव. यथाभणितं further on also will be meaningless. She has not said any where that she would kill herself (although like Sâgarikâ she says it further on; see p. 24.). So यथाभणितं must be taken to mean ' as ordered by the Queen '; and this she proceeds to do in what follows. महार्घे—महान् अर्घः यस्य; lit. of high value; hence noble, exalted. का गतिः—What course or help is there ? this must be done. गुल्म—a thicket or cluster. निर्भरं—filled with, full of (at the end of a comp.).

P. 16. Sl. 4. Now he shows how the four senses (the fifth, tongue, being excluded) are gratified by the several things connected with the tank. सुखयति—Denom. fr. सुख; सुखं करोति, according to the Ganasûtra तत्करोति तदाचष्टे ।. नूपुराह्लाद०—*v. l.* is not good; in the first place नूपुर will have to be taken in the secondary sense of नूपुरनाद; 2ndly the word आह्लाद is redundant as the idea is expressed by सुखयति; thirdly the word occurs in the fourth line and such repetition is not poetic. सौधपाली—सुधा (chunam paint) अस्यास्तीति सौधः (also सौधं) a mansion (अण् i. e. अ being added in the sense of possession); पाली a row or series of; or rather पाली may mean 'the skirt or edge of'. परिमलपटुना—strong, or excellent by, or clearly perceived owing to, its perfume.

Sl. 5. कान्ति—Splendour, beauty;-हारिणी—(1) Attractive or charming by; (2) attractive like. By a bold metaphor the दीर्घिका is compared to the दृष्टि of the goddess of the garden. For a similar comparison *cf.* कृष्णसारछविर्योसौ दृश्यते काननश्रिया । वनशोभाव-लोकाय कटाक्ष इव पातितः ॥ Vik. IV. 31. कुसुमपरिमल०—This and the other epithets apply both to स्त्री and वनदेवता; for these see com. परिमलेन सुगन्धा; the reading सुगन्धि is bad; for we canrot have the final इ as the smell is not invariably connected with the *Veni*; now see com.; a row of bees was attracted by the perfume of flowers in the braid of hair. This is clear from the use of the word अपरे (मधुकराः) further on; see p. 19. In the second case ०वेणिरिव मधुकरावलिर्यस्याः having the line of bees for her braid of hair. उज्ज्वलन्ती—Glowing, bright, radiant. The comparison of the tender and slender arm of a woman to a creeper is common enough in Sans. literature. विकल्प—Different thoughts or surmises. यत्सत्यं—Which is the truth; treated as an indec. meaning 'to tell the truth, to be sure, surely.'

P. 17. Śl. 6. भुवन—The world of mortals, the earth. ०परा—लोकनं परं यस्याः सा. पर at the end of a comp. means having 'anything as the highest object; hence solely devoted to, intent on, &c.' *Cf.* परिचर्यापर Ragh. I. 91. नागकन्या—A Nága damsel. In the Nágá. it is the Vidû. who wonders if Malayavati can be a goddess or a Nága maiden; &c., see p. 18. and *cf.* I. 15 The Nágas, according to the Purânas are a race of semi-divine beings, inhabiting the nether world or Pátala. They are generally identified with serpents, the offspring of Kadru, a wife of Kásyapa; as in the Nágá., where Vásuki is spoken of as their king, though the Bhg. makes a difference between them; see X. 28 (सर्पाणामस्मि वासुकिः); 29 (अनन्तश्चास्मि नागानां). They are described as having a human form with the expanded hood of a cobra, and sometimes as having the tail of a serpent. See Nágá. V. 17. Their females are described as exquisitely beautiful (*cf.* Nág. I. 15 where the face of a Nági is said to be as lovely as the moon), and as sometimes intermarrying with men (*e.g.* Ulûpî marrying Arjuna).

Historically the Nâgas were a race of people who have left many traces behind them. Nâgadwîpa was one of the seven divisions of Bhâratavarsha. Kings of this race reigned at Mathura, Padmâvati, &c. and the name, survives in Nagapur., They were probably a race distinct from the Hindus. See Dowson's Cl. Dic. p.213.

मिथ्या &c—*i. e.* She is superior to a नाग॰ in beauty. दृष्टं मया—This alludes to Vatsarája's visit to the Nága-world, described in Bṛh. K.manjari (II. 56-60) and referred to in Act IV (नागलोकाद्गृहीतविषविद्यः &c.). मूर्ती-having a bodily or corporal form; p. p. p. of मुर्च्छ्, (in this sense; मूर्च्छित fainted). कमलेन—उपलक्षिता marked by; the instrumental cannot be taken हेतौ (हेतुना) she looked like Lakshmî not because she had a lotus in her hand, but because she was beautiful like her and also had the lotus in her hand. Lakshmî is represented as having a lotus in her hand; *cf.* Kád. श्रियमिव हस्तस्थितकमलशोभाम्; p 24 उत्फुल्लारविन्दहस्तया आलिङ्गितो लक्ष्म्या; p. 92, &c. कमलिनी—कमलान्यस्या विद्यन्ते इति a lotus-plant, explain similarly नलिनी. संलाप इव व॰—*cf.* अये दक्षिणेन पुष्पवाटिकायामालाप इव श्रूयते। Śâk. I. p. 22

P. 18. यदा एषाहं—I, to whose care the maiden was committed. यदेषा &c.—This refers to the king's words यदा वरयोग्या &c at p. 10 *ante.* पर्याकुल:—Solely engaged in, busy with. मुषिताः—Deceived, deluded; *cf.* शीघ्रं न यात यदि तन्मुषिताः स्थ यूयं; Rat. IV. 3. निर्दोषदर्शना &c.—*cf.* निर्दोषदर्शना हि कन्या भवन्ति। Nágá. 1 p. 17. सरोषं—असम्बद्ध &c.—It is natural for a Hindu maiden of high birth (see the king's remark below) to display outward anger and to blush at the talk of her marriage by a friend; *cf.* Śa'k. 1. शकुन्तला-(सरोषं)...इमामसम्बद्धप्रलापिनीं प्रियंवदां &c. p. 34. धीरतया—gravity, firmness of mind; hence dignified demeanour. धन्यः खलुः—The same thought is expressed by Káli. in rich poetic strain when he makes Dushyanta say—अनाघ्रातं &c. न जाने भोक्तारं कमिह समुपस्थास्यति विधिः। Śak. II. 10. विस्तृतेन—Used as a noun for विस्तारेण the spreading lustre or splendour. विच्छुरितेन *Vl.*-is bad, as विच्छुरण would add to the beauty of the lotuses.

P. 19. Śl. 7. अच्छिन्न—Uninterrupted, continuous. अमृतबिन्दु-The Moon's body also sheds nectar. दृशा—By her sight *i. e.* glances or looks. दृशां—*v. l.* to the eyes of the beholders. The former is better as it furnishes the cause of pleasure. She gives delight by the succession of glances as the Moon does by the shower of nectar. Read in the text दृशा for दृशां which has remained through oversight. विगलत्पयो॰—Owing to the breast-garment slipping off; (2) owing to the drifting of the screen (*Lit.*

cloth) of clouds. **चन्द्रमसस्तनोः**—The poet says तनोः and not चन्द्रमसः and very happily, as he wants a fem. noun to correspond with तस्याः For it is the sensation of pleasure caused by the touch of a male or female that makes the other close the eyes ; hence the use of पद्म in the *mas.* also ; *cf.* निमीलताक्ष एव स्पर्शं रूपयित्वा Vik. IV. p- 110; शृङ्गेण च स्पर्शनिमीलिताक्षीं मृगीमकण्डूयत कृष्णसारः । Kum. III. 36.

करस्पर्शा॰—कर (1) Hand ; (2) rays. **मुकुलीभवन्ति**—A *Chvi.* formation; assume the state of buds, *i. e.* close up.

भ्रमरसंबाधां—This is doubtlessly suggested by the scene in Sa'k. where Śaku. is troubled by a bee. The influence of Káli., not only on the thoughts and ideas but on the language also of Harsha is observable in many places in this play. **अपरे**—*i. e.* other than those that gathered round her braid, attracted by the smell of flowers worn thereon ; see above p. 16. **समापतन्तः**—Coming in groups. **परिभविष्यन्ति**—The sense of 'defile or pollute me' by their touch is also implied. **गर्भदास्याः**—A born slave; see com. **सुता**—This is Vidu.'s humorous way of referring to maid-servants ; see note on दास्याः पुत्रं above, p. 6. **शब्दश्रुतेन**—for सूचितेन is not a good reading as it gives rise to an awkward comp. (॰शब्दात् श्रुतेन) and ॰संचार has to be taken in the secondary (La'kshaṇika) sense of संचारशब्द.

P. 20. **लघु**—Quickly, without loss of time; for this sense *cf.* एतां लघु परित्रायतां भवान् Śak. II. p. 72 लघु उत्थितापि *Ibid.* IV. p. 130 readings. **राजानमव॰**—This she did without turning back. **आरण्यिकोत्तरीयं** &c.—As the king clasped her round the neck A'ra. took off her upper garment from her head in order to ward off the bees by its hem, as women are wont to do.

Śl. 8. **परिमल॰**—परिमले यः रसः fondess for, love of; now see com. The परिमल may be of the flowers in her Veṇi, or better still, of her breath; *cf.* यदि सुरभिमवाप्स्यस्तन्मुखोच्छ्वासगन्धं &c. Vik. IV. 22. This will also indicate her पद्मिनीत्व. **भूयः**—Abundantly, profusely. **आयताक्षी**—Sans. poets describe long eyes as a mark of beauty in the case of females. *Cf.* तदेतदुन्मीलय चक्षुरायतं Vik. I. 5; संभावयत्याननमायताक्षि । Ragh. XIII. 16.

कुवलय॰—see *supra.* p. 19. l. 6. कुवलय is a beautiful water-lily (कोः पृथिव्या वलयमिव शोभाकरत्वात्) and is given in A. K. as a synonym of उत्पल. But it is generally used in the sense of a blue lotus ; श्यामं शितिकण्ठनीलं कुवलयमिन्दीवरं च नीलाब्जम् । नाममाला.

साध्वसं—Agitation, perturbation; or fear.

सकलपृथ्वी &c.—*Cf.* Śak. हला अशरणास्मि । उभे—पृथिव्या यः शरणः स तव समीपं वर्तते । p. 80. पक्षपात:—A strong leaning towards or liking, hence partiality; here choice.

P. 21. तव वदनस्यायं दोष:—*Cf.* for a similar thought अत्र आत्मनो यौवनं उपालभस्व । Śak. I. p. 26 कदलीगृह॰—In the Sa'k. Śâkuntalâ addresses the bower of creepers where Dushyanta lay concealed at the approach of Gautamî; see p. 89. ऊरुस्तम्भ:—numbness or benumbing of the thighs. स्तम्भ—Complete inactivity or torpor of limbs is one of the eight Sâtvika *bhâvas* due to strong emotion, for which see Sâh. Dar. III. 135. The ऊरुस्तम्भ was really due to the thrill caused by the touch of the king's hand, but A'ran. hides the truth by saying that it was due to the benumbing effect of the water. This was a ruse used by her in order to be able to look longer at the king in the Kadalîvana; *cf.* Śak. अभिनवकुशसूच्या परिक्षतं मे चरणं &c. p. 39 readings. न खल्वविघ्नं &c.—*cf.* अहो विघ्नवत्यः प्रार्थितार्थसिद्धयः । Śak. III. p. 116

P. 22. Śl. 9. कण्टकितं—कण्टकाः संजाता अस्य; इत added by तदस्य संजातं &c. Pán. V. 2. 36. Having thorns on; with the hair bristling, horripilated; and hence कथयतीव. कमल॰—Here कमल stands for पद्म *mas.* This is the effect produced on a lover by the touch of the loved one; *cf.* आसीद्वरः कण्टकितप्रकोष्ठः Ragh. VII. 20; and Vástyáyana–कन्या तु प्रथमसमागमे स्विन्नाङ्गुलिः भवति पुरुषस्तु रोमाञ्चितो भवति । Kámasútras.

मम मूर्खस्य—*V. l.* is perhaps better; he says so because the king had called him a fool above; see p. 16 *ante.* अलीकपाण्डित्य॰—This is a retort flung at the king by Vidû. for having called him a fool. He means-you only affect learning (पाण्डित्य); you do not possess it. विदग्ध is what is well burnt, burnished, or polished; hence refined, learned, wise; दुर्विदग्ध one not really skilled or learned, vainly proud. *cf.* अलीकशास्त्रग्रहणदुर्विदग्ध Ven. III. समाश्वासनं—something encouraging or comforting, निर्भर्त्सनं—Reproach, a chiding. अस्तमय:—setting (of the sun); fr. अस्तं and अय (from अय् to go)—अभिलाषी—desirous of, *i. e.* about to set; this has occurred before.

Śl. 10. प्रियतमेव—Like the beloved one (A'ran.), the splendour of whose lotus-face surpassed (eclipsed) that of the lotuses. The idea occurs in Rat. देवि त्वन्मुखपङ्कजेन शशिनः शोभातिरस्कारिणा पश्याब्जानि विनिर्जितानि सहसा गच्छन्ति विच्छायताम् । I. 25. राग:—(1) passion, love; (2) redness.

P. 23. **चक्राह्वः**—चक्र इत्याह्वा name यस्य; the bird usually called चक्रवाक (which also means the same thing—चक्र इत्युच्यते); hence it is also called रथाङ्गनामन्, रथाङ्गाह्वय, &c. It is the ruddy goose generally described in Sans poetry as condemned to pass the night in separation from his mate. Hence separated lovers are compared to a pair of Chak. birds at night. **अन्धकाराः**—used here as an adj., अच् (अ) being added मत्वर्थे by Pán. V. 2. 127; see com. अन्धकारै आसां विद्यते dark, void of interest. **जाताः**—*cf.* for a similar thought differently expressed.—राजा—सखे वैयर्थ्यमिव चक्षुषः सम्प्रति (after the departure of Urvási); Vik. II. p. 122 and 'And leaves the world to darkness and to me;' Gray's Elegy, stanza I. There is a succession of similes in this Śl. Mark how the king falls a victim to the influence of love at the very first sight of the heroine. Káli does not make his heroes yield so easily and helplessly to the power of love.

ACT III.

—:o:—

सांकृत्यायनी—appears from this play to be a lady of high rank and learning as she speaks in Sans. and is treated with respect even by the Queen. That she composed the Mimic play in a good style is clear from the Queen's speech below; see p. 30. The part played by her in this play is similar to that of the Parivrâjiká in the Mâl. She is mentioned as a friend of Vâsavadattâ in the Kath. Sar.; see Tar. XIV. 71 (ततः प्रव्राजिकां तस्याः सखीं पितृकुलागताम् । स सांकृत्यायनीं नाम शरणं शिश्रिये नृपः ॥) **नाटकोप०**—नाटके उपनिबद्धः made the subject matter of a play, dramatised, same as भवभूति's 'अभिनेयार्थः कृतः । Uttar. IV. p. 119. **कौमुदीमहोत्सव**—The great autumnal festival celebrated on the full-moon day of A'svina, when the moonlight is very bright, the sky being clear after the cessation of the rains and the disappearance of the clouds. It corresponds to the Kojâgarî festival and has been often referred to by poets; see Mudra. III. p. 166 It precedes the Vasantotsava or spring festival referred to in Rat. I. कौमुदी moon-light is derived as कुमुदानामियं प्रकाशकत्वात्; fr. कुमुद and अण् (अ) with the fem. affix ई; it is also derived as कौ on earth मोदन्त जना यस्यां तेनासौ कौमुदी मता । Malli. on Ragh. III. 1 (where the reading is कौमुदीमहं also). **नर्तितव्यं**—Here नृत् has the technical sense of 'acting, representing on the stage, and does not mean simply dancing.' अन्यथैव नर्तितं—*Cf.* for a similar mistake in acting the slip of tongue of Urvasî when acting the part of Lakshmî, in the Vik. when she said पुरूरवसि instead of पुरुषोत्तमे. विश्रब्धज०—A talk in full confidence that it would not be overheard by any one.

P. 24. प्रविशति आसनस्था—This might appear strange; but प्रविश् has a technical meaning. It simply means to appear on the stage. So this means A'ra. is discovered seated, the curtain being removed or lifted up. हृदय दुर्लभं जनं &c.—So Sâgarikâ—हृदय प्रसीद प्रसीद किमनेनायासमात्रफलेन दुर्लभजनानुबन्धेन । Rat. II. p. 48 हृदय निरवलम्बावृतिभूमिलंघिनो मनोरथाद्विरम । किं मामायासयसि । Mâl. III. p. 82 अभागधेयता—misfortune, ill-luck. नास्ति भागधेयं यस्याः सा अभागधेया तस्या भावः; धेय is added स्वार्थे to भाग; *cf.* रूपधेय and नामधेय. आभिजात्यसदृशः &c.—Kâli., however, makes Priyamvadâ congratulate her friend in language more elegant and impressive when he makes her add सागरं वर्जयित्वा कुत्र वा महानद्यवतरति &c.; see S'ak. III. p. 100 सह्यवेदनमिव दुःखं &c.—*Cf.* स्निग्धजनसंविभक्तं हि दुःखं सह्यवेदनं भवति । Śák. III. p. 96 हृदयनिर्विशेषा—not differing from, identical with, my heart (like my second heart). *Cf.* expressions like सुतनिर्विशेषं (Ragh. V. 6), अपत्यनिर्विशेषाणि (Śak. VII. p. 266), जातनिर्विशेषाः (Uttar. III. p. 78). तस्या अपि—*Cf.* कुतो विभवः स्निग्धजनस्येमं वृत्तान्तमाख्यातुम् । न जाने &c. Mal. III. p. 74 सर्वथा मरणं &c.—*Cf.* दुर्लभजनानुरागो...प्रियसखि मरणं शरणं Rat. II. 1.

P. 25. अतिभूमिं—The highest point or pitch; climax. हृदयस्यापि—*i. e.* of me who am your very heart—refers to A'ra.'s speech हृदयनिर्विशेषा &c. पर्याकुल :—Solely engaged in thoughts about. अयं सखीजनः &c.—This speech ought to be स्वगतं; or we should adopt the reading in the foot-note सखीजनपक्षपातेन &c. पक्षपातेन—*Cf.* सौहार्दमेवं पश्यति, and प्रिया खलु अहं तव Mál. III. pp. 80, 94. देवीगुणनिगड &c.—*Cf.* सखि देवीं विचिन्त्य न खलु मम हृदयं विश्वसिति । Mâl. III. p. 94. कमलिनीबद्धानुरागः &c.—This is doubtless an echo of अभिनवमधुलोलुपः Śak. V. 1. मालतीं प्रेक्ष्य—&c. मालती Jasmine; so—मालविकापि...अनुभुक्तमुक्तेव मालतीमाला म्लायमाना लक्ष्यते । Mâl. III. p. 66 लज्जालुका—लज्जालु is to be derived like कृपालु by adding उ (लु) to लज्जा + ला (as in the case of मितद्रु) by the Vártt. on Pàn. III. 2. 180 (see com.); क is added to express pity. आत्मा प्रच्छादयितुम्—Mark the use of the inf. with verbs like युज्, शक् &c., the cons. being आत्मा प्रच्छादयितुं न युज्यते । *Cf.* युक्तं नामायमशोको वामपादेन ताडयितुम्, Mal. III. 100 She means-you should not dissimulate; do not say शरदातपेन say मदनातपेन ;

I know it. For the difference between torment caused by आतप and मदन *cf.* Śak. III. 7 (न तु ग्रीष्मस्यैवं सुभगमपराद्धं युवतिषु ।). **अविश्रम्भशीला**—One not habitually confiding; because A'r. only hung down her face and did not admit the truth in plain words. **निश्वासनिभ**—Here निभ has the sense of pretext or guise of. **दिवसं रात्रिमपि**—may have been suggested by मम पुनः कामो दिवापि रात्रावपि । तपति अङ्गानि । Śak. III. 14. The reading दिवसरात्रं is grammatically inaccurate. **कुसुमशर**—Kâma is often spoken of as कुसुमशर-सायक, पुष्पसायक &c. **न भणति**—a question; does it not say, not proclaim your true state? Śree. reads this passage in a metrical form; see the foot-note. This is perhaps better and more poetical-as if it is the sound *Hum* (due to &c. and implying your love-torment). **नलिनीपत्राणि**—Lotus-leaves and lotus-stalk-rings are among the cooling remedies used for allaying love-fever ; *cf.* सखि अपनयेमानि नलिनीपत्राणि मृणालवलयानि च । Rat. II. p. 70. कस्येदमुशीरानुलेपनं मृणालवन्ति च नलिनीपत्राणि नीयन्ते । Śák. III. p. 86

P. 27. **परित्यक्तराज०**—So पत्रं राज्यकार्याण्युज्झित्वा । Sâk. II p. **विनोदयति**—*i. e.* he finds pleasure in nothing else. **अपि नाम**—would that; I hope that. **तथा भवेत्**—*i e.* यथा मे मनसि वर्तते—may it be like that, *i. e.* can it be that he has been sent to search for A'ra. by the love-sick king? **आरण्यिका सत्यमेव** &c.—*i. e.* has become really a forest-maiden by not acting like a city-maiden ; else she should have known that the king was smitten with love for her and been within reachable distance; or, has she gone to a forest? The reading सत्यमेवारण्यिका is simpler. **निस्सह**—Quite unnerved, drooping.

P. 28. **अस्वस्थवचनेन**—*V. l.* is bad. अस्वस्थ० cannot directly qualify वचन; so it will have to be taken as a Gen. Tat. (अस्वस्थस्य वचनं); it has no propriety after ०निस्सहस्य. **वासवदत्ता०**—Padmávatî, the second queen of Vatsarája was the sister of Dars'aka (also called Harshaka), king of Magadha and a contemporary of Udayana. The story of her marriage is given by Bhása in his Sva. Vás. The kingdom of Udayana was usurped by a king named Aruṇi, a rival of his. To regain it Yaugandharáyaṇa wanted to secure the assistance of the powerful king of Magadha; and Yau.'s subtle intellect suggested to him a stratagem. He caused a report to be spread that Vàsavadattâ perished in a fire at Lávaṇaka and thus paved the way for the marriage of his master with Padmávati. When Udayana visited R'ájagṛha, the capital of Maghadha, to seek the help of Dars'aka,

Padmávatî was offered to him in marriage and he readily gave his consent.

अन्यासां च &c —The Kathá. does not refer to any other queens of Udayana. **यत्र तदपि**—The cons. is यत्र यस्मिन्स्थाने तदपि स्थानम्. Or तद् may be translated as तां (दीर्घिकामपि). **करतल** &c — This indicates the intensity of the king's passion; any thing connected with the object of his love is comforting to him. Dushyanta similarly derives consolation from the sight of the arbour occupied by the love-sick Śakuntalá. See Śak. III. 24. Dissolve करतलस्पर्शेन द्विगुणितं यथा तथा सुखानि च तानि शीतलानि च; सुख is an adj. here; *cf.* मरुतो वबुः सुखाः, Ragh III 14; also 19. सुख may be derived as सुखयतीति सुखं from सुखय् denom. from सुख; or better still सु सुखानि खानि इन्द्रियाणि अनेन.

अहं ते ज्ञापयामि—Vasa. misunderstands her and thinks that she will tell the Queen that he was in search of A'ran. and that there was some love-intrigue.

P. 29. **सावेगं**—Because her love-affected state was brought to Vidû.'s notice by Manoramá. Śree. omits द्विगुणतर; see readings.

कर्णे कथयति—Mark the dramatic device used here to avoid an early disclosure of the plan which is set forth later on, (see *infra* p. 34 where the king repeats what Manoramâ whispered into Vasan.'s ear, mentioning also the name of the play that was to be enacted) that the interest of the audience in the incidents to follow may be well sustained. The plan suggested was that the king himself should act his part in place of Manoramâ in the Garbhanâtaka, A'raṇ. playing the role of the princess Vásavadattâ. **अपवार्य**०—This stage direction (opposed to प्रकाशं) is used when a character says something *aside* so as to be heard only by the person addressed excluding others with the *tripatáka* hand (*i. e.* all the fingers except the thumb and the one near the little finger raised so as to form three banners as it were). **नेपथ्यग्रहणं**—Here नेपथ्य means the costume proper for a particular character.

अतिकोपने—This she says because A'ra. got angry with her for saying येन स्वयमेव नलिनीपत्राण्यपनयति above. **प्रेक्षागृहं**—प्रेक्षार्थं गृहं *lit.* a house for exhibition or representation; a play-house. It was a hall or a house attached to the palace, usually used for instruction in music, singing and dancing and occasionally for the exhibition of dancing or the respresentation of plays. It is also referred to in the Mál. I; see p.

P. 30. अहो—expresses admiration. This praise of course refers to the first part of the play that had been already acted. See p. 23. The 2nd part it seems was not seen by the Queen, as she finds much in it to be found fault with, as will appear from the subsequent representation. गूढ़इ०—qualifies आर्यपुत्रचरितं. सानुभवमपि—and so likely to prove insipid and without interest. इव for अपि is quite out of place. आर्यपुत्र०—The husband is addressed or referred to in dramas as आर्यपुत्र (the son of the father-in-law). आयुष्मति—This is a sort of blessing. Young people are to be addressed by elders as आयुष्मत् or-ती.

आश्रयगुणः &c.—आश्रय the subject, the person or thing on which anything depends or rests; here the King and the Queen. *Cf.* पात्रविशेषन्यस्तं गुणान्तरं व्रजाति शिल्पमाधातुः । Mal. I. 6. क्रिया हि वस्तु-पहिता प्रसीदति Ragh III. 27.

असारम्—Lacking excellence; सार pithy sentences, charming sense; *cf.* for this sense वचांसि वाचस्पतिमत्सरेण साराणि लब्धुं ग्रहमण्डलीव । मुक्ताक्षसूत्रत्वमुपैति यस्याः; and गिरां प्रवृत्तिर्मम नीरसापि मान्या भवित्री नृपते-श्चरित्रैः । Vik. Ch. I. 7; 28.

Sl. 1. यत्किंचित्—Trifling, unimportant or uninteresting. आश्रयान्म०—*Cf.* गुणवज्जनसंसर्गाद्याति स्वल्पोऽपि गौरवम् । पुष्पमालाऽनुषङ्गेण तृणं शिरसि धार्यते ॥ Kshemendra. कुम्भतट—The surface or skirt of; or तट like भित्ति may be प्राशस्त्ये; the large temples. It is difficult to see the propriety of the epithet मत्त; perhaps the poet means that an infuriated elephant only is likely to butt against a heap of ashes and get his temples besmeared with the same.

वल्लभो जामाता भवति—It is not clear from the play whethe Sámkr. was some elderly near relative of the Queen or simply one held in such reverence by her as to be called a mother· नर्तितव्यं—is used here in the sense of dramatic representation. प्रेक्षणीयता—used to correspond in sound with प्रेक्षा (गृह).

Sl. 2. शातकुम्भ—See I. 11. अवसक्त—hung up, festooned with. युवतिभिः—It seems the performance was to be witnessed by the fair of the city; hence Manoramâ was to play the role of the king and not a male. सुरविमान०—Which is also रत्नशतशोभित and occupied by the nymphs of heaven. It may mean an aerial car, or a large house (विगतं मानं यस्मात्). The houses in great ancient cities were large, and were decorated with strings of gems and crowded with beauties that rivalled the nymphs of heaven. *Cf.* सद्रत्नमुक्ताफलवज्रभाञ्जि विचित्रधातूनि सकाननानि । स्त्रीभिर्युतान्यप्सरसामिवौघै-र्मेरोः शिरांसीव गृहाणि यस्याम् । Bhatti. I 7.

P. 31. **पिनद्ध**—(also अपिनद्ध) **fastened, *i.e.* worn on.** *Cf.* **यस्या** पिनद्धं मण्डनं (*v. l.*) मे प्रसाधीकृतं &c. Rat. III. p. 61. **मनोरमे** &c.—**Manoramá** was chosen to act the king's part as her features very closely resembled those of the king. See *infra,* p. 36. sl 7.

नडागिरिं—(called नडागिरि according to Kathà. ; see Lam II. Tar. 13) was a powerful elephant in the possession of king Mahásena. It was riding this elephant that Pálaka, a son of Mahâsena, pursued king Udayana, after he had fled with Vásavadattá, under cover of night having mounted a she-elephant. **ग्रहण**—It is said that Nadagiri once bolted away tearing off the post to which he was tied and made terrible havoc in the city, when king Udayana was asked to arrest his progress by the magic influence of his lute; see Meg. I. 34.

कञ्चुकी—This is the Kanch of Mahâsena, king of Ujjayinî' appearing in the mimic-play, part of which had already been acted before Vâsavadattâ.

Śl. 3. In this by using epithets having a double application the Kanchikî says that he discharges a duty similar to that of a king. **अन्तःपुराणां**—(1) The inmates of the harem; (2) पुराणामन्तः in the cities of his kingdom. **स्खलितानि**—(1) Mistakes or breaches of duty through carelessness; रक्षन्—preventing or not disclosing or giving out; *cf.* सर्वत्र स्खलितेषु दत्तमनसा यातं मया नोद्धतं; Veni. II. 1. A good king also (विनेता) prevents his subjects from going astray ; *cf.* Ragh. VI. 39. **जरातुरः**—When referring to a king may be taken in the sense of जरायां प्रशंसायामातुरः eager to win praise. But it is not necessary to do so.

P. 32. **दण्डनीत्या**—*Cf.* Śak. V. 3 आचार इत्यवहितेन मया गृहीता या वेत्रयष्टिरवरोधगृहेषु राज्ञः । काले गते बहुतिथे मम सैव जाता प्रस्थानविक्लवगतेरवलम्बनार्था ॥ (1) By being guided with a stick; having to support myself on a stick; (2) दण्डनीतिः दण्डो नीयते अनया इति politics or the science of government; administration of justice. It is one of the four lores or Vidyàs by which punishment is meted out to culprits. *Cf.* आन्वीक्षिकी त्रयी वार्ता दण्डनीतिश्च शाश्वती । विद्या ह्येताश्चतस्रस्तु लोकसंस्थितिहेतवः ॥ आन्वीक्षिक्यां तु विज्ञानं धर्माधर्मौ त्रयीस्थितौ । अर्थानर्थौ तु वार्तायां दण्डनीत्यां नयानयौ ॥ Kâm. Nît. This Śl. is the same as Nág. IV. 1.

विमानित—Discomfited, put to shame; hence defeated, overpowered. **०सैन्येन**—should rather have been ०सेनेन (सेना येन) and so महासेनेन (महती powerful, superior, सेना यस्य). The Kanch. being an elderly person simply says महासेनेन without any honorific epithet. **उदयनोत्सवं**—A festival instituted to celebrate the capture of Udayana or rather his marriage with Vâsavadattâ; or perhaps the reading may be वयं मदनोत्स० and hence the order to go to मन्मथोद्यान. रूपस्य योग्यः अनुरूपः अनुरूपः वेषः &c. **प्रेक्षा**—Representation.

तद्देतदादेष्टव्यं—Here we expect the stage-direction (अन्तःपुरं विलोक्य)

Śl. 4. **नूपुरिभिः**—नूपुरौ एषां विद्येते इति नूपुरिणः तैः having anklets on. Explain केयूरिभिः, कुण्डलिभिः, &c. similarly. **नितम्बफलकैः**—नितम्बाः फलकाः (broad and extensive) इव, or प्रशस्ता नितम्बाः नितम्बफलकाः; Karm. comp. Words like फलक, तट, भित्ति (*e. g.* कपोलभित्ति), &c. express प्राशस्त्य or excellence when forming the second member of a Karm. comp. **शिञ्जान**—tinkling; pre. p. of शिञ्ज् 2 A. to sound (like anklets). **काञ्चीगुण**—the girdle bands. **आपादित**—reduced, generated. **सस्वस्तिकैः**—स्वस्तिक a kind of mystic diagram denoting good luck and auspiciousness; स्वस्ति कायति इति स्वस्तिकः fr. स्वस्ति+कै to sound I P. and affix (अ); Pân. III. 2-3. Hence anything like a Sva., as a house, &c.; here a kind of head-ornament; or a particular symbol made with scented rice-flour and triangular in shape. स्वस्तिकः मङ्गलद्रव्यं तत्तु तण्डुलचूर्णनिर्मितत्रिकोणाकाराधिवासद्रव्यमिति कल्पद्रुमः।" Pandit Krishnamachariar. **परिचारिका०**—परिचारिकाः the maids in immediate attendance on the queens. **एतेषु**—*scil.* अन्तःपुरेषु.

अपूर्वं—Because adornment of the person in the case of the inmates of the harem was an ordinary thing.

केवलं &c.—The sentence may end with समादिष्टः; I was ordered by the King because the royal command must be given; or the constr. may be समादिष्टोहं स्वाम्यादेश इति मत्वा &c.

P. 33. **वीणा**—Popularly called Bîṇa or the Indian lute is a stringed instrument with a large round hollow bowl, a body of thin wood and a neck with tuning pegs and metallic strings, and with a hollow gourd attached to it on the other side of the body.

काञ्चनमाला—was the attendant of Vâsavadattâ in the palace of Mahâsena and followed her as her principal maid also after her marriage with Udayana. In the Garbhanâtaka she herself plays her own part **गन्धर्वशाला**—the same as the प्रेक्षागृह. **प्रविशति आसनस्था**—प्रविशति is discovered, seated. See notes p. 24. **वीणाचार्यः**—*i. e.* Vatsarâja. **एक उन्मत्तः**—This undoubtedly refers to Yaugandharâyaṇa, the devoted minister of Vatsarâja, who in the guise of a mad man, with Vasantaka, saw his master in his prison in order to effect his release and gave him instructions as to how that was to be done. **चित्रं**—wonder, astonishment. **भावित:**-seized completely, or entirely overpowered by.

सुहेवं &c.—The reading in the foot-note is better. **सदृशा सदृशे** &c.—*Cf.* सर्वः सगन्धेषु विश्वसिति । द्वावप्यत्रारण्यकौ । Śak. V. p. 184

राजपुत्र्याः &c.—This speech is addressed to Vâsavadattâ.: we expect here the stage-direction—वासवदत्तां प्रति. **तन्त्री**—The string or wire of a musical instrument. **घोषवती**—a Vîṇâ. Here the name of the Vîṇâ. presented to king Udayana by Vâsuki, See Katha. XI. 3. See, however, Intro., the legend about Udayana.

सारयति—Adjusts, puts into tune; or strikes to see if they were in good order. **रमणीयं भवेत्**—Because she could not have waited for the king very long.

Śl. 5. **संतापं** &c.—Construe शीतांशुः यथा प्रथमं संतापमकरोत्तथा अद्येव न कुरुते; similarly उष्णा निःश्वासा यथा पूर्वमजस्रमधरमग्लपयन् तथा &c. **अजस्रं**—Constantly or continually, fr. जस् with न (न जस्यति) and aff. र which is added to नम्, कम्प्, स्मि, जस्, &c. (Pân. III. 2. 167); नम्र, कम्प्र, &c.; जस् is always preceded by अ (नञ्) जसिर्नञ्पूर्वः क्रियासातत्ये वर्तते । अजस्रं संततमित्यर्थः । Sid. Kau. This is an अव्यय. **मनोरथेषु संचि०**—Thought of as being near accomplishment. *Cf.* for a similar thought आशंसापरिकल्पितास्वपि भवत्यानन्दसान्द्रो लयः । Mâl. Mâd. V. 7. त्वदुपलभ्य समीपगतां प्रियां हृदयमुच्छ्वसितं मम विक्लवम् । Mâl. III. 45; and for the idea somewhat differently expressed अभिमुखीष्विव कांक्षितसिद्धिषु व्रजति निर्वृतिमेकपदे मनः । Vik. II. 9. For an opposite idea *cf.* तीव्रः स्मरसंतापो न तथादौ बाधते यथासन्ने । Rat III. 10.

सर्वं तच्चरितेनैव &c.—तच्चरितेन—his own deeds. शिक्षितव्यं to be learned by way of acting. She means—As the king knows his own acts then, it will be easy for him to play his own part without instruction. Nothing will go amiss; and the Queen will not detect the fraud.

P. 35. **दास्यापि नर्त्यन्ते**—This speech of the Vidu ought to be taken as अपवार्य (meant to be heard by the king alone). **गुरुता**-Weightiness, importance (which makes a king humour maid-servants even); for, मनस्वी कार्यार्थी गणयति न दुःखं न च सुखम् । Bh Nit. 81. Sree. reads दास्य इव and explains दास्यो गणिका इव नर्त्यन्ते नर्तनंभाजः क्रियन्ते । **निभृतेन**—Adv secretly, being concealed; or silently; or it may be an adj. qualifying भवता. **चित्रशाला**—A picture gallery; seems to be here one adjoining to the concert-hall. **आरण्यिका**—तिष्ठतु तावत्

&c.. This speech of A'ra. is to be read directly after उत्सङ्गे वीणां कृत्वा सारयति । The entrance of Monoramâ, the king and Vidu., the participants in the intrigue being considered as *aside*. उद्देशः—Part of the story, context (so that he may know where his part begins).

अपहरति मां—Transports me with joy, fascinates or infatuates me. The king overhears her and understands अपहरति in the sense of 'takes me away.' **मुञ्चामि**—the object being तम्. **प्रविश्य**—*i. e.* on the stage of the Garbhanátaka unseen by A'ra. Vása. and Kán. **ग्रथितं बध्नाति**—It seems from this to have been an old custom, which still prevails in many parts of India, to tie a knot generally at the end of a garment when there is some pronouncement or an auspicious omen in favour of one's desired object, and is therefore called शकुनग्रन्थि (शकुनगांठ in Maráthi). It is also tied when one is determined or definitely undertakes to do a thing (निश्चयसूचकं) and wishes to be reminded of it.

Śl. 6. **अपहरामि**—अपहरिष्यामि, pres. in the sense of immediate future. अपहरामि इति पश्यामि the whole line, however, is metrically faulty; but it is so found in almost all the printed editions. Śreenivasachariar reads.—ताहरणं न चिराद्देवेति पश्यामि; but this seems to be a conjectural emendation, and is also syntactically inaccurate. We cannot connect उपनीय with अपहरणं unless we supply स्थितेन—उपनीय स्थितेन मया. अहं after पश्यामि is dropped as a useless addition, that might have originally got in through the carelessness of some scribe. **सुसंनिहितं सर्वं** &c.—Well arranged and brought within reach, *i. e.* made practicable. **यौगन्ध०**—युगन्धरस्य अपत्यं पुमान्; the son of Yugandhara, who was the chief minister of Vatsa.'s father, Sahasránîka. Similarly the fathers of Rumanvat and Vasantaka also were his father's servants. See Br. K. M. II. 12, 13; सुतो युगन्धरस्यासीच्छ्रीमान्यौगन्धरायणः । रुमण्वान् सुप्रतीपस्य द्विजस्य च वसन्तकः ॥ यौगन्धरायणो मन्त्री रुमण्वान्वाहिनीपतिः । वसन्तको नर्मसुहृद्राजसूनोरभूत्ततः ॥ *Ibid.* 38, 39 Yaugandharáyana was the devoted minister of Vatsarâja, the purpose of whose life was to see his master elevated to the rank of an emperor. When he heard that his master was put into custody he, leaving the cares of the kingdom to Rumaṇvat, came to Ujjain with Vasantaka to concert a plan for his master's escape. There he entered the cemetery and by the help of a friendly Brahmarákshasa, called योगेश्वर, he changed his own form into that of a dwarfish old hunch-back, and gave Vasantaka a deformed shape with a protuberent belly and projecting teeth and found access by that means to the apartment of the Princess. There the two made themselves known to Vatsarâja. Then Yaugandharáyaṇa informed the king of the arrangements made for his escape with Vásavadattá (see *ante* notes p. 6 foot-note) and keeping Vasantaka there for his amusement returned to Kaus'ámbî.

वासवदत्ता (सहसोत्थाय)—Vásav. forgets that she was one of the spectators and that A'ranyiká was playing her part in the mimi. play and suddenly rises at the sight of the king. This of course has a different effect on the king who has a guilty conscience. He thought that the fraud was detected. **संभ्रमेण**—संभ्रम hurried respect or hurry to show respect. *Cf.* for this meaning गृहमुपगते संभ्रमविधिः Bh. Nît. **कथं प्रत्यभि०**—So Vása in the Ratnávalî—कथं ज्ञातास्मि (p.124) when she goes disguised as Ságariká to the rendezvous.

प्रेक्षणीय०—Śamk. means—why do you rise in a hurry; this is not the real king.

P. 36. **उच्छ्वासितोस्मि**—I am made to breath a sigh of relief; life is put in me (by Śamk.); this he says because he dreaded the anger of the queen. **सविलक्षस्मितं**—विशेषेण लक्षयनीति विलक्षं विलक्षेण स्मितेन सहितं यथा तथा; with a smile of amazement or wonder; विलक्षो विस्मयान्वितः Amara.; or विगतं लक्षं यस्मात् तद्विलक्षं; with a smile of embarrassment or bewilderment.

Śl. 7. **तद्**—*i. e.* of Vatsarája. **नयनोत्सवा०**—श्लाघ्याग्वयेति नयनोत्सवकारिणीति; Mál. Mâd. VI. 17; also II. 3. **सा**—*i. e.* which characterises king Vatsa. **मत्तद्विरदो०**—*i. e.* a stately and majestic or dignified gait. **सत्त्वं**—dignity; or firmness, vigour, substance (inferrable from one's outward bearing or deportment). *Cf.* क्रियासिद्धिः सत्त्वे भवति महतां नोपकरणे Sub.; सत्त्वोत्कर्षस्य धात्रा निधय इव कृताः &c., Mud. III. 22. **ऊर्जितं**—great; p. p. p. of ऊर्ज् 10 cl. to become strong or powerful. **सान्द्र**—Dense, filled with water. **जलदह्लादानु०**—A deep loud sound is the characteristic sign of a great man; *cf.* एष च दुन्दुभेरिवातिगम्भीरः स्वरयोगोऽस्य रुदतः श्रूयते । Kád. p. 123; नवजलधरध्वानगम्भीरया गिरा Ibid. p. 129; Uttar. VI. 17. **बद्धेन**—see *ante* I. 5, and Vidû.'s speech on p. 6. **नीलोत्प०**—**निगलनं**—निगलनं same as निगडनं chaining, fettering; *n.* from the denom. verb निगडयति.

P. 37. **निष्पादितं** &c —This speech of the king is of course स्वगतं. It is not heard by A'ran. or Kánch. **तदाऽस्माभि०**—The अभिल० was that Vása. should secure Vatsa's love. The reading आलपितव्यं for अभिल० is not so good as it does not agree well with निष्पादितम्.

Śl. 8. **घनबन्धन०**—This epithet is श्लिष्ट; the sl. having a side-meaning; see I. 5 *supra*.—(1) covered or occupied by a dense line of clouds; (2) hidden from view by the compact or closely hemmed in prison walls. Sreekri. takes गगनं in the sense of the dark prison (गगनसदृशं तमसा नीलं चारकं); in this case घन० will mean well secured by the close fastened prison doors. **मानसं**—(1) the lake Mánasa* on mount Kailása to which swans are described as migrating at the approach of the monsoon; see Meg. I 11; Ragh. XIII. 60; (2) the mind. **मानसमेतुं**—*cf.* मानसमुपैति केयं चित्रगता राजहंसीव । Rat. I. 9. **राजहंस**—(1) A swan; (2) the best of kings, Vatsarája. *Fig.* अप्रस्तुतप्रशंसा.

स्वप्तुं न ददासि—For a similar use *cf.* बाष्पस्तु न ददात्येनां द्रष्टुं चित्रगतामपि Śak. VI. 22. लज्जेव वक्तुं न ददौ Kád. p. 280.

रात्रिंदिवं—A Dwandwa comp. the nasal added to रात्रि is by निपातन (irregular); see Pán. V. 4. 77; यदा प्रभृति—**निद्रा न दृष्टा**—Vidu.'s fondness for sleep is often referred to by poets; *cf.* Śak. II. रात्रावपि निकामं शयितव्यं नास्ति । He sometimes betrays the secret of his master and thus puts more impediments in his way by his prattlings in sleep, as here. *Cf.* in this respect his speech in the Mal. IV p. 150—**विदू०**-(उत्स्वप्नायते) भवति मालविके &c. For an instance of prattling in sleep comp. the scene wherein Vásavadattá sleeps in Bhá'sa's Sva. Vas. V.

Śl. 9. **अभिनव**—New, hitherto unknown. **क्षिप्ता**—hurled into, *i. e.* caused to be suddenly or forcibly smitten by passion. **वामकेन**—Káma is represented as वाम acting perversely, as making a person love one that is unattainable. *Cf.* सखि वामः किल कामः Das. Ch. ; and वामः कामो मनुष्याणां &c. Rámá. Sund. K. XXII. 4, where the Com. says वामः क्रूरः इत्यर्थः । सव्ये क्रौर्ये सुन्दरे च वामः। इति कोशः ।

मधुकरिका—Sans. poets represent even a female bee as longing for the company of her lover and enjoying amorous sports; *cf.* Kum. III. 36. and एषापि कुसुमनिषण्णा.........भवन्तमनुरक्ता प्रतिपालयति मधुकरी &c. Śak. VI. 19. **उत्ताम्यति** &c.—*Cf.* for the same thought differently expressed Mala.'s words नाथ मां पराधीनां त्वयि गणय सतृष्णाम् । Mâl. II. 4. Herein also we have the अप्रस्तुतप्रशंसा as Vása.'s longing for the king is indicated by implication.

अहो—expresses astonishment at the skill shown by Vâsa in playing on the Vînâ and at her proficiency in singing. **वादित्रं**—Performance or playing on the lute; fr. वाद् and the Unâdi affix

---

* So called being created by Brahmá with his mind. कैलासपर्वते राम मनसा निर्मितं परम् । ब्रह्मणा नरशार्दूल तेनेदं मानसं सरः ॥ – Râmâ.

इत्र by भुवादिगृभ्यो णित्रन्. Properly वादित्र, also called आतोद्य, refers to the four kinds of musical instruments, *viz.* (1) stringed instruments such as the Viṇá, wind-instruments such as वेणु, instruments with mouths covered with hide, such as the मुरज, and instruments beaten, such as cymbals (कांस्य, &c.).

P. 38. Śl. 10. This contains many technical terms of music. व्यञ्जनधातु—one of the four modes of playing on a lute. These are विस्तार, करण, आविद्ध and व्यञ्जन; see com.; read विस्तारकरणाविद्ध &c. धातु—Properly an element that produces anything; here the act of producing musical notes or tunes by striking the strings of a musical instrument; see com. For its ten forms distinguished by the different ways of striking the strings with the fingers, see com. वृत्तिः—*V. l.* for व्यक्ति means the relation between the vocal and instrumental music as the one or other is principal or subordinate; see com. Mr. Gadre quotes Rághavabhatta on तवास्मि गीतरागेण (Sâk. I) who says गीतरागेण श्रीरागादिना धातुना and says that धातु may mean Rága, the Rágas being ten, according to some authority. लयः—seems to be used here for ताल though there is a technical difference between the two. ताल is musical measure or time (तालः कालक्रियामानं) while लयं is the union or agreement of song, dance and instrumental music. लय, however, falls under the general category of ताल—*cf.* लयो दशतालप्राणान्यतमस्तालान्तरालवर्ती लयनात्मकः कालविशेषः । उक्तं च प्रस्तारे—कालो जातिः क्रियाङ्गानि मार्गग्रहकला लयः । यतिः प्रसारकश्चेति तालप्राणा दश स्मृताः ॥ quoted from the com. on the Mallikâmaruta by Gadre. The three kinds of लय or tempo are द्रुत or rapid (allegro), मध्य or middle (moderato) and विलम्बित or slow (adagio) corresponding to which are the three pauses समा, स्रोतोगता and गोपुच्छा. See Nát. śa. 31. 331-333. गोपुच्छ०—Read गोपुच्छाप्रमुखाः; गोपुच्छा (so called because it resembles the tail of a cow—see com.) प्रमुखा यासां ता गोपुच्छाप्रमुखाः. तत्त्व, ओघ and अनुगत are the three modes of playing on a वीणा (वेणं); see com.; read in the com वाद्यमथौघो instead of मयोघो For other particulars see the extract from Śivaráma's com. on this sl. in the Nágánanda, given on p. 60. उपाध्यायः—See com.; fr. इ with उपाधि and aff. अ (घञ्). Properly a spiritual teacher. See Śak. V. p. 164. एकदेशं तु वेदस्य वेदाङ्गान्यपि वा पुनः । योऽध्यापयति वृत्त्यर्थमुपाध्यायः स उच्यते ॥ Hence a teacher or preceptor in general

यदहमिच्छामि *&c.*—This apparently means—may you be an adept in music as I wish you to be; the real meaning is—may you be my queen as I wish you to be. This is probably suggested by Kás'yapa's words यदिच्छामि ते तदस्तु in Śák IV. p. 154.

P. 39. विद्यामानेन—By being honoured for her proficiency in the art. पीठिका—seat. शिष्याविशेषा—शिष्यासु विशेषा distinguished among pupils; an excellent pupil. *Cf.* अधिविशेष Śak. I. आकृतिविशेष &c. कार्यं—Subject matter. अधिकं—exceeding or not in the original; कृतं you have overdrawn the original This brings out the extreme modesty of Vásava, as a high-born and well-bred girl. She does not like to be so represented even before the inmates of the harem.

P. 40. अधिकमेतदपि—*Viz.* making the king seize her hand. काव्येन—काव्य composition, hence poetic art. She means—Káncha. may be deceived and speak in the way she is made to speak, but I cannot bear to see such false representation. Some read the two words as compounded. Then the meaning is—by the words put in Kán.'s mouth. I should not be placed in a false position by Kanch.'s speech. The Queen does not appear to have suspected any intrigue yet, to which Sámkri. could have been a party. This she does later on, when she discovers that it was the king who acted his own part. कार्यं भविष्यति—She means poetic art requires such additions for stage effect. आर०-सरोषमिव—A'ran., as was becoming a princess whom she was representing shows outward anger, seeing a hint to the king to seize her hand in Kanch.'s speech—तत्समाश्वस्ता भवतु मुहूर्तं above. A'ran., however, was innocent as she did not know that it was the king himself who was playing his part, as is clear from her speech below—एतां मनोरमां स्पृशन्त्या: &c. Also because the plan was arranged without her knowledge by Manoramá, who whispered into Vasantaka's ear what was to be done and Vasantaka's suggestion to her was *aside*. See p 29.

Śl. 11. अवश्याय:—dew. व्यतिकर—contact. पद्मकोश:—A lotus bud The hand with its fingers closed and covered with drops of perspiration is compared to a lotus-bud drenched in dew-drops. ह्लादित्वं &c —Construe—अस्य (पद्मकोशस्य) ह्लादित्वं सदृशं न मन्ये । यत: अस्य पद्मकोशस्य पीतातपस्य उषासि एव इदं (*i. e.* which is now felt by me) ह्लादित्वं भवति । The reading पीतातपस्य is bad as there is no आतप at dawn. नखरजनि०—The comparison of nails to the moon is unusual if not unpoetical. स: अपि—*i. e.* हिमौघ: (shed by the moon.) दाही—Burning; of course to love-sick persons; or to persons in separation. *Cf* ।विसृजति हिमगर्भैरग्निमिन्दुर्मयूखै: । Śak III. 3; and अमृतसृजोऽपि विरहाद्भवतो यदमूं दहन्ति हिमरश्मिरुच: । Śis IX. 68. अपदेश—Pretext, guise. *Cf.* कुतोऽन्यथा स्रवत्येष स्वेदच्छद्मामृतद्रव: । Rat. II. 18. The figures in this śl. are संदेह, अपह्नुति, रूपक and उत्प्रेक्षा.

Śl 12. बाल—tender. अपहारदक्षेण—Clever in robbing *i. e.* fully resembling. रागः—(1) redness; (2) passion.

P. 41. अनर्थमिव कुर्वन्ति—*i. e* feel an overpowering thrill through them. This was because it was the touch of a real male.

अलीकं—False. She feels that the scene was purposely so arranged. गान्धर्वो वि०—A marriage brought about by mutual consent; it was much in vogue among the ancient Kshatriyas. It is one of the eight forms of marriage recognised by Hindu law-givers. *Cf.* As'.v. Gṛh. I. 6 5 |मिथः समयं कृत्वोपयच्छेत स गान्धर्वः। and Manu. III. 26, 32 quoted in the com.

अस्थाने—*Lit.* at an improper place; when there is no occasion for it. रस—the interest awakened by the acting. अन्यथेव—देव्या—*i. e.* thinking that I might have allowed the king to act in my place. अन्यथेव—*i. e.* thinking that it was a simple question, not having the sagacity to divine the Queen's real object. आकुलीकृतं—For the fact that Monoramá was waiting there showed that she was acting in league with the king. बटुकेन—क implies censure (कुत्सायां कन् ।); the foolish fellow having no common sense. एतेन खलु &c.—Mark how ready-witted Manoramá is. She casts the net on Vidú.; full sure that he would save her even at the risk of incurring the queen's displeasure.

P. 42. मूर्खनिर्घोषा०—*V. l.* is bad. For मूर्ख can only refer to Vidû ; but then if not Mano.'s cries, the loud voice of Vidû. would have attracted attention. सूत्रधारः—*i. e.* he has arranged the whole business. कुत्र आरण्यका कुत्र &c —कुत्र repeated like क-क shows the great disparity between the two. Where is Ara., your servant, and where poor Vasantaka How can he dare take part in such an intrigue? प्रेक्षणीयमस्य &c.—Let me see how he enjoys the acting he has arranged. I shall just go to the king and expose the whole affair. Mr. Gadre compares the Marâthi expressin याचा आतां तमाशा पहाते. हताश अनुभव &c.—Mark again how the sagacious Manoramá says this to lull all suspicion on the part of the Queen that she was in the intrigue. बन्धितः—caused to be bound or fettered; p. p. p. of बन्ध् cau.

P. 43. कथं विज्ञातोस्मि—The king is surprised as he did not expect that Manoramá would be seen by the Queen and the ruse discovered. अभूमिरियं—Sámkrityáyanî wants to show that she being a holy personage should not be in a place where deceit was practised.

Sl. 13. वीक्षितं—P. p. p. used as a noun (वीक्षणं); *cf.* with this भ्रूभङ्गे सहसोद्गतेपि वदनं नीतं परां नम्रतामीषन्मां प्रति भेदकारि हसितं नोक्तं वचो निष्ठुरम्। अन्तर्बाष्पजडीकृतं प्रभुतया चक्षुर्न विस्फारितं कोपश्च प्रकटीकृतो दयितया मुक्तश्च न प्रश्रयः॥ Rat. II. 21.

अपूर्वोयं कोपप्रकारः—*Cf* प्रिये अपूर्वोयमुपचारः। Mal. IV. p. 162

आरण्यिके त्वं कुपितेति—Here Vása.'s jealousy is well brought out. In this scene she is represented as ईर्ष्याकषायिता. Bhása does not degrade her down to the level of ordinary women. But the cannons of dramaturgy require the chief queen in a Nâtiká to be jealous at every step. See Intro. p. 9. आरण्यिका—नाहं &c.—This was true; see *supra* note on सरोषमिव p. 40. गृहीतेनां—In the Rat also Ságariká and Vidû. are similarly treated. See Act III. p. 79. भवति अद्य कौमुदी &c.—This defence of the King by his friend, though ridiculous in the eyes of the Queen, has some point in it from Vidú.'s own stand point. He means--This being the time of the Kaumudî festival some liberty of action may be allowed to men. And so my friend acted that way just to see how you would take it and thus to enjoy the fun. Hence the king finds in this a crutch on which to lean. See sl. 14, last line.

P. 44. दुर्नयं—ill-advised course of conduct, mischievous or wrong policy, misbehaviour. She says युष्माकं because she knows that Vidû. (whom she has already called आरण्यिकानाटके सूत्रधार) is the King's principal accomplice in love-intrigues. विकल्पित—P. p. p. used as a noun; wrong supposition, suspicion (of a thing).

Sl. 14. भ्रूभङ्गैः—भ्रुवोः भङ्गः भ्रूभङ्गः the knitting of the eye-brows; a frown. भ्रूभङ्गाः the repeated knittings or frowns. The frown disfiguired her fair face.

ललाटशशिनः—०शशी that is now spotless and so superior to the moon. The comparison shows that the moon meant here is the moon of the 8th day of the bright half of a month; *cf* अष्टमीचन्द्रशकलाकारं ललाटदेशमुद्वहन्तं Kád. p. 19, 26. बन्धूजीवसमतां—The बन्धु० flower is bright red and hence the lip is compared to it; see *supra* p. 13, note on बन्धूक. मध्यः खिद्यते—suffers pain, is oppressed with the burden of; for the idea *cf.* क्रीडन्त्याः पीडयेव स्तनभरविनमन्मध्यभङ्गानपेक्षम्। Rat. I. 16.

अकृत्वैव प्रसादं &c.—The king uses the same words in the Rat. when Vása leaves him without minding his prostration at her feet; see Act III. p. 77.

Śl. 15. **भिन्न**—Broken through, streaked with; or mixed with; qualifies मुखं. एकं-*i. e.* of the Queen. अपरं—*i. e.* of A'ranyiká उत्प्लुत्यो०—bounding repeatedly, *i. e.* with great force and speed; the same as Káli.'s उदग्रप्लुतत्वात् Śak. I. 7. The वीप्सा (repetition) shows the intensity of the action. उत्पश्यन्—As I look up to. इदं—this, *i. e.* standing before my eyes as fancied or pictured by my mind. The cons. is इदं रुषौ स्वेदाम्भः &c. एकं, त्रासेन ०त्पलमपरं मुखमुत्पश्यन् &c. Compare with this the concluding Sl. of Rat. III.

भीतश्च-च—Here the two चs have the sense of 'and yet' or at the same time. **तथावत्**—And so the king in the Ratnávali—देवीं प्रसादयितुमभ्यन्तरमेव प्रविशामि । Rat. III. p. 146

ACT IV.

P. 45. **दीर्घरोषता**—दीर्घो रोषो यस्याः सा दीर्घरोषा तस्या भावः दीर्घरोषता । **एतावन्तं**—एतत्परिमाणमस्य एतावांस्तम् । **अङ्गारवती**—Queen of Mahâsena and mother of Vàsavadattá. She was the daughter of the Asura Amga'raka and the most beautiful maiden of the time. By a boon conferred upon him by the goddess Durgá Mahâsena got her for his wife after killing the demon. *Cf.* किं चाङ्गारवतीं नाम कन्यां त्रैलोक्यसुन्दरीम् । अङ्गारकासुरसुतां शीघ्रं भार्यामवाप्स्यसि ॥ Kathâ. II. 39; and for the story the s'lokas 43–73

P. 46 **या मम भगिनी**—The name of Angáravatî's sister, the wife of Drdhavarman, is not given here; nor is mention made of her in the story alluded to above. So she seems to be a creation of the poet—this serves a double dramatic purpose. It makes the Queen readily give up her anger towards the king and also paves the way to the marriage of Aranyiká (who turns out to be Priyadarshika', the daughter of the Queen's aunt) with the king.

विज्ञापयितव्यः—should be told. Mark the use of the verbs आज्ञापय् and विज्ञापय् which are used respectively when something is said by a person superior in rank to one inferior in rank, and by one inferior in rank to one superior in rank.

अनुवाच्य—Mark the sense of अनुवाचय् which means to read to oneself before reading aloud. *Cf* उभे तामसुद्राक्षगण्यनुवाच्य &c. Śak. I. p. 48 देवी-अनुवाचय तावद् यद्यविरुद्धं श्रोष्यामि । Vik II. p. 126

दन्तवलभ्यां— वलभि-भी is the uppermost room of a house; (here of the palace and built of ivory). It is also mentioned in Rat. III.

एष खलु भर्ता...दन्ततोरणवलभ्यां तिष्ठति । p. 62. It is written with a short इ (as in तां कस्यांचिद्भवनवलभौ Meg. I. 41) or long ई (as in दृष्टा दृष्टा भवनवलभीतुङ्गवातायनस्था । Mâl. Madh. I. 15) where Jagaddhara says—सौधोपरिकुटीं वलभीं विदुः ।) अत्याहितं—अतिशयेन आधीयते तन्निवारणार्थं मनो यस्मिन् a great calamity; or a rash deed endangering life. अत्याहितं महाभीतिः कर्म जीवानपेक्षि च । Amara. भवेत्—This gives a hint which prepares the audience for A'ra.'s swallowing poison further on in the Act;. see p. 54.

P. 47. नेदृशः—not such i. e. indifferent. The scene opens while Sâm. and Vâsa. are conversing. This is a reply to Vásavadattâ who in her previous speech must have charged her husband with being indifferent to the calamity that had overtaken her aunt's husband. विज्ञाय—not only ज्ञात्वा; when he knows very well. तादृशि न—i. e the sole object of his love. तत्र पुनः&c.—She means—you have seen how the King has transferred his love entirely to A'ranyiká.

यत एव मे प्रत्यक्षं—Sâmkr. means—Because I witnessed it myself I know what it all really was. Vatsarája wanted to enjoy a joke by playing his part himself and telling you in the end how you could not discover who the real actor was and thus to make you laugh. Had there been a love intrigue he would have taken care to keep Vasantaka and Manoramá out of the way. Of course this does not convince the Queen.

हासितास्मि—The Queen puns upon the word हासिता which means 'made to laugh' and 'caused to be laughed at', using it in the latter sense. लज्जया—Because the King manifested his love for Aranyiká so openly· Even her maid-servants knew that she was no longer loved as before by the King. एतावतीं भूमिं &c.—is ironical. She means—I have been reduced to such a sad plight. वासव० says—these are your sweet fancies; what does the King care for me now? This she says as प्रणयकुपिता. Similarly Dushyanta says to Vidu. in the Śâk. मनोरथा नाम तटप्रपाताः (V. 10).

P. 48. संघट्ट—Collision, close or hard fight. समुद्धितः—possessed of; or rendered more powerful (*lit.* elevated, lofty)· कुपीहितं कृत्वा &c.—This suggestion of the Vidû. which is ridiculous on the very face is meant to stir laughter. कुब्जवामन &c.—These with the Kirâtas (see Rat. p. 36.) formed the usual male attendants of the harems of ancient kings. For their bravery *cf.* Rat. II. 3. मासोपवासं—मासमुपवासः मासो० Acc Tat. देवी चण्डी—There is a pun on the word चण्डी which means wrathful and is also an epithet of the fierce goddess Durgá whose favour is also obtained by fasting.

धृष्ट:—has here the sense of 'shamelessly bold; *cf.* कृतागा अपि निःशंकुस्तर्जितोपि न लज्जितः । दृष्टदोषोपि मिथ्यावाक् कथितो धृष्टनायकः ॥ Sah. D. चाटु—Pleasing or coaxing words; flattery; words of blandishment (especially those addressed by a lover to his beloved). *cf.* प्रियः प्रियायाः प्रकरोति चाटुम् । Rit. VI. 12 विरचितचाटुवचनरचनं चरणरचितप्रणिपातम् । Git. 11प्रपञ्च—extension; fr. पच् (पञ्च्) 1 A. to be clear or manifest (प्रपञ्चते इति); and aff. अच् (अ)

P. 49. सखेदं—खेदेन (fatigue, languor) सहितं यथा तथा ।

Sl. 3. मयि—मद्विषयं; with regard to me; for me; the loc. is वैषयिकी. मम-मदर्थम्. तान्त—wearied, languid; p. p. p. of तम् 4 p., to be exhausted, &c.; *Cf.* ललितशिरीषपुष्पहननैरपि ताम्यति यत् । Mâl. Ma'd, V. 31; and as the fatigue may be due to slenderness तान्त may secondarily mean 'slender.' दृष्टिप्रसाद &c–For a similar idea *cf.* प्रसादमाकाङ्क्षति यस्तवोत्सुकः स किं त्वया दासजनः प्रसाद्यते । Vik. III. 13. विलक्ष:—abashed or put to shame; or embarrassed.

आर्यपुत्र विलक्षः &c.—is ironical. She means—you are not विलक्ष ashamed but विलक्षः embarprassed, being an admirer of Âranyiká.

सत्यमहं विलक्षः—*Cf.* देवि एवं प्रत्यक्षदृष्टव्यलीकः किं ब्रवीमि । आताम्रतामपनयामि विलक्ष एषः &c. Rat. III. 14.

P. 50 Sl. 3. भ्रूभङ्ग—This is the first sign of anger. *Cf.* Śak. V. 23. स्तिमितः p. p. p. of स्तिम् 4. p. to become fixed or rigid; steadied, held up, not allowed to manifiest itself, and hence causing pain inwardly. गूढप्रहारो०—गूढश्चासौ प्रहारश्च गूढप्रहारः स उपमा (in the sense of उपमानं) यस्य.; or उपमाति इति उपमः (क i. e. अ being added to मा कर्तरि); ०प्रहार उपमः यस्य; प्रहारस्य or–रेण उपमा यस्य is inadmissible, as Pân. does not sanction such a Vyad. Bah. A third way is ०प्रहारेण सदृशः, उपमा being treated like संकाश, निभ, &c.—a Nityasamâsa.

सुखितः—सुखमस्य संजातमसौ सुखितः; explain similarly दुःखित. विकारयासि—torment, afflict. सिद्धे एवास्मिन्न०—As that would have caused the Queen surprise and given her greater satisfaction.

Sl. 4. तैः—*i. e.* so well known for their bravery. बाह्यविषयः—*i. e.* the territory outside the fortress. दुर्गं &c—Constru अशरणः सहसा दुर्गं प्रविश्य स्थितः (which must be supplied) असौ कलिङ्गहतकः प्राकारमात्रशरणः कृतः । प्राकारः (here the rampart of the fort) एव प्राकारमात्रं; now see com.

P. 51. Sl. 5. निर्दिष्टा०–निर्दिष्ट-mentioned above. आक्रान्तं attack (p.p p. used as a noun आक्रान्ति which is also a variant here) तेन मन्ये

discomfited, with his power crippled (विहतप्रताप). निर्दिष्टाक्रन्दमन्दं *V. l.*—here आक्रन्द means a battle; see com. दासेरा:—Servants दास्या अपत्यं दासेयः by affixing एय (ढक्) which is added to words of two syllables ending in a fem. affix. (द्व्यचः Pân. IV. 1. 121 द्व्यचः स्त्रीप्रत्ययान्तादपत्ये ढक् Sid. Kau.); क्षुद्राभ्यो वा। Pân IV. 1. 131; when the female is of a low character ढ्रक् (एर) is optionally affixed; so दासेरः and दासेयः; क्षुद्राः अङ्गहीनाः शीलहीनाश्च ताभ्यो वा ढ्रक्। Sid. Kau. दासेर thus etymologically means a person of a low origin; and then a servant; and it is in this sense that the word is used here. See A.K. quoted in the com. The word दासेर is used for alliteration. वृत्तं—The working of, *i. e.* the schemes or activities of. The comp. may also be taken as वीराश्च ते दासेराश्च (his slavish warriors) according to कुत्सितानि कुत्सनैः। Pân. II. 1. 53. But that will not do here, as the king, who is an admirer of the heroic deeds of his enemies even, is not likely to speak disparangingly of the warriors here. नरः foot soldiers. अप्रतिविधाय—that is—without taking measures to avenge the wrong done to Dṛdhavarman. ततः प्रवि० कञ्चुकी च—This is the chamberlain attached to the court of Dṛdhavarman, who had been serving his master in his captivity (see p. 5) now coming to see Vatsarája with a message from his royal master. अद्य स्वामिपादाः—यमनुभवामि—*Mark* the contrast this gives with Śl. 8 Act I. The reason is given in the next sl. by the Kanchukî. Vijaya. feels happy here, because he has achieved a great military feat that was sure to be hailed with great delight by the King and Queen. The conquest of Vindhyaketu was a comparatively insignificant matter. *Cf.* Rat. IV. बाभ्रव्यः—वसुभूते अद्य खलु चिरात्स्वामिनं द्रक्ष्यामीति यत्सत्यमानन्दातिशयेन किमप्यवस्थान्तरमनुभवामि। p. 100

Śl. 6. निर्भरः—Excess; निःशेषः भरोऽत्र इति निर्भरः; now see com. अन्यथा—Even when he has not executed a command; ordinarily. निर्व्यूढ—Fully carried out; completely executed. नियोगभरः—The responsibility of a duty; hence, an onerous task or momentous business, entrusted to him.

Sl. 7. देवस्य समादेशः &c.—This reading is preferable to देवस्य समादेशाद्रिपुजयिना &c. as it brings out more prominently the signal service rendered by Vijayasena. ०देशोऽवस्थापितः *V. l.*—violates the metre and also is not appropriate.

पत्रिका—पुत्रिकायुगं *v. l.* is bad, as we are not told anywhere in the play why the two girls were sent, nor is there a reference to them in what follows. गुरुपूजा—Here he refers to the King as Vásavadattá's Guru

सर्वबंधनमोक्षः—It was customary to set prisoners free on an occasion of great joy, such as the birth of a son and heir to a King, a great victory over an invading powerful enemy, &c.; *cf.* Hemadri on Raghu III. 20—युवराजाभिषेके च परचक्रावमर्दने। पुत्रजन्मनि वा मोक्षो बद्धस्य हि विधीयते॥ *cf.* Mal. V. p.194, where the king, on hearing of the victory gained by his son (sl. 15) says—मोद्गल्य मुच्यन्तां सर्वे बन्धनस्थाः। Also IV. p. 130, where Vidû. says—देवचिन्तकैर्विज्ञापितो राजा सोपसर्गं धो नक्षत्र सर्वबन्धनमोक्षः क्रियतामिति। see also Mrch X. p.

छोटिका—Snapping the thumb and the middle finger together.

P. 53. कथं त्वं &c.—The impatient Vidû. wanted Va'savadattá to give the order for the release of A'ra. at once. सम्बन्धः—Family connexion. वासवदत्तायाः परिणेत्रा &c.—The pain is removed at the thought that you, as the husband of Va'sava. are connected with our family. संचिन्त्य—Thinking it to be a wise step. स्मर्तव्यतां नीतं–reduced to the condition of being remembered, made a matter of memory—a phrase often used in the sense of 'utterly destroyed'. *Cf.* अवगम्य कथीकृतं वपुः Kum. IV. 13. For this see the Chamberlain's introductory speech in Act I.

P. 54. विजयसेन किं &c.—The king asks Vijayasena significantly. He knew that A'ranyaká was meant. प्राणसंशये वर्तते—is in imminent danger (of life). This speech of Manoramá is so introduced as to be taken in connection with and serve as a reply to the Kanchuki's words न ज्ञायते क वर्तते इति। It is not known where she is—she is in great danger of life. This is a kind of what is called in dramaturgy a Patákásthána. Four different kinds of it are mentioned in the Sah.-D. One occurs when a speech is so arranged that it should serve as a reply to one preceding it, though uttered in a different context. See Sah. D. VI. 48.

प्रियदर्शना—seems to be another name of Priyadars'iká. कल्य-wine; see com. दुःखमन्तरितं—Not because she was inclined to love Priyadar. but because she feared that people might suspect her hand in the matter of the administration of the poison. अतिदुर्जनः खलु लोकः—*Cf.* Uttar. I. यथा स्त्रीणां तथा वाचां साधुत्वे दुर्जनो जनः। (s'l. 5); सूत्रधारः—अतिदुर्जन इति वक्तव्यम्। नागलोकात् &c.—It is not mentioned in the Katha that Udayana was taught the art of curing snake-bites and other kinds of poisons by means of incantations and drugs, when in Pátála. It is probably an invention of the poet to enable the king to resuscitate the heroine and thus to assist in the *denouement* in the last Act.

विषवेग—The circulation or effect of poison. **अन्धकारं प्रवेशयसि**—As her brain was affected by the poison her sight was bedimmed and all things appeared to be dark to her.

P. 55. **विपद्यते**—dies; *cf.* for this sense त्वमनाथा विपद्यसे। Uttar. I. 44; हा तात एष ते नरेन्द्रचिन्ताराधनोपकरणं जनो विपद्यते। Mâl. Mâd. V. p. 107.

Śl. 8. **गतश्च—दग्धा च**—The repetition of च here expresses the simultaneous occurrence of two actions. **हिमेन—दग्धा**—These apparently appear to be contradictory terms or to be wanting in what is called योग्यता (fitness or power to express a meaning) as अग्निना सिञ्चति which is absurd. But here हिमेन दग्धा is quite intelligible, as the effects of extreme cold and heat on plants, foliage, flowers &c. are similar; *cf.* हिमसेकविपत्तिरत्र मे नलिनी पूर्वनिदर्शनं मता। Ragh. VIII. 35. **वाम**—Adverse, unfavourable; *cf.* for a similar description—आपूर्णश्च कलामिरिन्दुरमलो यातश्च राहोर्मुखं संजातश्च घनाघनो जलधरः शीर्णश्च वायोर्जवात्। निर्वृत्तश्च फलेग्रहिर्द्रुमवरो दग्धश्च दावाग्निना। &c. Mâl. Mâd. IX. 39.

किं ते बोध.–Have you consciousness, are you aware of anything?

P. 56. Śl. 9. The poison was working on Priya., the effects were produed on the King, as he says. This was because their hearts were linked together by love; *cf.* स हि स्नेहात्मकस्तन्तुरन्तर्मर्माणि सीव्यति। Uttar. V. 17. This indicates the intensity of the King's passion. The *fig.* of speech here is असङ्गति which occurs when a cause and its effect are represented as totally different, or separated (or in which there is an apparent violation of the relation between cause and effect). विरुद्धं भिन्नदेशत्वं कार्यं हेत्वोरसंगतिः। विषं जलधरैः पीतं मूर्च्छिताः पथिकाङ्गनाः। Kuva; भिन्नदेशतयात्यन्तं कार्यकारणभूतयोः। युगपद्धर्मयोर्यत्र ख्यातिः सा स्यादसङ्गतिः॥ Kav. P. X. **वेदना**—Feeling or sensation, power of perception. **विषमा**—Adverse, alarming. **मन्त्रस्मरणं**—mental recitation. **नाटयति**—*i. e.* by the movement of the lips, looking at the person &c., accompanied by the sprinkling of water on the person operated on.

P. 57. **नरेन्द्रता**—The word नरेन्द्र here is श्लिष्ट (paronomastic). It means a king and also a विषवैद्य a physician skilled in curing poisons; *cf.* सुनिग्रहा नरेन्द्रेण फणीन्द्रा इव शत्रवः। Sis. II. 88, where the word is used in both the senses. **इदानीमपि**—Even now, *i. e.* although revived.

राजा-(सस्मितं)—Because the king knew that her bewildered condition was due to the action of love at the sight of her lover. For the effects mentioned in the śl. are also due to love affection; *cf.* Mâl. Mâd. III. 8.

अलीकशीले—Falsely observing reserve or affecting modesty, has here the force of 'thou naughty or obstinate girl.'

P. 58. कुतोऽस्मात्परमं प्रियमस्ति &c—In the Rat. the King says—को देव्याः प्रसादो न बहुमन्यते । अतोऽपि परं &c.—This is the usual expression marking the close of a drama (the Sans. dramas always having a good end). This is called काव्यसंहार.

Śl 11. Another feature of the Sans. drama is to enumerate good results attained in the stanza preceding the Bharatavákya; *cf.* Rat. IV. 21. त्वं कोपेन &c.—So in Rat. देवी प्रीतिमुपागता.

P. 59. भरतवाक्यं—*Lit.* The speech of the actor (भरत)' technically called प्रशस्ति. It is a sort of stage direction. It refers to the concluding śl. of a play containing an expression of good wishes put in the mouth of the chief actor, as a member of the dramatic party and not in the role of a dramatic personage, all acting being over or the Vákya enjoined by Bharata, the founder of dramatic art.

Śl. 12. This Śl. occurs as the closing stanza of the Ratnâvali also with some variations in the last two lines उद्दाम—दाम्न उद्गतानि उद्दामानि Prádi Tat.; growing unchecked, *i. e.* luxuriantly or abundantly; now see com. वासवः—A name of Indra. It is variously derived as—वसोः अपत्यं पुमान्; or वसवो देवा वसूनि रत्नानि वा अस्य सन्ति; ज्योत्स्नादित्वात् अण् (अ) being added to वसु in the sense of possession (मत्वर्थे). Indra is the ruler of the firmament and the dispensor of rain. *Cf.* तव भवतु बिडौजाः प्राज्यवृष्टिः प्रजासु. Śak. VII. 34. इष्टां—as desired, *i. e.* timely and sufficient for the growth of corn. इष्टैः—By sacrifices; here इष्ट is used as a noun in the sense of इष्टि, त (क्त) being added to यज् भावे (to form an abstract noun). त्रिविष्टपाः—The gods; see com. प्रीणनं—gratification, pleasure. This is done by offering oblations to them in sacrifices. *cf.* इष्टान्भोगान् हि वो देवा दास्यन्ते यज्ञभाविताः । Bg. III. 12. and Śâk. त्वमपि विततयज्ञो वज्रिणं (स्वर्गिणः the gods *v. l.*) प्रीणयस्व । VII. 34.

विप्राः—Learned Bráhmaṇas; जन्मना ब्राह्मणो ज्ञेयः संस्कारैर्द्विज उच्यते । विद्यया याति विप्रत्वं त्रिभिः श्रोत्रिय उच्यते ॥ आकल्पान्तं—Kalpa is the period of the duration of creation. It extends over one thousand cycles of the four yugas. स्थिरसङ्गु०—In the Rat. we have समुपचितसुखः संगमः. वज्रलेपाः—see com.; sticking hard to the mind; leaving a permanent impression on the mind. वज्रलेप also is a kind of glue, so called because things joined by means of it remain stuck together permanently. For it see Vara's. Brh. ch. 57.

APPENDICES

I

The Subhāshitas occurring in the Play

(*The figures refer to the pages of this edition*)

प्रविशन्ति शङ्कमाना राजकुलं प्रायशो भृत्याः । 8

गुणैकपक्षपातिनां रिपोरपि गुणाः प्रीतिं जनयन्ति । 9

नास्ति खलु दुष्करं दैवस्य । 15

न खल्वविघ्नमभिलषितमधन्यैः प्राप्यते । 21

प्रायो यत्किंचिदपि प्राप्नोत्युत्कर्षमाश्रयान्महतः । 30

सदृशाः सदृशे रज्यन्ते । 33

दुःखं याति मनोरथेषु तनुतां सङ्कल्प्यमानेष्वपि । 34

अतिदुर्जनः खलु लोकः ।

वामे विधौ न हि फलन्त्यभिवाञ्छितानि । 55

II

The flowers and the trees mentioned in the play.

अम्भोरुह्—A lotus, or water-lily in general.

उत्पल—A lotus (Nymphaea*) in general, refers to कमल (see Ragh. III 36), कुमुद, &c. 44.

कदली—The plantain tree. 9, 21, 23, 27.

कमल—A lotus (Nelumbium Speciosum) in general; कं जलं अलति (beautifies); or काम्यते इति what is desired owing to its beauty; from कम् and Unā. aff. अल). 13, 14, 17, 18, 22, 55.

कुवलय—A synonym of उत्पल as given in Amarak; generally means 'a blue lotus' 20

तमाल—Name of a tree having a very dark bark and leaves but white flowers. 13

नलिनी—A lotus plant; a tank having lotuses in it. 17, 23, 26,

नीलोत्पल—The blue water-lily (Nymphaea cyanea) 19, 36, 42.

पङ्कज—A lotus. 16

पद्म—A lotus, generally one blooming at sunrise, 2, 13, 17, 19, 20,&c.

बकुल—Generally called Kesara, (Mimusops Elengi) 13

बन्धुजीव—Same as बन्धूक. 44.

---

* The L. names are taken from the Col. U. Ed.

बन्धूक—An erect growing plant (Pentapetes phoenicea) has large flowers of a bright red colour which expand at noon; their juice is cooling and is used in some diesases. 13, 14.

मालती—A kind of jasmine (Jasminum grandiflorum) called चमेली. 13, 26.

शिरीष—A fragrant but very delicate flower, also the name of the tree (Mimosa sirissa also called Acacia speciosa) 14.

शेफालिका—A charming small tree (Nyctanthes arbour-tristes) the flowers have a delicious fragrance which is evanescent. 13, 14, 15, 17.

सप्तच्छद
सप्तपर्ण } Alstonia scolaris. 13, 14.

III

The Metres used in the Play, their Definitions and Schemes.

1. Sanskrit verse is regulated by quantity, and not, as in English, by accent. A पद्य (stanza) consists usually of four पादs (quarters). A पाद is regulated either by the number of syllables (अक्षरs), or of syllabic instants (मात्राs). When the पादs are all similar, it is called a समवृत्त, to which type most of the metres conform. There are अर्धसम वृत्तs, wherein the first quarter corresponds to the third, and the second to the fourth, called respectively the *odd* (विषम) and *even* (सम) quarters. A third class comprises विषमवृत्तs, but these are very seldom used.

2. The vowels अ, इ, उ, ऋ and ऌ are short, and the rest long. The quantity of a syllable is determined by its vowel. A syllable with a short vowel is called लघु ('light'), and a syllable with a long vowel is called गुरु ('heavy'). But a लघु syllable is considered as गुरु if it is followed by an *anusvára*, or a *visarga*, or a conjunct consonant, or when it comes at the end of a पाद.[1]

3. A set of three successive syllables is called a गण (foot). Marking a short syllable as ⏑ and a long one as —, the different गणs,[2] which are 8 in number, may be exhibited as follows:—य ⏑ — —; र — ⏑ —; त — — ⏑; भ — ⏑ ⏑; ज ⏑ — ⏑; स ⏑ ⏑ —; म — — —; and न ⏑ ⏑ ⏑. In the definitions which are given below, a short syllable is indicated by the letter ल and a long one by ग.

4. The Priyadarśiká contains 49 slokas in all, of which two only are in Prákrit, and there are only seven different metres employed. So numerically and as regards the variety of metre, it is inferior to the other two plays. The Ratná· contains 7 Prákrit stanzas and 78 in Sans. in 13 defferent metres, while the Nágá has 123 stanzas in 12 different matres.

---

1 सानुस्वारश्च दीर्घश्च विसर्गी च गुरुर्भवेत् ।
वर्णः संयोगपूर्वश्च तथा पादान्तगोऽपि वा ॥

2 आदिमध्यावसानेषु यरता यान्ति लाघवम् ।
भजसा गौरवं यान्ति मनौ तु गुरुलाघवम् ॥

आर्या—Def. यस्याः प्रथमे पादे द्वादश मात्रास्तथा तृतीयेऽपि । अष्टादश द्वितीये चतुर्थके पञ्चदश साऽऽर्या ॥. This belongs to the class of metres which are regulated by the number of मात्राs or syllabic instants. The four *pádas* contain respectively 12, 18, 12 and 15 मात्राs. I. 5, 8; II. 5, 9; III. 1, 3, 9, 12; IV. 6, 7; Gitî—III. 8.

उपजाति—Def. [स्यादिन्द्रवज्रा यदि तौ जगौ गः उपेन्द्रवज्रा जतजास्ततोगौ ।] अनन्तरोदीरितलक्ष्मभाजौ पादौ यदीयावुपजातयस्ताः ॥ इत्थं किलान्यास्वपि मिश्रितासु वदन्ति जातिष्विदमेव नाम ।. An उपजाति is a mixture of one or more pádas of इन्द्रवज्रा [11 syllables, Scheme—त, त, ज, ग, ग], with one or more of उपेन्द्रवज्रा [11 syllables. Scheme—ज, त, ज, ग, ग], so as to form one stanza; a mixture of other metres also, in this manner, is called an उपजाति. The student should scan and find out in each case whether a páda is in इन्द्रवज्रा or उपेन्द्रवज्रा.

I. 4; III. 3.

मालिनी—Def. ननमयययुतेयं मालिनी भोगिलोकैः । 15 Syllables. Scheme—न, न, म, य, य. The pause occurs after the 8th syllable. II. 8.

वसन्ततिलका—Def. उक्ता वसन्ततिलका तभजा जगौ गः । 14 Syllables. Scheme—त, भ, ज, ज, ग, ग.

I. 10. III 2; IV. 2, 4, 8.

शार्दूलविक्रीडितं—Def. सूर्याश्वैर्यदि मः सजौ सततगाः शार्दूलविक्रीडितम् । 19 Syllables. Scheme—म, स, ज, स, त, त, ग. The pause occurs after the 12th syllable. This metre is very frequently used in this play.

I. 1, 3, 6, 7, 11; II 1, 3, 6, 7, 10; III 4, 5, 7, 10, 13, 14, 15; IV 1, 3, 9, 11.

शिखरिणी—Def. रसै रुद्रैश्छिन्ना यमनसभलाः गः शिखरिणी ।. 17 syllables. Scheme—य, म, न, स, भ, ल, ग. The pause occurs after the 6th syll. IV. 10.

स्रग्धरा—Def. म्रभ्नैर्यानां त्रयेण त्रिमुनियतियुता स्रग्धरा कीर्तितेयम् । 21 syllables Scheme—म, र, भ, न, य, य, य. The pauses occur after the 7th and the 14th syllables. This is the longest metre in ordinary use.

I. 2, 9, 12; II. 2, 4; III. 11; IV. 5, 12.

NOTE ON THE GEOGRAPHY OF THE PLAY.

The scene of the play is laid at the palace of Vatsarája in Kauśambī, the capital of the Vatsa country. Vatsa is thus described in the Kathâsaritsâgara—अस्ति वत्स इति ख्यातो देशो दर्पोपशान्तये। स्वर्गस्य निर्मितो धात्रा प्रतिमल्ल इव क्षितौ ॥ Kauśâmbî was a famous and very flourishing city in ancient times and is mentioned in the Râmâyaṇa of Vâlmiki. The Kathâ. thus describes its grandeur—लक्ष्मीनिवासवसतिर्भूतलस्येव कर्णिका। (II. 1. 5). ***Cf.*** **also Rat. I., 10. It was founded by Kuśamba (son of Kus'a), tenth in descent from Purūravas. In many Ceylonese books it is named as one of the nineteen capital cities of ancient India. Its decline began after the Christian era and its ruin was completed in the Mahammadan times ; and now it is represented by the comparatively insignificant village of Kosam on the river Jamunâ, about thirty miles above Allahabad.**

Anga—The kingdom of Anga was situated on the right bank of the Ganges and to the south of Kaus'ika Kachcha. Its capital was Champa', also called Angapurî, Lomapâdapuri (after King Lomapâda), Karṇapurî (capital of Karṇa) and Mâlinî. According to Hiouen Thsang it stood on the Ganges about 24 miles west of a rocky island and is, therefore, considered to be the same as or situated very near the modern Bhágalpur.

Kalinga—The country of Kalinga lay to the south of Odra or Orissa, along the Bay of Bengal, between the Mahânadî and the Godavarî. It is identified with the Northern Circars. Its capital, Kalingapur, was at some distance from the sea-coast and was probably at Râjamahendrî, See Ragh. IV. 38.

INDEX OF IMPORTANT WORDS.

(The figures refer to the pages of this Edition).